JESUS AND THE GOSPEL
Volume 2

JESUS AND THE GOSPEL
Volume 2

By
Pierre Benoit

translated by
Benet Weatherhead

A Crossroad Book
The Seabury Press · New York

The Seabury Press
815 Second Avenue
New York, N.Y. 10017

First published in Great Britain 1974 by
Darton, Longman & Todd Ltd
English translation copyright © 1974
Darton, Longman & Todd Ltd

This is the second volume of a translation of
selected articles from the second volume of *Exégèse et Théologie*
published by Editions du Cerf in 1961

Library of Congress Catalog Card Number: 72–94303
ISBN: 0–8164–1147–6

Printed in Great Britain by
Western Printing Services Ltd, Bristol

Contents

BS
2 555, 2
B 473
v. 23

4460

List of Abbreviations

AAS	Acta Apostolicae Sedis
Ang	Angelicum. Rome.
Bibl	Biblica. Rome.
BiZ	Biblische Zeitschrift. Paderborn.
CBQ	Catholic Biblical Quarterly. Washington, D.C.
CSEL	Corpus Scriptorum Ecclesiasticorum Latinorum. Vienna.
DTC	Dictionnaire de Théologie Catholique. Paris.
FRL	Forschungen zur Religion und Literatur der Alten und Neuen Testamente. Göttingen.
HThR	Harvard Theological Review. Cambridge, Mass.
JBL	Journal of Biblical Studies. New Haven.
JThSt	Journal of Theological Studies. London.
NRTh	Nouvelle Revue Théologique. Tournai.
PG	Migne. Patrologia Graeca.
PL	Migne. Patrologia Latina.
RBibl	Revue Biblique. Paris.
RHE	Revue d'histoire ecclésiastique. Louvain.
RHL	Revue d'histoire et de littérature religieuses. Paris.
RHPR	Revue d'histoire et de philosophie religieuses. Strasbourg.
RHR	Revue d'histoire des religions. Paris.
ROC	Revue de l'Orient Chrétien. Paris.
RSPT	Revue des sciences philosophiques et théologiques. Paris.
RSR	Revue de science religieuse. Paris.
RT	Revue Thomiste. Paris.
ThBl	Theologische Blätter. Leipzig.
ThLZ	Theologische Literaturzeitung. Leipzig.
ThQ	Theologische Quartalschrift. Tübingen.
TWNT	Theologisches Wörterbuch des Neuen Testaments.
ZkTh	Zeitschrift für katholische Theologie. Innsbruck.
ZNW	Zeitschrift für die neutestamentliche Wissenschaft und die Kunde der älteren Kirche. Giessen.

The Theology of St Paul

1. The Law and the Cross according to St Paul*
Romans 7:7 – 8:4

In the four major epistles which date from the middle of his career, especially in *Romans* and *Galatians*, Paul explains his conception of the part played by the Law in the plan of salvation. What was the value of this temporary dispensation and what was its relation to the new one of Righteousness through Faith, instituted by Christ and preached in the Gospel? Was it a useful and even necessary preparation, or rather a divine experiment which came to grief? But if the Law was from God, how can one talk of failure? and if, on the other hand, it was good, why did it serve only to increase the power of sin? We can sense how the problem haunted St Paul, harassed as he was by the objections and protestations of the Jews, but above all stimulated by his own desire to penetrate into the depths of the 'mystery of God'. One of the classical texts is chapter 7 of the epistle to the Romans. But elsewhere too there are many fleeting allusions which suggest that this problem was always present at the back of his mind[1]. These are eager and unconditional expressions which it does not always seem easy to reconcile with one another: sometimes the Law is sacred, good and just (*Rm* 7:12), sometimes it is the 'administering of death' or of 'condemnation' (*2 Co* 3:7–9).

Exegetes are in general in agreement on a first, negative, aspect of the Law: it is unable to impart life. Being an external rule, it lays down what should be done, but does not give the power to carry this out. It enlightens man as to his sinful condition, but without helping him to emerge from it. This first fact is obvious and for the moment it does not call for discussion though it is capable of being enriched later. There is, however, more. On several occasions, St Paul

* This article was first published in the *Revue Biblique*, 1938, pp. 481–509.
[1] In Romans itself, before the formal development in ch. 7, the problem is already hinted at in 3:20, 3:31, 4:15, 5:13, 5:20, 6:14. See KUEMMEL, *Römer 7 und die Bekehrung des Paulus*, Hinrichs, 1929, p. 6f.

12 THE LAW AND THE CROSS ACCORDING TO ST PAUL

attributes to the Law a positive part in the aggravation and the multi-
plication of sins (*Rm* 5:20; 7:13; *Ga* 3:19): it is the 'power' of
sin (*1 Co* 15:56), it brings about 'law-breaking' and hence punishment
(*Rm* 4:15). In what way are we to conceive this active participation
of the Law in the establishment of the power of sin? It is customary
to employ two considerations, to which too often an equal importance
is attributed: on the one hand, by enlightening the mind with *moral
knowledge* the Law makes the sinner fully responsible for his action;
instead of being a simple, more or less conscious, dislocation of
order, this becomes the formal transgression of divine order, i.e. a
rebellion against God himself, and hence takes on a far greater
culpability; on the other hand, the Law, with its numerous prescriptions and prohibitions, is an *occasion* of further sin. And this
in its turn can be conceived as taking place in two ways: first, by
enriching the mind and widening the material possibilities of sinning,
whether it is a question of morally indifferent acts which the natural
law would permit but which a positive commandment forbids, or
simply of ways of satisfying his desire which man would not have
invented by himself; secondly, by rousing desire, which is irritated
by the imposed prohibition and is more drawn to the sin as it takes
on the attraction of forbidden fruit. Here, in the opinion of many
exegetes, the active part played by the Law ends. For, as far as death,
which follows, is concerned, St Paul says formally that it is the direct
consequence of sin (*Rm* 7:13), the part played by the Law having
been quite indirect and confined to providing occasion.

The place of the Law in the design of providence is conceived
accordingly: God willed that it should be through the Law that man
came to realise his fall, recognised the gravity of his sins, succumbed
under their increased weight and augmented numbers, and in consequence ceased to expect salvation elsewhere than from God alone.
This divine scheme is presented sometimes as a lucky hit by which
God restores a plan which the Law has 'thwarted'[1], – in virtue of
what autonomous action does not appear – sometimes as the intention he has had all along, from the first commandment given in the
earthly Paradise[2].

[1] F. PRAT, S.J., *La Théologie de Saint Paul*, Beauchesne, I[19] (1930), p. 279; but in
II[16] (1929), p. 124, he writes more exactly that the first (good) purpose of the Law
'was thwarted by the hard-heartedness of the Jews'.
[2] See especially Jülicher (*Die Schriften des N. T.*, Göttingen, 1908, pp. 265-70)
who, with a courage bordering on audacity, formulates the thesis in all its rigour:
God, foreseeing that man would sin, decided to lead him towards good through
evil and gave him a law it was impossible for him to keep, in order that the flame

There is a good deal of truth in these views. But to me they appear inexact and insufficient – inexact, in that they attribute too much importance to the Law as an *occasion* of sin, where this is secondary with regard to its role as giver of moral knowledge, and insufficient, in that in practice they ignore another role of the Law which is of prime importance, that of the sentence of death for Sin. To show this we shall have to return to the texts, first to *Romans* 7:7–13, which is the principal source here.

There are few passages of Paul which have given rise to so much discussion[1]. It is impossible here to resume every aspect of it and I shall content myself with recalling certain main points which seem to be proven and which must govern our understanding of the text.

St Paul is not talking here about man in the earthly Paradise[2]. There are two principal difficulties opposed to this view. First, the expressions concerning sin, which is 'dead' and which 'comes to life' (vv. 8f), cannot be understood without violence of the personification of Sin which is powerless as long as man lives in innocence and establishes itself in him through his transgression of the commandment. In the second place, and more particularly, νόμος can only mean the Mosaic Law which has been troubling St Paul since v. 4[3]. The alteration of this word with ἐντολή presents no difficulty[4]. It merely shows that νόμος is being used in the formal sense of a positive commandment laid down by God. On this point the great majority of exegetes are in agreement.

The same cannot be said of the 'I' who appears in the passage. Not that the hypothesis of the man who has been justified, the Christian, can still be upheld with much success. Since νόμος means the Mosaic Law, ἐγώ must represent the man who is subject to this Law, the Jew.

---

of sin might be lit (in the earthly Paradise) and then burn up more fiercely, and man, with his back to the wall and convinced of his own powerlessness, might aspire to righteousness as a gift from God.

[1] Useful information about the different positions taken up by recent exegesis is to be found in the monograph of Kuemmel, cited above.

[2] This exegesis was proposed formerly by St Methodius, Theodore of Mopsuestia, Theodoret, taken up again by Cajetan, and put forward in our own day by Jülicher, Lietzmann . . . See KUEMMEL, *op. cit.*, pp. 85ff. P. Lagrange also came close to it, but with nuances which are too often ignored.

[3] After speaking of our death to sin (ch. 6), Paul goes on to our death to the Law, both being due to our mystical union with Christ. The assimilation of these two deaths to one another then poses the difficult question – are ἁμαρτία and νόμος identical (v. 7)? In the verses which follow Paul applies himself to making his thought more exact concerning their distinction and their relationship.

[4] See KUEMMEL, *op. cit.*, pp. 55f; SCHRENK, in Kittel's *Theol. Wört*, II, p. 547, 11.1–19; BANDAS, *The Master-Idea of Saint Paul's Epistles or the Redemption*, Bruges, 1925, p. 93, note 2.

But is this Paul himself, recounting his own experience and behind it the experience of all Jews? This is the opinion of many[1]. Ἐγώ would bring before our eyes the young Israelite who, after the years of innocence, reaches the age of reason and becomes conscious of the message of the Law: the Law opens his eyes to moral evil, and stimulates his desire which until then has been asleep or merely unconscious; he commits the forbidden evil and dies. This exegesis deserves well of the critics and the effort to refute it has been useful. Its chief defect in my opinion – and the same goes for other interpretations which more or less resemble it, e.g. Paul's period as a Pharisee before conversion – is that it places the whole of this text on the level of a personal experience. Not enough attention has been paid to the fact that Paul is reflecting on the main stages in the history of mankind, not on the spiritual development of the individual soul. What Paul conceives as a cosmic drama has been reduced to the description of a subjective crisis[2]. He is interested above all in the Νόμος, considered in itself and conceived as an actor who enters on the world stage to play his part (Rm 5:20). What is this part, and how does it fit in with those of the other actors who are already on the scene, Ἁμαρτία and Θάνατος (5:12)? Paul represents these abstract powers in a living and dramatic way, treating them as persons. This has long been observed for ἁμαρτία[3], but not always of its accomplice θάνατος[4]. This drama has to have a theatre, and evidently the theatre is man, since it is in him that the debate takes place. How then is he to be referred to? Ἄνθρωπος would have been possible but graceless; its character of an abstraction makes it unsuitable for this setting in which the whole point of Paul's writing is to present abstract realities as living persons. Ἐγώ on the other hand works splendidly. 'I' suggests man as such, visualised in his specific character as an autonomous and responsible being. This is indeed the battle-field where the figures of the play take on

[1] Cf. KUEMMEL, op. cit., pp. 76–84.
[2] LIETZMANN, An die Römer, 3rd ed., 1928, p. 73: 'The psychological process of the origin of individual sins in man is described'.
[3] At least as regards 5:12ff. Those who interpret 7:7ff as an inward experience of the soul are led to treat ἁμαρτία there as desire. I believe that 7:7ff maintains exactly the same viewpoint as 5:12ff and that ἁμαρτία is still regarded as a personified force which tries from outside to establish its dominion over man. From this point of view the exegesis which sees the espisode of the earthly Paradise here is closer to the truth.
[4] Cf. FREUNDDORFER, Erbsünde und erbiod beim Apostel Paulus, Münster, 1927, pp. 227ff – on the analogy between this procedure of Paul and the Diatribe, cf. BULTMANN, Der Stil der paulinischen Predigt und die kynisch-stoische Diatribe, Göttingen, 1910. p. 87.

one another. No one should be deceived by this rhetorical, or rather dramatic, device which was familiar both to Paul and to his contemporaries[1]; and least of all would the readers of *Romans*, arriving at verses 8f, think that Paul was talking about himself, since the key-text, 5:13, would still be ringing in their memories and they did not have the subtleties of modern exegesis at their disposal to persuade themselves that the Jew Paul, before reaching the age of reason, was living without the Law.

Now that we have put Paul's thought back in its proper framework, what is the part which Paul gives the Law to act? or rather what are the parts, since the situation is complex?

Let us take first the Law as the *occasion* of sin, on which so much stress is laid. This aspect must be restored to its proper place, which is secondary, but not eliminated altogether. It is implied by certain details of the text. In v. 5, the τὰ διὰ τοῦ νόμου which qualifies 'our sinful passions' must be understood of a kind of co-operation rendered by the Law to the unleashing of desire, whether this be through information about the possibilities of evil or the exasperating of desire by prohibitions. Similarly, when Sin 'takes advantage' of the Commandment to mislead the 'I' and produce all kinds of covetousness (vv. 8 and 11), the reference is to the same unhappy, but accidental, effect of the rule imposed on man. It is possible that the same idea underlies v. 7b, but the principal significance of this passage is to be found elsewhere. Before proceeding to this, to show that the rest of the elements of the text under consideration are to be understood of the two essential roles of the Law, information and condemnation, I want just to emphasise again the secondary and accidental character of its role as an occasion of sin, by pointing out that this appears nowhere else in St Paul (it can be introduced into *Ga* 3:19 or *1 Co* 15:56 only by violence). Furthermore, in vv. 14–25, which follow on strictly[2] from what has preceded them and describe

---

[1] Cf. KUEMMEL, *op. cit.*, pp. 121–32. It is to be regretted that Kuemmel did not profit more from this excellent interpretation and remained attached to the subjective explanation from Paul's experience, though it is true that at the same time he tried, by a kind of compromise, to combine the formal, objective interpretation with it. See especially Stauffer (in *Theol. Wört.*, II, 355,39–356,13) who brings out most felicitously the *heilgeschichtlich* sense of this passage.

[2] It is inadmissible to separate vv. 14–25 from 7–13 in any way whatsoever, and, for example, to suppose that the subject has changed, that it has become man under Grace instead of man under the Law (St Augustine's interpretation after the Pelagian controversies). The setting remains exactly the same. The only difference is that between two succeeding scenes of the same act; first, the disturbance produced by the entrance of νόμος (7–13), then the resulting situation (14–25).

the battlefield of the 'I' and the respective positions of the adversaries facing one another, Νόμος is ranged beside νοῦς and notifies him of the verdict of moral responsibility and condemnation, while, opposed to them, Ἁμαρτία holds sway over σάρξ. Not a word is breathed of any support Ἁμαρτία might find from Νόμος. The latter no longer has anything of the accomplice, not even an involuntary one; it is nothing but teacher and judge. This particularly tragic scene would however have provided a magnificent opportunity for Paul to demonstrate the part played by the Law in the development of sin, if that had indeed been one of its principal roles, willed, or at least recognised and legitimised, in the designs of God. Nothing shows more clearly how secondary is the importance which Paul attributes to this aspect than the fact that he here passes over it in silence.

Let us turn next to the aspect of *moral knowledge*. This has been very generally recognised, and it could not have been otherwise. There are texts of Paul of which this is only too evidently the meaning. But the exaggerated attention paid to the preceding aspect has very often prevented this one being given the importance which is its due, particularly in *Rm* 7:7–13, the text we are considering. This time, however, it is a matter of the direct and formal effect of the Law. It is the Law which furnishes the true knowledge of sin (ἐπίγνωσις *Rm* 3:20), still more, which gives it its essential character of a rebellion against God. Out of what was lack of moral order, unrecognised by a conscience still ignorant or asleep, it makes a breach of the revealed will of God, a formal 'transgression' (παράβασις), and an offence against God himself. Without it there is no transgression (*Rm* 4:15).

This doctrine is expounded especially in 5:12–14 and is taken up again in 7:7ff, a passage which remains on exactly the same general level of the history of salvation as 5:12–14 and continues as though it were the second act of the drama[1]. These two texts must be explained in strict association. The first act involved the entrance of two characters Ἁμαρτία and Θάνατος, who introduce themselves into humanity under cover of man's transgression of the first divine command; from then on they occupy the scene, Sin remains in the world (ἁμαρτία ἦν ἐν κόσμῳ) and all men are subject to Death (vv. 1,2 14; cf. *1 Co* 15:21f). But there is as it were an interlude marked by

[1] This I hope will appear from my exegesis. The two descriptions cannot therefore be opposed to one another as the 'historisch-empirisch' and the 'immanent' (FREUNDDORFER, *op. cit.*, p. 223). It will be noticed that the intervening ch. 6 remains on this same level of historical personifications when it opposes Sin and Grace (or Justice) as two masters disputing over man's service.

the absence of any commandment revealed by God: the ἐντολή given in the earthly Paradise no longer operates and the νόμος has not yet been promulgated. In the absence of a divine command, the two actors find themselves deprived, so to speak, of what gives them their character and their power. From Adam to Moses men sin, but their sins do not resemble the transgression of Adam (v. 14). They die, but this is in consequence of Adam's fall, not their own[1], for their sins, not being formally such, are not counted (ἁμαρτία δὲ οὐκ ἐλλογεῖται μὴ ὄντος νόμου, v. 13), that is to say, they do not incur their normal punishment, Death[2]. This is exactly what is restated, in another form, in 7:8b–9a: without the Law Sin is 'dead', the de facto lack of order has not acquired its malignant character as an offence against God, and man 'lives', now with a fullness of life such as that of grace, but in the relative sense that he is not in open rebellion against God and especially that he is not under the yoke of Θάνατος, which is imposed solely through formal Sin[3]. Then comes the turn of events which leads to the second act: the Law makes its entrance (ἐλθούσης δὲ τῆς ἐντολῆς, v. 9; cf. v. 20 παρεισῆλθεν). Its light unmasks 'Αμαρτία, which then appears to the 'I' in its true colours as the enemy of God;'I should not have known what sin was except for the Law' (v. 7a)[4];

---

[1] This must be the idea which underlies the reasoning of 5:12–14: Paul wants to prove that all men have sinned in the person of Adam (ἐφ' ᾧ πάντες ἥμαρτον); in fact, all men die, even those who are not under the Law (v. 14); but sins committed outside the Law do not incur death (v. 13); therefore this death which they nevertheless undergo must be due to something other than their own personal failings, that is, to Adam's transgression; see also vv. 15 and 17. – It is true that many exegetes see in ἐφ' ᾧ πάντες ἥμαρτον the assertion of men's personal sins; this idea is true in itself (v. 13a), but it cannot be read into these words without making the reasoning incomprehensible. (Cf. LAGRANGE, in loc., BANDAS, op. cit., pp. 31–39; FREUNDDORFER, op. cit., pp. 239–54). This can be felt in the embarrassed explanation given by Bultmann (Theol. Wört., III, 15,11. 20ff); and Lietzmann (op. cit., p. 62) says: 'Die Bezugnahme auf die Tatsünden der Einzelnen ist doch ein mehr störender als fördernder Nebengedanke, weil er aus dem Parallelismus herausfällt'.

[2] Cf. Preisker, in Theol. Wört., II, 514f; GRUNDMANN, ibid., I, 313f; FREUNDDORFER, op. cit., pp. 249f.

[3] ἔζων which is opposed to ἀπέθανον (v. 10) can only be understood in the strong sense of 'being alive', and not merely 'existing, being without the Law'. But this strong sense does not necessarily imply life in the fullest sense, the life of complete innocence, such as that of Adam before the Fall, or the Jewish child before the age of reason; its relative sense of life is defined precisely through its opposition to ἀπέθανον: man had not fallen under the sway of Θάνατος.

[4] Γιγνώσκω normally carries a connotation of intellectual knowledge, and this seems preferable here. The majority of exegetes however adopt the meaning of practical or experimental knowledge, appealing to 2 Co 5:21. Although this translation seems to me to be arguable and to sacrifice too much to the conception of the text as a description of experience, it is to be noticed that my exegesis can make room for it: from the moment that ἁμαρτία is seen to refer not to desire but to Sin personified as a power hostile to God, it is only by informing man as

similarly, that insatiable source of desires, ἡ ἐπιθυμία, whose spur he has long sensed but of which he has yet seen almost nothing but the attractions, is manifested as condemned by God; for the Law says, You shall not covet (v. 7b)[1]. In throwing this pitiless light on all the evil that was seething in man, the Law did something which was 'sacred, just and good' (v. 12), something which is the essential function of all law; it acted 'towards life' (v. 10) and yet Ἁμαρτία profited from its intervention to take possession of man definitively. How did this happen? Was it by making the Law an accomplice who would connive at Sin and 'thwart' the plans of God? This is an inadmissible notion which we have already rejected. Was it by overplaying the severity of its message and maddening wretched mankind's desire still further? Yes, if you like, up to a point; but this remains a secondary aspect. The truth is different: what Ἁμαρτία owes to the Law is that it can now play its part openly. From now on man no longer gets the benefit of his irresponsibility: when he yields to the temptations of Ἁμαρτία he will be declaring himself knowingly and willingly against God. He will, in the strongest sense of the word, be choosing his own master and entering quite freely into slavery under him. From being dead, the enemy has come 'back to life' (v. 9); he has profited from the message God sent to mankind, which was good in itself (διὰ τοῦ ἀγαθοῦ, v. 13) and which unmasked him, to show himself for what he is, to reveal himself as Ἁμαρτία (ἵνα φανῇ ἁμαρτία) and to act accordingly, that is, to strike the death-blow (μοι κατεργαζομένη θάνατον). And in fact man dies as a result ἐγὼ δὲ ἀπέθανον, v. 10). From now on, as though identified with the slave he has conquered and who has become his thing, Sin becomes 'utterly sinful', ἵνα γένηται καθ' ὑπερβολὴν ἁμαρτωλὸς ἡ ἁμαρτία[2]. And it is by using the divine command in its most formal aspect as moral knowledge that Sin has won (διὰ τῆς ἐντολῆς) (v. 13)[3]. Its victory means death.

to the true nature of his adversary that the Law gives Sin its hold on man and the latter his formidable practical knowledge.

[1] Here especially it is customary to take εἰδέναι to mean only experimental knowledge and to quote 2 Co 5:16. But is it true that man had to wait for the Law before evil desires sprang up in him? He carried them in himself, he even satisfied them, but he did not know clearly and formally that they were evil. This was the knowledge that the divine prohibition brought him.

[2] καθ' ὑπερβολήν 'to excess' must be taken in a qualitative sense, not a quantitative one, as if the Law, functioning as the occasion, had merely increased the number of sins. Cf. Ga 1:13, 1 Co 12:31, 2 Co 1:8, 4:17.

[3] It is this de facto association of the two antagonists that Paul expresses in realistic terms when he identifies in practice 'being ὑπὸ νόμον' and 'being ὑπὸ ἁμαρτίαν' (Rm 6:14f, Ga 3:22f, 5:18f).

At several points we have come across the close link between Sin and Death. This is a cardinal point of doctrine, particularly in connection with the part played by the Law in the history of the world. There are numerous texts in which Paul juxtaposes ἁμαρτία and θάνατος. But one of the principal difficulties raised by the interpretation of them comes from the indeterminateness of the second.

Physical or spiritual death? Actual or eschatological death? In some cases it is clear which of these alternatives is meant. More often it is better not to choose but to leave all these possibilities included in one fundamental reality which Paul personifies. This is *Death* conceived as a great cosmic force (*Rm* 8:38; *1 Co* 3:22), as a monarch who reigns over humanity (*Rm* 5:14, 17), as a hostile power, 'the last enemy' (*1 Co* 15:26), whose yoke Christ has shaken off in regard to himself through his Resurrection (*Rm* 6:9) and for his faithful too in advance (*1 Co* 15:54f). This Tyrant wants to establish his dominion over the whole man; over his body in the first place, and this is physical death, but over his soul too, by depriving him of the true Life which consists in peace with God. The first of these victories he acquired in the earthly Paradise (*Rm* 5:12ff) and he will not lose it again until the end of the world (*1 Co* 15:26). But this does not apply to the second, the conquest of the soul, which has to be renewed endlessly, in each individual case. But to make certain of this conquest, as previously in the subjection of the body, Death absolutely has to have the services of his ally, Sin. It is only through Sin that Death gets a grip on man, that it can wound him with its 'sting' τὸ δὲ κέντρον τοῦ θανάτου ἡ ἁμαρτία, *1 Co* 15:56)[1]. Sin is Death's indispensable accomplice, who introduces him into the world (*Rm* 5:12) and into the individual soul (7:13) and is his middleman (7:5); and this complicity is reciprocated, since Sin is no less inseparable from Death: it is through Death that Sin reigns (*Rm* 5:21); Death is the normal end of Sin (6:21), the 'wage' paid by Sin to its victim (6:23), and to submit to the slavery of the one is to become the slave of the other (6:16).

This dramatic picture – which merely resumes the exact mode of expression adopted by St Paul – is based on the legal principle that sins merit punishment, and that this punishment is death: this is the order of divine justice, τὸ δικαίωμα (*Rm* 1:32). And this gives us the essential clue to the part which the Law takes on in this matter[2]. Man

---

[1] Cf. L. SCHMID, *Theol. Wört.*, III, 667, 4–30.
[2] Cf. GRUNDMANN, *Theol. Wört.*, I, 313, 27ff and *ZNW*, XXXII (1933), p. 57f.

can incur this punishment only if his sin is formal and mortal, that is, only if it is performed in conscious opposition to God and his command; it is necessary for man to know the rights of God and his δικαίωμα condemning their infringement (*Rm* 1:19ff and 32). This was the case in the earthly Paradise, where the ἐντολή was laid down under pain of death (*Gn* 2:17). In the period which followed, during which man lived without law, he did not have the necessary knowledge and his sins were neither formal nor mortal, as we have seen[1]. But when the Law was given (7:7ff), and with it the knowledge which brought ἁμαρτία to life, it also brought back in force the penalty of death. If man dies, it is because the 'sting' of death has regained its deadly venom thanks to the Law and the moral knowledge it brings: τὸ δὲ κέντρον τοῦ θανάτου ἡ ἁμαρτία, ἡ δὲ δύναμις τῆς ἁμαρτίας ὁ νόμος (*1 Co* 15:56). It is fully understood that of itself the Law does not kill; this false and blasphemous conclusion is strongly rejected by St Paul (v. 13). Nevertheless it is the necessary intermediary without which Sin would not have come to life again and been able to kill. The Law does not have a principal causality in the death of the sinner, but neither is it a mere occasion, quite accidental; it exercises a real instrumental causality. This can be seen in the expressions Paul uses: ἡ ἁμαρτία . . . δι' αὐτῆς (i.e. διὰ τῆς ἐντολῆς) ἀπέκτεινεν (v. 11); ἡ ἁμαρτία . . . διὰ τοῦ ἀγαθοῦ μοι κατεργαζομένη θάνατον (v. 13).

To the part therefore which the Law plays in giving moral knowledge there is added the part it plays in passing sentence of death. Not only does it teach man that his sin offends God and that his most inward covetousness is reprehended, but it also asserts that through these irregularities he becomes liable in law – and since he continues to commit them, it decides that he is liable in fact – to the sentence which abandons him to destruction, to separation from God. Or, to resume the dramatic style, the new character Νόμος, the teacher who enlightens and the judge who sentences, having informed man

---

[1] Paul is not unconscious of the fact that man could have an awakened and responsible moral conscience without being instructed by the Mosaic Law. The Hebrew before Moses, or the pagan at all times, can find sufficient light in his own conscience where the natural law is engraved (*Rm* 1:32, 2:14f). But this source of information is highly subjective and varies according to the individual, and falls outside this panoramic view of the objective stages of the history of salvation. The broad outlines of the picture Paul is drawing impose a certain schematisation on him. He is not denying these individual illuminations any more than he is ignoring the action of grace in the souls of the righteous, but he is abstracting from them so that he can draw the general situation better. By accepting hypothetically that before the Law it was impossible to sin either formally or mortally, he has shown up in strong relief the new element brought by the Law into the world – full responsibility and condemnation.

('Εγώ) and established that he continues just the same to do wrong, declares that man has willingly made himself the slave of 'Αμαρτία and delivers him into the hands of the latter and his partner Θάνατος. I have not returned to this scene for the pleasure of a piece of picturesque description which could very well be tiresome, but because it brings out much better the very real difference which exists between the Law as informing and the Law as condemning. If the subjective, experiential interpretation is maintained, these two points of view are almost fused: for man to learn that his fault offends God and for man to realise that his fault is threatened by punishment, are virtually one and the same thing. The one appears to be ordered to the other; the penalty serves only to show how serious the fault is. In the end, it is hardly thought of in any way except as threat, the sense of its reality is lost. And this is normal as long as one remains on the subjective level: this Death is not experienced. But the sinews of Paul's thought have been destroyed. For him, this Death is a reality, and by decreeing it the Law has struck a second blow, distinct from its first duty as informant, and much more grave. With this, the world has entered a new phase; after the period of irresponsible immorality, when man was the beneficiary of his own ignorance, comes the stern epoch of responsibility, condemnation and death.

We can understand now the full meaning of the expression which he applies to the Law, 'administering death' (διακονιά τοῦ θανάτου), 'administering condemnation' (διακονία τῆς κατακρίσεως) (2 Co 3:7, 9). When he says that 'the written letters bring death' (τὸ γὰρ γράμμα ἀποκτείνει, ibid., 6), this is not to be understood in the softened sense, which has unfortunately become traditional[1], that the Law taken materially, without spiritual discrimination, above all without the light which is thrown on it by its fulfilment in the New Covenant, is incapable of imparting life. It is to be understood rather in the strong sense that the Law, being only written, that is, an external rule, does not have the power to infuse the inward principle that would permit man to keep it, and can only make prohibitions and bring down the sentence of death on its now fatally culpable subject[2].

Vv. 14–25 describe the tragic situation which results for the latter.

---

[1] As early as St Ambrose; see Aug., Confessions, vi, 4.
[2] See the excellent remarks of SCHRENK, Theol. Wört., I, 765ff. Also BULTMANN, ibid., III, 16,4; BANDAS, op. cit., p. 118 – the ἀποκτείνει of this text corresponds therefore to the ἀπέκτεινεν of Rm 7:11 (contrary to B. WEISS, Comm., 1891, p. 309) with this difference alone that the instrumental cause figures as principal. Compare too this text with Ga 3:21, the Law, by its very nature, is unable ζωοποιῆσαι.

The wretched creature is as it were torn in two, forcibly detained, in his guilty half, his σάρξ, by the master Sin, to whom he has given himself and whose slave he has become, while through his νοῦς, which knows and accepts the Law, he realises that he is condemned and handed over to death. On him there weighs a κατάκριμα (8:1) which is added to that already drawn down by Adam's sin (5:16, 18) and reinforces it with all the weight of the 'transgressions' which the Law causes him to commit in the likeness of Adam's (cf. 5:14). This is a state of hopelessness[1] in which the definitive penalty has not yet been encountered (it is of the eschatological order), but appears no whit less inescapable, unless some providential turn of events comes and upsets things . . . And this is what happens in the person of Christ, as we learn from Paul's exclamation: 'Thanks to God through Jesus Christ our Saviour!' On the Cross the threatening κατάκριμα is going to be borne and its good effect will be released, destroying Sin and saving the sinner. This is what we are told in ch. 8, vv. 3–4.

But since the interpretation of this text is one of the most argued over and many exegetes refuse even to see it as referring to the death of Christ, it is preferable to examine first some other passages which deal indisputably with the sacrifice on Calvary and, in my opinion, present it as the carrying out of the sentence passed by the Law.

The first one to come to mind is surely *Ga* 3:13; 'Christ redeemed us from the curse of the Law by being cursed for our sake, since Scripture says: *Cursed be everyone who is hanged on a tree*'. The reference to the Cross is unmistakable. Dying upon the Cross, Christ bears the curse of the Law in our stead (ὑπὲρ ἡμῶν). It would be as useless as it is contrary to the text, to see in this a special curse laid by God on Christ, quite distinct from that of the Law. Nor will it suffice to suppose that the Law, conceived as a power hostile to God, is using this murderous curse to take vengeance on Him who has come to destroy its dominion[2]. There are other texts which assert too plainly that the initiative for this punishment comes from God himself (*Rm* 3:25; *2 Co* 5:19, 21). The obvious meaning therefore is that the Law, as a code of retributive justice established by God, finds in the person of Christ an opportunity to carry out the sentence of condemnation which it passes on the sinner, or, better still, on all those who live under its rule and count on it alone (*Ga* 3:10). For

---

[1] Deissmann (*Neue Bibelstudien*, p.92f) had brought out very well this suggestion of a state, of a penalty which is lasting and which is always binding; some papyri use the word κατάκριμα to refer to the 'servitude' with which a country is burdened.
[2] Cf. BÜCHSEL, *Theol. Wört.*, 1, 451.

this to happen it was necessary for Christ to become one of them, to submit to the yoke of the Law (γενόμενον ὑπὸ νόμον *Ga* 4:4) or rather to be placed beneath it by God: it is God who is pursuing his plan of salvation in the person of his Son, at the moment in the history of the world when he judges it suitable to inaugurate its third and last act: 'but when the appointed time came, God sent his Son, born of a woman, born a subject of the Law, to redeem the subjects of the Law' (*Ga* 4:4f). To redeem them from whom? Not from Satan, there is no question of that. Simply from the Law conceived as a person who, faithful to the stern mission given by God, keeps those who have infringed it bound fast by its demands for justice and reparation. The way in which God, himself just, brings this earlier dispensation to a close is by satisfying the requirement of punishment which he himself established[1]. This is, of course, only an image which fits in well with the dramatic scene we have already drawn attention to several times and which we risk over-weighting and falsifying as soon as we try to translate it into logical terms.

Another image is the χειρόγραφον of *Col* 2:14, which was outstanding against us and which Christ wiped out and suppressed by his Crucifixion. This is not a reference to the Law itself which, if this were the case, would be 'cancelled, nailed to the Cross'[2], or presented as a contract signed by the Israelites at Sinai. What is meant is again its sentence of condemnation here conceived as an IOU, a 'debit note'[3], which the Law brandishes in the face of its debtor as long as the latter has not settled his account. Under a different image it is in fact the same reality as the κατάρα of *Ga* 3:13 and the κατάκριμα of *Rm* 8:1[4]. By dying on the Cross, Christ pays off this debt and in strict justice 'cancels' the record, or, to use an even more realistic expression, nails it to the Cross in his own person[5]; he takes upon

---

[1] Büchsel (*ibid.*, I, 126ff) brings out very well the true nature of this 'activity of God with us in the history of salvation' (128, 1. 4f). The fundamental conception is 'an idea of representative punishment' (*ibid.*, 451, 1. 13). 'The claim of the law is satisfied' (127, 1.2).

[2] PRAT, *op. cit.*, I, 278; II, 275ff – against this is P. DE LA TAILLE, *RSR*, 1916, pp. 468ff.

[3] This is the translation of P. Huby (*Les Épîtres de la Captivité*, Paris, 1935 pp. 71ff) who, following P. de la Taille, takes τοῖς δόγμασιν as a dative of attribution (here of disadvantage): 'in place of the commandments', and not as a dative dependent on γεγραμμένον understood (Prat). In fact, *Col* 2:14 is not by any means identical with *Ep* 2:15 (ἐν δόγμασιν).

[4] Like the curse and the condemnation, this χειρόγραφον is the action of the Law, punishing its transgressor; the legend of Satan binding Adam to himself with a pact like this provides only a distant analogy (cf. MEGAS, *ZNW* XXVII (1928), pp. 305–20).

[5] This last image is inspired only by the fact of the Crucifixion; there is no reason

himself the payment of the χειρόγραφον just as he does the incurring of the κατάρα.

In *2 Co* 5:18–21, at any rate as far as the letter goes, the Law does not play a part in the sacrifice of Christ. But it is only necessary to look a little closer at the thought and even the expressions to see that it is there nevertheless. The διακονία τῆς καταλλαγῆς instinctively reminds us, by contrast, of the διακονία τοῦ θανάτου or τῆς κατακρίσεως which have been mentioned very shortly before (3:7, 9)[1]. μὴ λογιζόμενος αὐτοῖς τὰ παραπτώματα recalls the πάρεσις τῶν προγεγονότων ἁμαρτημάτων of *Rm* 3:25, which denotes that time under the Law when the condemnation had been incurred and sentence passed, but not yet rendered effective because God was waiting for the Victim who alone could undergo it in a way profitable for salvation. Lastly, for God to make Christ into ἁμαρτία for us, although we had committed no sin himself, comes to the same thing as saying that he placed him under the rule of the Law (ὑπὸ νόμον, *Ga* 4:4), since in point of fact this latter, in the history of salvation, had become the rule of ἁμαρτία (συνέκλεισεν ἡ γραφὴ τὰ πάντα ὑπὸ ἁμαρτίαν, *Ga* 3:22; and see *Rm* 6:14f).

If, having read these texts which are indisputably talking about the death of Christ, we return to *Rm* 8:3f, we shall be struck forcibly by the parallelism of the thought. Τὸ ἐξαπέστειλεν ὁ Θεὸς τὸν υἱὸν αὐτοῦ of *Ga* 4:4, there corresponds here ὁ Θεὸς τὸν ἑαυτοῦ υἱὸν πέμψας. Τὸ τὸν μὴ γνόντα ἁμαρτίαν ὑπὲρ ἡμῶν ἁμαρτίαν ἐποίησεν of *2 Co* 5:21 we now have corresponding ἐν ὁμοιώματι σαρκός ἁμαρτίας καὶ περὶ ἁμαρτίας. It seems therefore perfectly natural to pursue the similarity and to see in κατέκρινεν τὴν ἁμαρτίαν ἐν τῇ σαρκὶ a synonym in practice of the καταλλαγή which is brought about on the Cross (*2 Co* 5:18ff and *Col* 1:21f; cf. also *Ep* 2:16) and of the redemption effected by the bearing of the curse upon the tree (*Ga* 4:5 and 3:13). Many exegetes however take exception to this; some are hesitant and regard Paul's words as too uncertain[2]; others prefer deliberately to understand the condemnation of sin in the flesh as effected by Christ's life of innocence on earth[3]: he showed that it was possible, even while living in

to suppose, as used to be done, that contracts were annulled by being pierced; cf. DEISSMANN, *Licht vom Osten*, 4th ed. 1923, p. 283.
[1] Cf. *Ep* 2, 14ff, where the annulment of the Law by the death of Christ on the Cross brings about the reconciliation ἀποκαταλλάξῃ) not only of Jews and pagans with one another (v. 15) but also of both with the Father (v. 18).
[2] LIETZMANN, *loc. cit.*: 'Paul's words are not enough for a certain decision to be made'. Similarly BAUER (*Wört.*, c. 685), KUEMMEL, *op. cit.*, p. 72.
[3] Zahn (*Comm.*, 1910, p. 383) gives as his reason for adopting this solution the

the flesh of sin, to resist sin's tyranny and live free of any fault. This model which it is impossible to imitate makes a very odd kind of condemnation. It seems that in practice the force of ὁμοίωμα has been forgotten. It is however very strong. The assimilation of Christ to the sinner remains wholly external; it is perfectly valid even if it remains on an objective and juridical level; the innocent flesh of Christ can suffer the penalty in place of the guilty flesh as long as God has declared the substitution valid[1]. But if, as this exegesis does, you place yourself on the subjective, moral plane of resistance to sin, the 'likeness' loses all reality, and the innocence of Jesus remains the incommunicable privilege of his transcendent person[2].

An especial objection is based on the word πέμψας[3]. It is said to refer of itself only to the Incarnation, the coming of Christ on earth, and not his death, It would be possible to answer this somewhat pedantically by pointing to the grammatical character of this participle, the connotation of chronological priority and not of concomitant instrumentality. But this is not the real solution. What is wrong with this way of looking at it is that it forgets that in the primitive Christian catechesis Incarnation and Redemption make up one thing. The Son of God took human flesh only that he might die on the Cross. In the sermons in Acts, just as in the letters of Paul, there are no passages at all where the actions of the life of Christ are considered for their own sake and elaborated in their function as lessons or examples. At the very most a word will recall his miracles as a proof of his mission. But this mission was to die and rise again. Even in

supposed fact that in none or the numerous passages in which he speaks of the death of Christ does Paul consider it from the viewpoint of a condemnation by God. The texts which we have just examined hardly bear out this extraordinary assertion. It is enough if we do not forget that behind the verdict of the Law it is God who condemns or who curses. – Kuemmel (*op. cit.*, p. 72) writes in the contrary sense that the interpretation through the death of Christ 'undoubtedly corresponds . . . most closely to Paul's other ideas about redemption'.

[1] B. Weiss (*op. cit.*, p. 337) faces those who see the death of Christ here with some very real difficulties, which can be summed up in the crude formula of P. Prat (*op. cit.*, II, 196): this explanation 'implies the existence of sin in the flesh of Jesus, which formally contradicts 2 Co 5:21; it imputes to St Paul the absurdity that the death of the sinner destroys sin in himself and in others'. This objection has real force against many exegetes, because they have mistaken the indispensable part played by the Law in this condemnation. But from the moment that one perceives this, and the juridical substitution which allows its satisfaction, everything becomes clear and there is no difficulty in understanding it of the death of Christ.

[2] The objection of Weiss and others (see the preceding note) can therefore be turned to some extent against their own interpretation.

[3] Even Büchsel (*Theol. Wört.*, III, 953), who caught the implications of κατέκρινεν so well /see especially 11:26–31) does not dare to restrict it to the fact of the Cross, because of the too general sense of πέμψας.

the famous text of *Ph* 2:5ff, where Paul uses the obedience of Christ
to give his readers a moral lesson, he jumps straight away to the
supreme manifestation of that obedience, the death on the Cross.
This text offers us a new and striking parallel to *Ga* 4:4f and *Rm* 8:3;
in all three cases the descent of Christ to earth terminates immediately
at the Cross, without the attention's pausing on any of the intervening
stages of the hidden and the public life: γενόμενον ὑπὸ νόμον¹ is
followed immediately by ἵνα... ἐξαγοράσῃ, which as I have said takes
place on the Cross (cf. *Ga* 3:13); the 'emptying' by which he humbles
himself to the likeness to human nature (*Ph* 2:7; here, in a new form,
we find again the idea we have already met in τὸν μὴ γνόντα ἁμαρτίαν
κτλ. in *2 Co* 5:21 and in ἐν ὁμοιώματι σαρκὸς κτλ. in *Rm* 8:3) leads
him directly to the ultimate annihilation of the death on the Cross.

From this it seems clear that κατέκρινεν κτλ in *Rm* 8:3, which
follows on from πέμψας refers to the fact of the Cross and it would
be strange if, on this one occasion, Paul were to dwell on Christ's
life among us in a way in which he does nowhere else².

Once this is admitted, we can demand from this text the specific
teaching which it gives us more clearly than any other: the strict
connection between that death and the sentence passed by the Law.
It is suggested already by the verbal sequence of the context alone. In
the whole of ch. 7, the issue has been the rule of the Law, and v.4 has
already said expressly that the death of Christ delivers us from it;
this idea is going to be taken up again in 8:1ff. And this sequence is
manifested in the linking of the words: the κατάκριμα of v. 1 is
answered by the κατέκρινεν of v. 3. The Law condemned the sinner.
God condemns Sin in the flesh of his Son. Between these two facts,
the sentence and the execution, there is a close relation, the key to
which is given by the words τὸ γὰρ ἀδύνατον τοῦ νόμου, ἐν ᾧ ἠσθένει
διὰ τῆς σαρκός. How is this?

The grammatical construction of v. 3 is somewhat rough and it
is possible to debate the nominative or accusative absolute which

¹ We can be quite sure that Christ, born under the Law, observed it 'from his
birth onwards, in the circumcision, the presentation in the Temple, the annual
pilgrimage, etc.,' /PRAT, *op. cit.*, II, p. 192). But it seems quite as certain that Paul
is not thinking directly of this in the present text.
² In these different texts there is to be found the same linking together of certain
essential and identical ideas. It is possible even to sense the presence of a quasi-
official catechetical schema, accepted by the earliest Christian preachers. If
one absorbs its structure such as it emerges from the text of *Ga*, *2 Co* and *Ph*
and then goes back to that of *Rm*, it seems to me that the similarity is inescapable.
It too describes the coming of Christ in the flesh in order in it to suffer the redemptive death.

occurs at the beginning, or the active or passive sense of ἀδύνατον. This matters little to us now. The overall sense of the thought is plain: what the Law could not do God has done . . . But what is it that the Law could not do? We are referred back to 7:14–25; it could not prevent sin from reigning in the flesh; it gave an enlightenment which was received gratefully by the νοῦς (7:16, 22), but not the inward power which would have allowed it to subdue the rebellious σάρξ. Hence the interpretation of κατέκρινεν given above: God brought about a victory which was impossible for the Law in the person of his Son; perhaps πέμψας even hints at the principle of this victory – the sending of the πνεῦμα (Holtzmann).

This solution is coherent but weak. It is the logical and necessary consequence of the kind of exegesis we have been attacking in regard to ch. 7, an exegesis which understands everything on the subjective, experimental level, while all the time Paul is talking *heilgeschichtlich* and describing the stages of world-history marked out by the crises of the struggle betweeen the personified Powers who are fighting for dominion over man.

Let us look at things again from this point of view. At the end of 7:7–25, the Law has been shown to us as passing sentence of death on its transgressor. But – and this is of the greatest importance if we wish to understand the thought fully – this sentence does not as yet achieve its definitive effect. Man is spiritually dead, if you like, but not yet totally possessed by Death, whose true kingdom belongs to the eschatological order. To put it in cosmic terms, the coming of this kingdom would mean the new age which is to follow the end of this world, and the annihilation of the rebellious creature, or rather the eternal and definitive damnation of guilty humanity. But the Law does not carry out this sentence which it promulgates. It cannot do so, for two main reasons, which are connected with one another. The first is that it is merely a law and does not possess executive power; it announces, in the name of God, the punishment which is deserved, but only God can carry out this verdict. And this He will not do, because of a second imperfection in this instrument, the Law. Death, as demanded by this latter, would be a dead loss. It would restore the external order and satisfy the justice of God in the strict sense, but death would have no power to restore the sinner inwardly, to bring about the renewal of his being in a state of righteousness, his return to Life, in short any of those things willed by the δικαιοσύνη Θεοῦ in its wide sense of compassionate and saving justice. The Law is not only powerless to assist in the avoidance of evil, but it is also powerless to repair it in a manner that is useful and constructive. The Death which it decrees is a death which does not give life, and God will have nothing of it[1]. What then? He suspends the execution of the sentence: this is the πάρεσις τῶν προγεγονότων ἁμαρτημάτων of Rm 3:25. God waits until he himself has provided the Victim, whose divine nature, penetrated through with the πνεῦμα, alone will be able to cause Life to spring up out of Death. On the Cross Christ remedies the profoundest weakness of the Law. What the Law could not do (τὸ ἀδύνατον τοῦ νόμου) was to condemn sin *in the flesh*, σάρξ here standing for that part of man which is possessed by the tyrannical dominion of 'Αμαρτία. Against this σάρξ which shares in the quasi-spiritual, but demoniacal power of its master, the condemnation of the Law could do nothing; it reached the body but was unable to destroy the evil Power which ruled it (ἐν ᾧ ἠσθένει διὰ τῆς σαρκός)[2]; but the death of the Son of God destroyed the tyranny of 'Αμαρτία, condemning it in a way that was at last efficacious, on the very ground where it exercised its power (κατέκρινεν τὴν ἁμαρτίαν ἐν τῇ σαρκί).

It is possible to carry the exegesis of the text on in the same direction and to see in the δικαίωμα of v. 4 this sentence of death which the Law passed and which Christ fulfilled while at the same time giving it a

---

[1] As a matter of fact, the religion of the Old Testament and Judaism had a presentiment of this transformation of death-as-a-punishment into a penalty which would expiate for the sinner himself (Cf. G. F. MOORE, *Judaism*, 1927, I, 547f; BONSIRVEN, *Le Judaïsme palestinien au temps de Jésus-Christ*, Paris, 1935, II, 96.). Attention has been drawn to this doctrine especially in regard to a rabbinic axiom which Paul knew and appropriated (Cf. KUHN, *ZNW*, xxx (1931), pp. 305–10; SCHRENK, *Theol. Wört.*, II, 222). And it is to be found also behind the sacrifices of the old dispensation. But this conception arises rather from the whole system of worship and belief than from the Law as a principle of retribution, the aspect which was under formal consideration in Paul's controversies with contemporary Jews. And moreover these reparations are only negative and insufficient sketches: these animal victims could not really expiate human sins before divine justice (an idea which is developed in *Heb*); and if man himself dies, he quits the struggle of the moral life on this earth; the most his death can do is make amends for the past, it cannot give him a new life in which he will triumph over sin in the flesh, since it has destroyed both the sin and the sinner. Christ was needed in order that the impossible might be realised – a death which destroys sin, but which gives life to the sinner and makes him righteous, a beginning of the new, eschatological era, although the present era continues! – It remains true that Paul keeps to the line suggested by the old dispensation when he uses the old moulds to pour the new reality into: thus ἱλαστήριον and ἀπολύτρωσις in *Rm* 3:24, and the axiom in *Rm* 6:7, etc.

[2] In whatever way one understands the weakness of the Law, this διά with the genitive cannot be intended to convey instrumental causality; it is therefore in practice equivalent to διά with the accusative, 'because of the flesh'. Thus BAUER (*Dict.*), RADEMACHER, LIETZMANN. – One might also suggest the διά of circumstance as in *Rm* 2:27; *2 Co* 2:4.

saving efficaciousness which the Law could not expect from its own power alone? We would have here expressed in juridical form the same reality that κατάρα and χειρόγραφον expressed in imaginative terms. One hesitates, truth to tell, in face of the unanimity – or so I believe – of the exegetes who take this word as the equivalent of the plural δικαιώματα, the term which is classical in the Septuagint to designate the 'commandments' or prescriptions of the Law, a term which is also taken up in this sense in the New Testament (*Lk* 1:6; *Heb* 9:1, 10) and by Paul himself in this very epistle (2:26). The singular form would have been used in order to gather all these commandments into a global unity, and the sense would then be:- in consequence of Christ's victory over sin (v. 3), the commandments of the Law are henceforth to be fulfilled by the Christians, who live by the spirit, a thing which was impossible for the Jews, who lived according to the rebellious flesh and under the old dispensation (7:14–25). In however broad a sense this interpretation is upheld, it seems to be disputable enough; it does justice neither to the general sense of the context nor to the precise force of the words. The matter remains open and deserves at least to be looked at again.

First of all, the general sense of the context. In this epistle, and especially from the beginning of ch. 7, Paul is talking about and giving stronger reasons than anywhere else for the abolition of the Law. He analyses the faults of the system in the most specific way and concludes by rejecting it. Christ has delivered us from it in order to establish us in the liberty of the Spirit. And now the end of this liberation, the purpose (ἵνα) of Christ's work, is that the Law should at last be accomplished – by Christians! It is, to say the least, a little odd. Certainly the exegetes add that it is a question only of the moral precepts of the Law which are always in force. And this restriction would in fact be inevitable although Paul does not state it explicitly. It is obvious too on the other hand that the dispensation of grace established by Christ also implies obedience to a law, the accomplishment of good works (cf. *Ep* 2:10); it is not we who deny this; we notice instead with interest that the Protestant commentators accept it here without hesitation, obliged as they believe themselves to be to recognise this truth in v. 4. But if the idea is legitimate in itself, the way in which it is formulated is still surprising. When, in 6:15ff, Paul wanted to combat the danger of a Christian licentiousness by insisting on the character of 'service' and 'obedience' which the Christian life must preserve, he used some very strong expressions –

he even felt the need to apologise for them in v. 19 – but he did not think of reminding his reader's consciences of the δικαιώματα τοῦ νόμου[1].

It is not enough for the sense to appear unexpected for one to be able to reject it. But do the words themselves render it inevitable? It is treating the singular too lightly if one takes it merely as a collective noun, without any special connotations. If Paul prefers it to the plural, might this not be because he wants to revert from the accepted, stereotyped meaning of the latter and return to the first, formal meaning of the term? Support for this comes from the discovery of three earlier texts in *Rm* (1:32; 5:16, 16) not one of which favours the translation by 'commandments'[2]; it is true that they do not include the words τοῦ νόμου, nevertheless they merit consideration since that can throw light on the meaning of 8:4. In 1:32, the δικαίωμα τοῦ θεοῦ is the decision by which God the Legislator attaches the penalty of death to certain crimes committed by pagans. It is in fact the verdict of the natural law, in so far as it issues from God the creator and is known to the human conscience. It is a verdict of condemnation and punishment whose object is death[3]. Surely exactly the same meaning can be postulated for 8:4, with this difference alone that in this case the verdict is pronounced by the Mosaic Law (τοῦ νόμου) in conformity with the whole development of 7:7–25. Besides, there is nothing unusual about this meaning of δικαίωμα; on the contrary, it is plainly its first and fundamental sense, and expresses the essence of the Mosaic Law and its prescriptions – a juridical disposition which decrees what is right, demands its observation, and, if it has been injured, claims reparation. Analogies of this can be found in secular authors[4]. This demand for justice, proclaimed by the Law

[1] P. Prat expresses this very well (*op. cit.*, I, 278); 'The Mosaic Law must . . . disappear in its entirety, for Paul does not make the distinction, so familiar to us today, between the ceremonial and the moral law. For him the Law is a unity; it stands or falls in one piece. It can be established that, in his moral exhortations, he never appeals to the Mosaic Law. All he asks of it, and scarcely even that, is a simple confirmation; he can sometimes quote it as revelation, but not as a binding code.' It is to be regretted then that this author (II, 195) compromises with the traditional exegesis: 'The effect of this condemnation is to allow us to fulfil the precepts of the Law'.

[2] Of the five occasions on which Paul uses δικαίωμα (*Rm* 1:32; 2:26; 5:16, 18; 8:4), four therefore are in the singular and only one in the plural, 2:26, when it is used in the classical sense of the Septuagint. The singular is found nowhere else in the N.T. This fact alone is significant and invites us to treat the nuance proper to Paul's thought with respect.

[3] Cf. SCHRENK, *Theol. Wört.*, II, 225, 15ff.

[4] PLATO, *Laws*, IX, 864e, envisaging the case of a crime accompanied by extenuating circumstances (sickness, age, youth . . .), demands reparation for

and satisfied by Christ through his death, is in the end identical with its condemnation, the κατάκριμα of v. 1. But this identification seems to give rise to a serious objection: κατάκριμα and δικαίωμα are surely opposed as contraries in 5:16. Indeed, but this new text is going to throw a valuable light on ours. First, the fact of their opposition alone shows that the two words belong to the same class of ideas, legal sentences passed by God on humanity; the one, a sentence of condemnation in consequence of the fall of Adam, the other, a verdict of acquittal in virtue of the work of Christ. But there is more. These two sentences are opposed in their effects on man, but they are united in the person of God who pronounces them. If from condemning he turns to acquitting and justifying, this is precisely because Christ has intervened. In the history of salvation, these are two stages whose meeting-point – whose turning-point, rather – is the Cross. This is exactly the same line of thought as that in 8:1–4, as we have tried to unfold it. Thanks to Christ, the powerless and inefficacious condemnation of the Law has been transfigured into a penalty which restores Life. Thanks to the fact of v. 3, the κατάκριμα of v. 1 becomes the δικαίωμα of v. 4. They are separated by the enormous fact of the Cross. There is no question then of admitting for a single moment that the sentence of the Law had any power of itself to effect salvation. The Law's verdict by itself remains a dead letter which can neither destroy sin effectively in the flesh (v. 3), nor, in consequence, bring justification (*Ga* 3:21). But Christ took it upon himself and realised it in his own person: this is the meaning of 5:18, in which we see the *action* by which he has succeeded in arresting the course of divine justice[1]. From then on, in virtue of their mystical union with Christ through faith and baptism, the verdict is realism in Christians (πληρωθῇ ἐν ἡμῖν) in all the fullness with which it was endowed in the divine plan but which the Law could neither effect nor even conceive:

the damage done, but dispenses with τῶν ἄλλων δικαιωμάτων, i.e. the other punishments foreseen by the law. – It would be possible also to adduce, at least for the analogy of the fundamental sense, the way in which δικαίωμα is employed to designate the just claims put forward by an individual or a group to win respect for their rights or, if this is appropriate, to demand reparation (cf. SCHRENK, *loc. cit.*, a). Despite an attractive approximation to χειρόγραφον, it seems more difficult to attribute to δικαίωμα in 8,4, the concrete sense of 'legal document', 'documentary proof', which is met with frequently in the papyrus. The verb πληρωθῇ appears to oppose this.

[1] B. Weiss and Sanday-Headlam want to keep the same sense as in 5:16. The sense of 'Rechtstat' is acknowledged by many (Zahn, Cornély, Lagrange, Lietzmann, Bauer, Schrenk). But instead of seeing in it, with some critics, the whole righteous life of Christ, I prefer to restrict it to the fact of the Cross as in 8:3.

in them Ἁμαρτία has really been put to death, that is, its rule over them has been destroyed, as is shown by the conduct of their lives: they walk no longer according to the flesh but according to the spirit (τοῖς μὴ κατὰ σάρκα περιπατοῦσιν ἀλλὰ κατὰ πνεῦμα). Notice the passive πληρωθῇ and the preposition ἐν which governs ἡμῖν: these turns of speech are much less favourable to the subjective, experiential exegesis (i.e. that Christians now succeed, with the help of the πνεῦμα, in conquering sin in their own flesh) than they are to the objective, *heilsgeschichtlich* one: the Christians are the theatre in which is played out the third act of the drama, which has been set in motion by the reversal wrought by the Cross: the tyranny of Ἁμαρτία has disappeared from them, because the sentence of the well-informed but weak actor Νόμος which until then has not been satisfied has at last been carried out.

It is obvious enough that this interpretation does not tend to allow the Law and its specific procedure any force at all in the new dispensation of salvation. It has even less of this tendency, if I may dare to say so, than the customary exegesis of 8:4. Once it has been accomplished in the person of Christ, the δικαίωμα τοῦ νόμου has only to disappear. It is eliminated and put aside like its equivalent, the χειρόγραφον of *Col* 2:14. But this does not mean that it has been rejected as something which has revealed itself as useless, it is merely being abolished as something that has served its turn. The Law has been abrogated, Christ has rendered it useless (καταργεῖν, *2 Co* 3:11, 13, 14; cf. *Rm* 7:6), but this was by giving it satisfaction, by fulfilling its demand. He is the 'end of the Law' (*Rm* 10:4), not only because he has abolished it, but because he has fulfilled and achieved it. And on the other hand, if it has found its fulfilment, it follows that it no longer has force. Through the body of Christ (and our mystical union with him) we are 'dead to the Law' (*Rm* 7:4). It is to be regretted that the realism of such expressions is habitually ignored and softened down by exegetes. It is normally understood to mean that, by the mere fact of our being mystically dead, the Law is no longer binding on us, in conformity with the rabbinic axiom of 6:7, and the secular example given in 7:1-3. But there is much more to it than this. The text of 6:7 applies to the death to sin; and the example in 7:1-3, is only an illustration[1], not a proof on which it is founded. The word

---

[1] We can compare it with a saying of Montesquieu (*Lettres persanes*, 76): 'I am obliged to follow the laws when I live under the laws. But when I no longer live under them, can they still bind me?'

ἐθανατώθητε 'you have been put to death' recalls the putting to death of Christ himself, in which we participate; Christ is the first to die to the Law by undergoing its sentence; in union with him we have undergone the same sentence and the same death[1]. This idea finds a clear commentary in the text of *Ga* 2:19; through his crucifixion with Christ (Χριστῷ συνεσταύρωμαι), the Christian dies *to* the Law *through* the Law (ἐγὼ γὰρ διὰ νόμου νόμῳ ἀπέθανον)[2].

From this study of the texts we can isolate some reflections which will complete our analysis of the original character of the conception of the role of the Law, proper to St Paul. The spirit which inspires it from end to end is to maintain the holiness of God's design and his goodness as manifested everywhere in his works. The Law in itself was good; if in fact it became a power of harm towards man, this was the fault of the latter; and besides, even in this it remained good. God demonstrated this by making use of the condemnation to produce salvation from it[3].

Paul, then, would not have admitted that from its very origin the Law was a yoke it was impossible to bear, which God had imposed on man in order to crush him. This romantic notion of certain modern exegetes does not do justice to God and ignores the holiness produced by the Old Testament. But neither would Paul have conceded that the Law by itself could give Life, as was thought by the Jews of his own time. In brief, he took it for what it really is, a code of retributive justice, neutral and objective, as ready to reward as to punish, and which ought to have favoured goodness, if one was wise enough to demand that only from it and to look elsewhere, in aid from above,

---

[1] Similarly in 7:6, we are exonerated (κατηργήθημεν) from the Law *because* we are dead to the Law: in fact, we should understand τῷ νόμῳ (or τούτῳ referring to it) after ἀποθανόντες it was by the Law that we were held bound, in a slavery linked to that of sin (*Ga* 3:22).

[2] This death to the Law is of the same order as the death to Sin, in that the two tyrannies are historically associated. With *Ga* 2:19, we may compare the two analogous texts of *Rm* 6:11 and 8:10, on the death of the Christian *to* sin (νεκρούς... τῇ ἁμαρτίᾳ) and *through* sin (τὸ μὲν σῶμα νεκρόν διὰ ἁμαρτίαν). In this latter text it is customary to see the natural death to which the body had been subject since Adam's sin. But the text has νεκρόν and not θνητόν as in v. 11. Is it not possible here again to understand that our body is mystically dead to sin in union with that of Christ (Lietzmann)? σῶμα would have been substituted for σάρξ because, once ἁμαρτία has been destroyed, one can no longer talk about σάρξ which of itself connotes the presence of that tyrant; σῶμα is a neutral term without moral overtones. – Notice should also be taken of the difference between διὰ τὴν ἁμαρτίαν and the διὰ νόμου of *Ga* 2:19; sin was the cause of the death of Christ but not the instrument of it as was the Law.

[3] Rightly has it been said that 7:7ff represents a defence of the Law rather than a prosecution. Cf. KUEMMEL, *op. cit.*, p. 9.

for the inward power to accomplish its commandments. We too often forget the presence of grace in the Old Testament and are apt to judge the old dispensation in the light of the later Judaism which had vitiated everything with its belief that it was possible to keep the Law by human effort alone. This is not Paul's way of talking about the Law, when he considers it according to its proper limits and playing that beneficial role it had in the primary intention of the Lawgiver. He does not claim to have achieved an impossible feat when he declares that previously he was faultless before the Law (*Ph* 3 : 6). And when he speaks of the just judgement of God, rendering to each according to his works (*Rm* 2 : 6), when he promises life to those who do good (*Rm* 7 : 10) and justice to those to fulfil the Law (7 : 13), this is not for the pleasure of indulging a hypothesis which is of itself unattainable, as Protestant exegesis habitually understands it. He is envisaging a very real possibility, but this is because he assumes the help of the divine grace without which, as he knows better than anyone, any good work is impossible[1]. Envisaged in this way, with the necessary and assumed complement of inward aid[2], the Law is no longer an infamous swindle and God is exonerated of the strange plot which is too easily attributed to him.

But it is true that, in its historical realisation, the system of the Law failed. This was the fault of the Jews who, instead of remaining faithful to the true tradition of the saints of the Old Covenant, ignored the need of divine help and looked for justification only from *their own* fulfilment of the Law, that is to say, in the final analysis, only from their own human efforts[3]. They truncated God's design and upset its equilibrium. By demanding from the Law what the Law by itself could not give, Life, they twisted this divine instrument. In the majority of his texts, Paul places himself on the level of his adversaries. When he repeats that 'no one can be justified . . . by keeping the Law' (*Rm* 3 : 20; *Ga* 2 : 16), he is speaking to men *who count on it alone*. This is why what was 'holy, just and good' in the intentions of God takes on such dark colours. Faithful to his historical view of the progress of the world, he talks about the Law such as

---

[1] This conviction is at the basis of everything he says about Abraham who was justified by faith before the coming of the Law and about the Promise which the intervening dispensation could not annul. At the basis of the Law and preceding it there is the will of God to lead man to true righteousness. This implies, of necessity and from the very beginning, the personal action of God, the help of his grace.
[2] Cf. PRAT, *op. cit.*, II, 123.
[3] Cf. BONSIRVEN, *op. cit.*, II, 24–6.

it has historically turned out, such as it is when misused by the Jews of his own time[1].

And besides, even then, he maintains that it does not injure the designs of God. It still plays its part, but this has become a terrible, because unilateral, one: now it can do nothing but condemn. Following its own implacable, objective logic of reward and punishment, it recoils on those who think that they can fulfil it by their own unaided efforts and awards their pretentions only what they deserve in reality, condemnation. 'Those who rely on the keeping of the Law are under a curse' (*Ga* 3:10). In their hands, the Law 'administers condemnation' and 'death'. The Law brings wrath (*Rm* 4:15). Man, by claiming a monopoly over it, has deprived it of the joy of bringing a blessing on him. But God can draw good from this curse, since his intention to save man remains and his plan must triumph.

The solution of the problem would be impossible to a Jew, always supposing that he was conscious of being in difficulties[2]. But the fact

---

[1] When he says that 'no one can be justified . . . . by keeping the Law' (*Rm* 2:20), he means, as do his adversaries, by that *alone*, and there is no contradiction there with 2:13, where he was speaking according to the intentions of God about a fulfilment of the Law which would not be an arrogant effort of Man by himself in the face of God.

[2] Did the Jew feel the need of a solution? Did he feel himself crushed under the yoke of condemnation? This has been suggested of Saul when a Pharisee, but it is not certain. To the degree to which, as a keen conscientious Jew, he believed himself faultless before the Law (*Ph* 3:6), he had no reason to think of its yoke as a curse. It is quite certain in any case that the great majority of his co-religionists rested happily and proudly on this Law which they flattered themselves they kept well enough, the goodness of which they were never tired of praising and which they thought of chiefly in its flattering aspect of a national privilege (Cf. BONSIRVEN, *op. cit.*, I, 302f.). To see it as 'administering condemnation' would have been for them impious and even unthinkable. Those among them however who were more religious and more sincere felt some disquiet when they saw it, fundamentally, somewhat badly observed, especially in what concerned its most inward and most important commandments; and they experienced considerable anguish at the thought of the condemnation which was waiting for so many transgressors, even among their own brethen. Too religious to reassure themselves with a presumptuous (*Rm* 2:4) and even insolent (3:5, 7) confidence in the election of Israel, they had to admit to themselves that justice would be done on the day of judgement and that it would be the Law itself that would accuse and condemn them. This is what we find in the authors who are nearly contemporary with Paul, the authors of the *Apocalypse of Baruch* and of *4 Esdras*. Cf. the *Syriac Apoc. of Bar.*, XV, 5f: 'It is true that man would not have known my judgement, if he had not received the Law and if I had not given him enlightened instruction on it. Now however since he has transgressed it knowingly, he must also undergo knowingly a penalty.' There is a striking parallel here with the ideas we have found in St Paul on the double function of the Law; moral information and judgement. *Ibid.*, XLVIII, 47: ' . . . thy Law, which they have transgressed, shall punish them on thy day'. The eschatological framework of the thought implies clearly enough that this punishement is eternal death. The same sentiments are to be found in *4 Esd*, VII, 18–24, 72; VIII, 56–9. The parallel is the more striking in that in the bulk of the Jewish tradition in which the sequence

of Christ came to change the face of things. From his light Paul received this radically new truth, that, in the design of God and through the intervention of his Son, Life was to issue from Death. And this revelation transformed his whole view of the former dispensation. If he could say that the Law had been a system of condemnation and death, and that God willed it to be such, this was because he had come to realise that this condemnation and death were to be fulfilled at last in the person of Christ and, that in him and through his Resurrection, they were to be transformed into a source of Grace and Life.

Hence those bold expressions which strike us with such force. It would be weakening the ἵνα of *Rm* 5:20; 7:13; *Ga* 3:22 (cf. too τῶν παραβάσεων χάριν of *Ga* 3:19) to take it as merely a Semitic turn of speech, denoting a consequence which God did not intend but to which he resigned himself. It does indeed express purpose and mark the divine intention. In producing this two-edged sword, which is what a retributive system is, God could not *not* intend the sentence of condemnation which is one of the possible solutions. But this was because he was waiting for the day when by making it effective he would also make it serve his purposes. Through the Cross, the condemnation of the Law would achieve its proper effect: the abolition of sin. Life would spring up out of death. But this was because a new character, the hero of the drama, would have appeared on the scene – Jesus Christ – and in him the plot would be unravelled and the whole design of God realised and achieved.

Death leading to life, punishment becoming expiation, sterile destruction turning into fruitful purification, this is the dramatic

---

ἁμαρτία – θάνατος is a commonplace, the Law never appears as a link. And in addition, even in the authors of *Apoc. Bar.* and *4 Rsd.* their loyal acceptance of the formidable part the Law can play leaves them with a view of the divine plan radically different from that of Paul. They do not have the Cross to throw light on the riddle. The author of *4 Esd* is invited by the angel Uriel to shut his eyes to this mass-damnation and to forget a problem which is the concern only of the divine wisdom: let it suffice him to think of the happy fate of the elect, of whom he is one (VIII, 51, 55; IX, 13). In short, he is not to speak as though the Law had been defeated; any failure lies on the side of the individuals who have not observed it. It remains good and truly leads to goodness, as is proved by those Jews who like himself are faithful to it. This is in fact the best solution that could be found by a Jew who did not know Christ, and doubtless the solution held by Paul himself before his conversion. As long as the new Revelation had not arrived, bringing fresh light, a religious Jew had to hang desperately on to two convictions, first, that the Law could be observed and could bring life, always assuming the divine compassion which assists in the performance of good and pardons the inevitable failings, and second, that in the history of the world, therefore, the Law remains a step forward, a stage of higher justice.

reversal at the heart of the history of man's salvation, the stroke of genius and paradox which was discovered by the compassionate justice of God, the δικαιοσύνη θεοῦ in its full Old Testament sense[1], and which lies at the foundation of Paul's message. He took it from the revelation of Christ and even from that very first contact, on the Damascus road, when he learnt and understood that the Dead, cast out and crucified, had become the Living, in glory. All his contemplation is in line with this first revelation.

From then on the Cross appeared to him as the link which reunites two dispensations which of themselves are totally unlike. Because it brings death to Christ and to all those who are mystically united to him, it declares the legitimate demands of the old dispensation to have been holy. But because the Cross draws life from the old dispensation, it declares the latter to be outdated and opens a new era which can be called eschatological because it is beyond death. What the Law was holding in reserve for the end of the world and which was to have been the punishment of eternal death, has happened now on the Cross in a form in which the dead rise to eternal life.In the person of Christ all the redeemed have undergone the same condemnation in a fruitful way, a way which has destroyed Sin and the flesh of sin in them and substituted the Spirit that gives life. And God willed that this should take place in line with the old dispensation, by the carrying out in them of the just sentence pronounced by the Law in his name[2].

By looking at things in this way, Paul manages to find an admirable harmony in the progress of God's designs. But it is firmly understood that he is providing a retrospective explanation of the hidden fitness

---

[1] That is to say, not only a strict, legalistic justice, but also the will to save, faithfulness, truth, . . . that whole range of sentiments that God maintained towards the people with whom he had allied himself. Cf. SCHRENK, *Theol. Wört.*, II, 197.

[2] In reply to A. Schweitzer, for whom eschatological mysticism and juridical legalism are juxtaposed in St Paul as two incompatible systems, Grundmann (*Gesetz, Rechfertigung und Mystik bei Paulus* in *ZNW*, XXXII (1933), pp. 52–65) has shown very clearly that the unity of Pauline thought is founded on the idea of death, where the two systems are joined and knitted together. Although he does not always push this far enough and seems sometimes to see in the death of Christ and of Christians in him nothing more than a negative liberation from the Law, he has seen plainly that this death which delivers us from the Law is at the same time the death which the Law claimed as a punishment for sin; cf. pp. 62–5 and especially this extremely interesting passage with which he accompanies the quotation of *Ga* 2:19 (p. 63): 'The Law gave death the force of Law by passing a sentence of death on sinners. Paul died this death in dying together with Christ in baptism and this death was at the same time also a liberation from the Law'.

of God's plan, and not claiming to express metaphysical necessities[1]. It would be blasphemous to say that God *had* to satisfy his justice with a sacrifice before being able to give his grace; and it would be ridiculous to attribute an assertion of this kind to Paul. Nor must we give the instrumental causality of the Law in the death of Christ and in ours a real importance which does not belong to it. If St Paul envisages it in the way which I think we have discovered from the texts, this does not mean, once again, that he grants the old dispensation the least particle of active collaboration in the present gift of justice through faith in Christ. The whole outpouring of forgiveness, grace and Life that comes to us from the Cross is entirely and uniquely due to the Son of God. In other words, if we view it from the inward dynamics of the work of salvation, it is understood that the Law contributed nothing by itself. This we have affirmed already in regard to the old covenant; *a fortiori*, it applies to the new one. And to attribute to the Law the least part of the efficacity of the Cross would be to falsify the thought of Paul, who links the Cross firmly to the *condemnation* of the Law[2]. It is the contrary rather which is true. In brief, in order to give their true sense to these ideas of St Paul, and to this study which has attempted to bring them out, it is essential to remain resolutely on the level of a historical explanation of the work of salvation, seen from outside. Paul wanted to explain the relation of the old and the new dispensations, not as the juxtaposition of two mutually exclusive systems, but as the linking of two economies by a central act, in which the second is substituted for the first in an elevation of infinite significance. This anxiety to preserve continuity in God's plan is shown in many a passage: 'Christ died for our sins *in accordance with the scriptures*' (κατὰ τὰς γραφάς, *1 Co* 15:3). And elsewhere: 'Do we mean that faith makes the Law pointless? Not at all: we are giving the Law its true value' (νόμον ἱστάνομεν, *Rm* 3:31)[3].

[1] Cf. BÜCHSEL, *Theol. Wört.*, I, 451, 1. 34ff.

[2] The classical opposition between the dispensation of the 'Law' and 'Faith' remains unscathed. They are two irreducible principles which do not belong to the same order. But their historical conjunction is a fact; it must never be forgotten that the Christian faith is faith *in Christ crucified*, and we have seen that Christ was crucified under the exigencies of the Law.

[3] This is usually meant to mean the Law in the wide sense, i.e. the Scriptures, whose 'true value' then is that they announce beforehand the new justice through faith (ch. 4). But it is possible to see more in these words: this new justice through faith in Christ crucified (cf. v. 25, where διὰ πίστεως is closely framed by ἱλαστήριον and ἐν τῷ αὐτοῦ αἵματι) gives the Law, for the first and last time, its true value as a useful remedy against sin, for life. 'Ιστάνω means more than merely 'to conform', it means 'stand upright', 'establish on a proper basis', here 'give value' as Bauer translates it (*Dict:* zur Geltung bringen), referring the reader to *Gn* 26:3; 1 Macc 2,27.

Finally to say that Christ is our δικαιοσύνη (*1 Co* 1:30), that he is 'the end of the Law for the δικαιοσύνη of whoever believes' (*Rm* 10:4), and that we are δικαιοσύνη θεοῦ in him (*2 Co* 5:21), is, at one and the same time, to set him in opposition to the former instrument which was incapable of giving righteousness and to show that he has come to substitute himself for it in the service of the same great cause, that is, the divine plan of salvation for humanity. This is the idea expounded in the fundamental text, *Rm* 3:21-6[1] and resumed in a striking manner in *Rm* 15:8; Christ became 'the minister of the Circumcision' (διάκονος . . . περιτομῆς; cf. *Ga* 4:4, γενόμενον ὑπὸ νόμον) in order to serve the truth of God (ὑπὲρ ἀληθείας θεοῦ; ἀλήθεια plainly reproduces the idea of the δικαιοσύνη θεοῦ of *Rm* 3:21)[2] 'to carry out the promises made to the patriarchs'. It pleased God that his plan should work out in a smooth and continuous way. He did not go back on the dispensation of the Law which he had established himself and which in itself remained good and holy; he did not reject it by a mere act abolishing it; he willed that his Son should suppress it only by fulfilling it, that he should submit to it and its just demands in order to destroy them only by satisfying them. The Law died on the Cross – because Christ died to the Law and through the Law.

[1] *Rm* 3:21-6; the Justice of God (δικαιοσύνη θεοῦ vv. 21, 22, 26), that is, both his demand for justice in the strict sense, through punishment for sin, and his compassionate intention to save mankind, which was attested by the Law (v. 21b), but could not be usefully served by it and had to suspend prosecution (vv. 25c–26a), can now manifest itself without the Law (vv. 21a, 25b, 26b), thanks to the Victim which God has provided for himself, the sacrifice of whose blood, carried out in the manner of the expiations of the old cult (ἱλαστήριον) (v. 25) but now at last efficacious owing to the quality of the Victim, communicates inward and saving righteousness to those who unite themselves to it in faith (vv. 24, 25, 26d), At last God can both be just and justify (v. 26cd). The Sacrifice of Christ has satisfied once and for all the demand for outward justice which God had deposited in the Law, and at the same time it has brought the positive gift of life and inward justice which the latter was unable to give.
[2] 'Αλήθεια must be understood in the sense of אמת, which it is often used to translate in the Septuagint, alternating besides with δικαιοσύνη: in holding fast to his will to save, to the Promises and to the Covenant in which it is expressed, God shows himself faithful, true and just . . . Cf. SCHRENK, *Theol. Wört.*, II, 197 1.30 and 44f. BULTMANN, *ibid.*, I, 239, 5ff. Notice that in *Rm* 3:1-7, πίστις, ἀλήθεια and δικαιοσύνη are in practice synonymous in God.

2. 'We too groan inwardly as we wait for our bodies to be set free*
Romans 8:23

The textual tradition of *Rm* 8:23 is not particularly certain. Leaving aside the opening, which already shows a number of variants, I want here to examine the second part, in which Paul expresses the object of the expectation which makes Christians groan in unison with the whole of the creation sin has enslaved: υἱοθεσίαν ἀπεκδεχόμενου τὴν ἀπολύτρωσιν τοῦ σώματος ἡμῶν. Such at least is the text furnished by the bulk of tradition: A B C K L P and all the minuscules, Vg, Pesh, Syrhcl, Boh, Sah, Arm, and quoted by the majority of the Fathers, Origen, Methodius of Olympus, Ambrose, Diodorus of Tarsus, Chrysostom, Jerome, Augustine, Cyril of Alexandria and Theodoret[1].

There are however some witnesses who form a group on their own by omitting the word υἱοθεσίαν: these are the representatives of the so-called 'Western' text, that is, the Greek/Latin codices D G d g, the Liber comicus toletanus, Ambrosiaster[2], Pelagius[3] and Ephrem[4]. Although these witnesses are of considerable authority they have not succeeded in making their voices heard by the critics. In recent years however they have received the support of a new and important witness, the Chester-Beatty papyrus[5]. It might have been thought that this new vote would have led to a revision of the case. It has done

---

* A contribution to *Mélanges Jules Lebreton*, *RSR*, 1951/1952, pp. 267–80.
[1] Origen, *PG*, xiv, 1115f; Methodius, *GCS*, ed. Bonwetsch, p. 299; Amb., *Ep.* 35, *PL*, xvi, 1078 and 1081; Diod., cf. Staab, *Pauluskommentare*, p. 95; Chrys., *PG*, lx, 531; Jer., Vulgate, ed. Wordsworth-White; Aug., *PL*, xxxv, 2075f. and passim, the text is quoted more than twenty-five times in his works and always with *adoptionem;* Cyr. Alex., *PG*, lxxiv, 824; Theodoret, *PG*, lxxxii, 137.
[2] *PL*, xvii, 125.
[3] Ed. Souter (*Texts and Studies*, ix, 2), p. 66: *adoptionem filiorum* is omitted by only two manuscripts, though these are among the most important: cf. *Texts and Studies*, ix, 1, pp. 213, 245 and 343.
[4] St Ephrem Syrus, *Commentarii in Epistolas D. Pauli . . .* a Patribus Mekhitaristis translati, Venice, 1993; cf. J. Molitor, *Der Paulustext des Hl. Ephräm*, Rome, 1938, p. 14.
[5] The omission is a necessary conclusion from the normal length of the lines (ed. Saunders, p. 41):

nothing of the kind. The critics have resolutely rejected this reading of P[46] [1], even when they have not quite simply neglected to take it into consideration[2]. The word υἱοθεσίαν continues to figure in modern editions of the New Testament[3] as it did in older ones[4], and recent commentators[5] exert themselves to explain it as their predecessors did[6].

This attitude does not appear to me to be justified, and I want, in this note offered as homage to the great exegete and theologian J. Lebreton, to focus attention on the difficulties presented by this current interpretation and to draw the conclusion that, on this point as on several others, the 'Western' text has no doubt preserved the original text of St Paul.

Exegetes have always been well aware that the occurrence of υἱοθεσίαν in v. 23 creates a difficulty. A little earlier the Apostle has said that we have received the spirit of adoption and are now the children of God (vv. 14–16). How can he write, after that, that we are still waiting for adoption and that the desire for it makes us groan in a way similar to the whole of the rest of creation? The exegetes, from the earliest Fathers to the commentators of our own time, get themselves out of the difficulty by explaining that the word has a shade of meaning, different here from that in v. 15. There, what was meant was an incipient adoption, a first gift which could be lost; here it means a possession rendered stable and definitive by the entrance into beatitude. Or again, the gift we received with the Spirit, according to v. 15,

[εχοντες ημ]εις και αυτου εν εαυτοις στεναζο
[μεν απεκδ]εχομενοι την απολυτρωσ[ιν]
[του σωματος] ημων

[1] H. LIETZMANN, 'Zur Würdigung des Chester-Beatty Papyrus der Paulusbriefe', Sitzungsber. d. Pr. Ak. d. Wiss., Phil. – Hist. Klasse, 1934, xxv; Sonderausgabe, p. 6) qualifies this omission with 'certainly wrong'. Similarly, M.J. LAGRANGE, R. Bibl, 1934, p. 483.
[2] Thus H.C. HOSKIER, A Study of the Chester-Beatty Codex of the Pauline Epistles, in JThSt, xxxviii, 1937, pp. 148–63. A. DEBRUNNER, Über einiger Lesarten der Chester-Beatty Pappri des N. T. (Collectanea Neotestamentica, xi, 1974), p. 34f. occupies himself only with the first part of Rm 8:23, and comes to the conclusion that the reading of P[46] alone preserves the original text here.
[3] MERK, VOGELS, SOUTER, BOVER. The 17th edition of Nestle (Greek text) does not even mention P[46] in its apparatus criticus; cf. G. D. KILPATRICK, JThSt L, 1949, p. 16.
[4] TISCHENDORF, SODEN, WESTCOTT-HORT, HETZENAUER.
[5] SCHLATTER, HUBY, CERFAUX, VIARD.
[6] St THOMAS, CAJETAN, CORNELIUS A LAPIDE, TOLET, B. WEISS, SANDAY/HEADLAM, GODET, CORNELY, LIETZMANN, JÜLICHER, ZAHN, KUHN, LAGRANGE, BARTH, BARDENHEWER, SICKENBURGER. Cf. also BAUER (Wört. z. N.T.); ZORELL (Lex. Gr. N.T.); the Bible du Centenaire, note in loco; BULTMANN, Theologie des Neuen Testaments, I, p. 274; BONSIRVEN, L'Évangile de Paul, pp. 193f, 331.
PALLIS, To the Romans, p. 104, is the only exegete I know of who opts for the omission of υἱοθεσίαν; but he makes the unhelpful suggestion that in the original text its place was taken by ἐν ὑπομονῇ or δι' ὑπομονῆς.

was still imperfect, regarding as it did only the soul; we can still
desire its full achievement, its consummation in a perfect sonship
which would make its effects felt in the glorified and incorruptible
body. Or, lastly, the adoption in v. 15 was only a *legal act* which conferred a *right*; what we are waiting for in v. 23 is a *state* in which we
would in *fact* possess all the privileges this right assures us[1].

All of these explanations, which are only distinguished one from
another by different shades of meaning, express one and the same
fundamental doctrine, a doctrine which is excellent and upon which
doubt cannot be cast, that the state of a Christian's salvation is
imperfect and precarious as long as he has not yet departed from this
world of sin and entered into glory and thus received the perfect and
final diffusion of it. But I doubt whether they do full justice to the
letter of the text and in particular to the force of the term υἱοθεσία.

In itself, this term, which Paul, and only Paul among the New
Testament[2] writers, borrowed from the legal vocabulary of the
Graeco-Roman world[3], does not convey the idea of a state subject to
growth and fluctuation[4]. It is an action which initiates a state, it is
a legal step, which is unique and in itself definitive: one cannot be
more or less of a son, one is either or is not[5]. It is evident that there
are degrees in which one can fulfil the obligations this new title implies
and degrees in which one can share the benefits it brings; but this is
not the meaning of the word υἱοθεσία, which by itself essentially
denotes the initial step, the legal act by which one is adopted as the
'son' of someone else.

But, it will be objected, the divine adoption to which Paul applies
this term drawn from mere human language is a very special case

[1] The interpretations of the different exegetes can always in practice be reduced
to one or other of these. Origen however in one of the solutions he proposes
(*PG*, XIV, 1115) envisages the possibility of restricting ἡμεῖς καὶ αὐτοί to the
Apostles and the first disciples of Christ, who received the 'firstfruits of the Spirit';
and what they are then waiting for is to see those whom they evangelise also
come to adoption. This interpretation cannot be retained.
[2] The word does not appear in the Septuagint either.
[3] The word υἱοθεσία does not appear until the Hellenistic era. It is found in
numerous inscriptions which use the formula: X . . . son of Y . . ., καθ' υἱοθεσίαν δὲ
son of Z . . . (DEISSMANN, *Neue Bibelstudien*, p. 66f.). Two acts of adoption from
the 4th century A.D. have been preserved for us in the Papyrus: *P.Lips.* 28 (381
A.D.); *P. Oxy.* 1206 (335 A.D.).
[4] ZORELL, *Lex.Gr.N.T.*, proposes, in addition to the active sense of *adoptatio*,
adoptio, a passive sense, *status seu condicio eius qui adoptatus est, dignitas filii
adoptivi*, but he does not quote any text to support this sense, and I do not know
what he founds it upon.
[5] Some exegetes have felt this implication of υἱοθεσία and tried to respect it. Thus
SANDAY/HEADLAM: 'Here (v. 23) υἱοθεσία = the manifested, realised, act of
adoption – its public promulgation'.

which cannot be confined in our earthly categories. This is true; and it will be opportune here to make some observations and bring out more exactly what we mean.

One of the characteristics of Christian salvation, one which gives it a paradoxical look, is that it takes place at one and the same time on two levels – that of the eschatological world which has already been inaugurated by the resurrection of Christ and that of the old world which has been condemned by the Cross but which continues until the renewal of all things at the Parousia. In regard to one part of himself, man, regenerated through union with Christ, is already living on the plane of the eschatological world, and from this point of view his salvation is acquired, certain and definitive; but in regard to another part of his being, he is still living on the perishable level of the old world which is subject to sin and death, and on this score his salvation is still imperfect and can be lost. These two worlds meet and intersect in man, and the result is an intermediate state, with a wholly original 'amphibious' character in which is to be found the 'tension' proper to the Christian life. To describe these things, no longer from the objective viewpoint of world-history, but from the subjective angle of the Christian's life, we can establish as it were three different levels: (1) the mystical, that of his union with Christ through which he lives even now in the eschatological world; (2) The physical, that of his natural being and particularly of his body, which is not dead and risen but keeps him stuck in the old world of flux; (3) the moral, where the tension between the two preceding levels is realised and where he has to struggle to achieve little by little in his physical being what has already been achieved on the mystical plane: having died in Christ through baptism, he must still die each day, preparing and realising little by little that natural death which will sever his belonging to the old world, while waiting for the moment when the latter will be brought to an end by the end of time and he can belong to the eschatological world even in his physical being. Paul's thought moves ceaselessly from one of these planes to the other; this gives it its richness, but also makes it difficult to grasp in all its fullness.

Now the different concepts of Pauline theology do not belong equally to the different planes. 'Being in Christ', 'new creature', are ideas proper to the mystical plane; they express the bond with the risen Christ, which operates on the level of being, and which is of itself definitive, since God does not annihilate what he has created.

This is what is taught by theology when it says that the 'character' conferred by baptism cannot be lost. There are other ideas which belong to the physical level, such as 'glory'. Although it is often spoken of as an anticipation which is already possessed (*Rm* 8:30; *2 Co* 3:18), glory of itself belongs to the eschatological realm and will not be granted us until our physical being has quitted the present and entered the future world (*1 Th* 2:12; *2 Co* 4:17; *Rm* 8:18, 21; *Ph* 3:21; *Col* 3:4; *Ep* 1:18)[1]. Lastly there are some ideas which pertain to the moral level and for this reason take on the aspect of 'tension', of growth and instability which is proper to it. Thus 'salvation' can be considered as already acquired (*Ep* 2:5, 8) and yet still exists only in hope (*1 Th* 5:8f; *Rm* 8:24; cf. 5:9f; 13:11; *1 Co* 5:5), since it will be the result of a struggle which is being fought out at this moment and whose issue is uncertain (*Ph* 2:12; notice the present tense in *1 Co* 1:18; 15:2; *2 Co* 2:15).

On which of these levels does adoption operate? On the mystical, for sure. It stands beside the 'new creation' which gives us our 'being in Christ', since this adoption is the equivalent of a new birth (παλιγ-γενεσία says Tt 3:5). It is because we are united to the Son in baptism that we become sons ourselves. And just as the new being we receive in Christ can of itself neither be lost, lessened nor increased, in the same way this sonship is a new relationship contracted with God on the eschatological level which of itself can be neither revoked nor modified. A man has to grow from childhood to adulthood, for all that he is not any the less 'man' from his first moment; a son can grow into a more and more intimate relationship with his father and benefit more and more from the advantages such a relationship brings, but for all that he is no less a 'son' from the first moment of his birth or adoption. Similarly, the Christian has to develop the divine life in himself, he can even lose it; but this does not mean that he has been any the less a 'son of God' from the moment of his baptism, and this new dignity is of itself an immutable gift, since the divine will which is its source is immutable[2].

[1] This entry will be fully realised only when the soul is reunited to its risen body. Thus the eschatological 'glory' Paul speaks of concerns the body in particular and is reserved for the moment of the Parousia. In the intermediate state of the 'separated soul' already united to Christ, one can speak of glory after a fashion, but this glory is not yet consummated. In actual fact, St Paul who gives little in the way of explanation of the intermediate state – to the point where exegetes have been able to cast doubts on it – never uses glory in this incomplete and provisional sense.
[2] T. WHALING, 'Adoption', *Princeton Theological Review*, XXI, 1923), forcefully

The examination of the texts in which Paul calls us 'sons of God' and speaks of our 'adoption' fully confirms this way of looking at it. In vv. 14–17 of this ch. 8 of *Romans* and in the parallel passage in *Ga* 4:6, the Apostle asserts that we are 'sons of God' from the moment that we have received the Spirit of the Son; and it is at baptism, through faith, that this Spirit has been given us (*Ga* 3:26f), that is, at the moment at which we have entered into the 'new creation'. Before that, we were 'slaves' of the Law and in general of the στοιχεῖα τοῦ κόσμου, the principles which govern the old world. Through the coming of the Son and through what he did on the Cross, we have been redeemed from this slavery to be raised to the dignity of 'sons' (*Ga* 4:3–5)[1]. This title is indestructible, like that of the 'First-born' in whom we have been begotten and whose brethren we have become. We can of course fail to live as sons and turn back to our former masters, but we shall then be sons living in slavery, a state contrary to nature, the state of the baptised living in hostility to God (*Ga* 4:9)[2].

Adoption appears again in *Ep* 1:5, but it cannot be treated as 'eschatological'[3] there, unless by that one means the new world of salvation in its total extension, which begins with the work of Christ, and not in its final realisation, which will be accomplished at the

emphasises this fact. P. 229: 'The υἱοθεσία can know no repetition or additions or subtractions'. P. 230: Adoption 'gives us an indefectible title to the immutable and changeless love and grace of God the Father, which in the nature of the case cannot suffer change or less'. P. 232: In contrast to sanctification which is a process, adoption 'is *ipso facto* and essentially complete and perfect in the one act by which is gloriously given the *status* of a son, upon the basis of Christ's perfect filial obedience . . . It is evident that nothing can be added to this legal status of sonship, with its sublime corollaries of heirship to God and joint-heirship with Christ. There is nothing which can be added, and no subtraction can be made since this legal status rests upon the perfect obedience of God's own Son.' It is significant that in this article which deals with the theology of adoption there is no mention of *Rm* 8:23!

[1] *Ga* 4:5b is obviously speaking of the gift of adoption which resulted immediately from the work of Christ on the Cross, and it is incorrect to relate this text to *Rm* 8:23, as JÜLICHER does (*Die Schriften des N.T.*, ed. Joh. Weiss, II, 1908, p. 282) and to see in it 'The full glory of sons of God . . . the enjoyment of all rights as sons' which remains reserved for the future.

[2] Adoption appears also in *Rm* 9:4, among the privileges of the Jewish people. It is in virtue of its being the people chosen by God that Israel is called son by God in many passages of the Old Testament. This makes plain how adoption is an initial act which is valid in itself independently of the human defections which belie it in practice, because it is founded on the divine pleasure whose gifts are given without revocation (*Rm* 11:29). – The adoption granted under the New Covenant is only the perfect realisation of the imperfect one given under the Old, which was a preparation for it (HARNACK, *Texte und Untersuchungen*, XLII, 3: 1918, p. 103), and it is useless to look for the origin of this Christian idea in the mysteries of the Graeco-Roman world (DIETERICH, *Eine Mithrasliturgie*, 1903, pp. 134–56).

[3] Cf. Dom J. DUPONT, *Gnosis*, Louvain, 1949, p. 499 note.

Parousia. For it is to this level of its total extension that we are raised by the description of the plan of salvation as contemplated in the mind of God with which the epistle to the Ephesians begins. Just as our call to a life of holiness and love in his Presence (v. 4) applies to the whole of our life as saved and not merely to our blessedness in heaven, so the precise determination of the mode of this salvation by our adoption as sons does not apply only to a state which is to follow the glorious consummation, but concerns in a general way a whole condition of life which flows immediately from our being united to Christ.

The result of all this is that the act of our adoption in Christ cannot be the object of anxious expectation on our part, as it is usually suggested of v. 23. From the moment that Christians have been re-generated in Christ and received his Spirit, as Paul repeats in v. 23 itself, τὴν ἀπαρχὴν τοῦ πνεύματος ἔχοντες, they are sons and there can be no question of their groaning with desire for a divine gesture, the benefit of which they have had from the moment of their baptism and which does not have to be renewed, since it has placed them in a new and definitive condition.

What is it then that they are waiting for, groaning? It is simply and only the deliverance of their body: τὴν ἀπολύτρωσιν τοῦ σώματος ἡμῶν. For this is indeed a benefit which they do not yet possess. If we refer back to the categories proposed above, we can say that ἀπολύ-τρωσις taken by itself is an idea which emerges from the moral plane like that, for example, of 'salvation'. For this deliverance from a world which is hostile to God, that is, from the world of Satan, sin and death, is an operation which is realised little by little and with many vicissitudes during the period of struggle which separates the initial union with Christ from the final triumph through death and resur-rection. Acquired in principle and in a definitive way in the person of Christ who has triumphed over sin (*Rm* 3:24f; *1 Co* 1:30), this deliverance is granted from the beginning, and as an already present benefit, to the man who is united to Christ through baptism: God 'has taken us out of the power of darkness and created a place for us in the kingdom of the Son that he loves', and for this reason 'we gain' from the latter 'our freedom, the forgiveness of our sins' (*Col* 1:13f; cf. *Ep* 1:7).

But this deliverance is as yet granted only to one part of our being. Our body, and with it our whole natural and physical being, remains plunged for the time being in the old world in which it still has to live and from which it will have to be delivered in its turn. And for this reason ἀπολύτρωσις can be regarded equally as a future benefit which is not yet possessed. It is with this meaning in mind that Paul can speak of the 'day of deliverance' as an era still to come, for which we are prepared by the 'seal of the Spirit', but which we still have to wait for *Ep* 4:30). Similarly, in *Ep* 1:14, the 'freedom for those whom God has taken for his own' (ἀπολύτρωσιν τῆς περιποιήσεως) is presented as the last stage in the divine plan of salvation[1].

Our complete deliverance therefore depends on the ultimate deliverance of that part of us which still remained subject to the old world, our body, a deliverance which actually takes place on the physical level and which St Paul is clearly referring to when he adds τοῦ σώματος to τὴν ἀπολύτρωσιν[2]. Here we have in fact a benefit which is truly eschatological and not yet possessed and which is a more fitting object of our anxious expectations than the already acquired title of sons of God.

But in addition we only have to examine the immediate context to be convinced that ἀπολύτρωσις τοῦ σώματος alone is opposite here. The whole of the opening of this chapter, which describes 'the liberation of fallen man by the communication of the Spirit'[3], is devoted by St Paul to showing us how this liberation has already been made present in the Christian's soul by the substitution of the new principle, the Spirit, for the old one, the Flesh. From now on man is introduced into the order of salvation, that is, of 'Life and Justice' (v. 10). It is on this plane that he has received a spirit of adoption, that he is a son (vv. 14–16). But this mystical renewal has not accomplished everything for him; his body is already dead mystically (νεκρόν, v. 10), but he has to realise his death on the moral plane by struggling against the flesh, which is still active (vv. 12–13); finally, he remains doomed to natural death (θνητόν) and can only expect later the final victory on the physical plane through resurrection in the Spirit (v. 11)[4].

---

[1] Notice in *Ep* 1:14, the mention of the Spirit, ἀρραβὼν τῆς κληρονομίας ἡμῶν which brings this text still closer to *Rm* 8:23 and its perspective which is properly eschatological.

[2] Origen (*PG*, xxiv, 1116) and Ambrosiaster (*PL*, xvii, 126) suggest the σῶμα here should be understood as the Mystical Body, the Church. But this is certainly not the primary meaning of the text.

[3] A. FEUILLET, *RBibl*, 1950, p. 375ff.

[4] On the way in which the Holy Spirit acts even in the present age on the body of the Christian in order to prepare this victory, notably by means of the sacraments, cf. O. CULLMANN, *La délivrance anticipée du corps humain d'après le Nouveau Testament*, in *Mélanges offerts à Karl Barth*, pp. 31–40 (cf. *RBibl*, 1947, p. 156).

Child and therefore heir, he has to wait to receive his inheritance
until he reaches glory through suffering in union with Christ (v. 17)[1].
Then, and only then, on the physical plane of the renewal of the
entire Cosmos, will there take place that revelation of the sons of
God (vv. 18–19)[2] which will mean liberation from the yoke of sin
for the whole of creation (vv. 20–21). This 'revelation of the sons of
God' and this liberation from corruption, which all creatures including man himself are waiting for so painfully ,will not consist for the
latter in at last becoming a 'son of God'[3], but in seeing the disappear-
ance of the last layer of the corruption which veiled this great dignity
received at baptism and impeded its exercise: in brief, it will be the
departure of the human body from the world of corruption and its
entry in the world of glory[4].

As I have said, the traditional exegesis of v. 23 cannot fail to
recognise this manifestation of Pauline thinking. But it imposes a
regrettable dislocation on it when it preserves υἱοθεσίαν in the text,
since this word has then to be taken as the principal complement of
ἀπεκδεχόμενοι and τὴν ἀπολύτρωσιν τοῦ σώματος as added in apposition to explain it[5]. But this is to invert the order of their importance
and to dismiss into second place what manifestly should occupy first
place in this context, that is, the deliverance of the body. If Paul had

[1] Cf. Rv 21:7; ὁ νικῶν κληρονομήσει ταῦτα, καὶ ἔσομαι αὐτῷ Θεός καὶ αὐτὸς ἔσται
μοι υἱός.
[2] Cf. 1 Jn 3:2; ἀγαπητοί, νῦν τέκνα Θεοῦ ἐσμέν, καὶ οὔπω ἐφανερώθη τί ἐσόμεθα.
It is in this sense, the full flowering in glory of our quality of son, that it is
legitimate to link our case to that of Christ, constituted υἱὸς Θεοῦ ἐν δυνάμει at
the moment of his Resurrection (Rm 1:4); cf. B. WEISS, in Meyer's commentary,
1891, p. 368; HARNACK, Texte und Unters., XLII, 3, 1918, p. 103. But, just as the
words ἐν δυνάμει describe a new state of the natural sonship which Jesus already
possessed in virtue of his birth and its confirmation by the Messianic declaration
at his baptism (Mt 3:17 and par.), in the same way the 'glorious revelation' of
the sons of God that we are will only manifest in its full extension the quality we
received at the time of our baptism through an initial act of adoption which is
υἱοθεσία properly so called. To signify this full and glorious achievement of our
adoption, as many wish to understand it, the word υἱοθεσία in v. 23 ought to have
been accompanied by a qualification of the same as ἐν δυνάμει.
[3] Cf. Heb 2:10; we are sons before being glorified; and it is as sons that God
now corrects us (Heb 12:5–8).
[4] ἀπολύτρωσις τοῦ σώματος certainly does not mean that we want to be delivered
from our body. This interpretation, which the Bible du Centenaire puts forward
as another possible alternative, is absolutely contrary to Paul's thought, as it
is to all Judaeo-Christian thinking. 2 Co 5:8, cannot be adduced in its favour,
since the perspective of this passage (vv. 1–8) is quite different: there it is a question of the intermediate period which separates the individual death from the
final resurrection, a period when the soul has in effect to live 'naked', without
its body, while waiting for the cosmic renewal at the end of time of which Rm 8:
18–23 is talking. As for the cry of Rm 7:24, it is calling for liberation not from the
body, but from the law of death which is crushing it.
[5] Cf. BARDENHEWER, Der Römerbrief, 1926, p. 127: 'explanatory addition'.

wanted to say, as he is made to, that we are waiting for the deliverance of our body and *consequently* the full flowering of the state of
sonship which results from this, he ought to have expressed himself
in a different way.

From the point of view of style, too, the tenor of the text, whose
preservation, with υἱοθεσίαν, is such an object, is strange. I cannot
see any real parallels in St Paul which can justify it.[1] The absence of
the article in front of υἱοθεσίαν especially is abnormal[2]. If we agree
to suppress υἱοθεσίαν the style becomes natural and the thought is
excellent. One becomes convinced of this, in addition, when reading
the commentaries of those who, like Ambrosiaster, omit this word
or of those who, like St Augustine, keep it in their text all right, but
more often than not dispense themselves from alluding to it in their
commentary[3].

The secondary character of a variant reading is only really proved
when one can explain its origin. Can we see here any reasons which
will permit to justify the addition or the omission of υἱοθεσίαν?

It can certainly be said that the omission would be explained by
all the very objections on which we have been laying emphasis. A
copyist could very well have felt how jarring the word is in its immediate context and how it contradicts the assertion in v. 15, and
suppressed it for these reasons[4]. But one can imagine the opposite
happening with more likelihood: not understanding the profound

---

[1] Of the analogous cases quoted by E. PERCY, *Die Probleme der Kolosser- und
Epheserbrief*, 1946, p. 24, the five most striking ones (*Rm* 7:14, 12:1; 13:4;
1 Co 4:13; *2 Co* 5:1) are not completely similar. Moreover, in them, the second
member always plays the role of an explanation in apposition which, as we have
seen, cannot be played here by τὴν ἀπολύτρωσιν τοῦ σώματος. A little further on,
p. 53, note 54, Percy appears to think he can justify the order of the words in
Rm 8:23, by contrast with that in *Col* 1:14, with the reflection: 'The different
word order is clearly based on the unwieldy' ἀπεκδεχόμενου. I must admit that
this explanation remains obscure to me.
[2] ZAHN, *Der Brief des Paulus an die Römer*, 1910, p. 409, n. 25, claims, surprisingly,
that the absence of the article in front of υἱοθεσίαν means that the υἱοθεσία in
v. 15 must be considered the essential, the fundamental, one. On the contrary one
would expect the definite article to indicate the reference.
[3] Thus *PL*, xxxvi? 471; xxxvii, 1145, 1750, 1781; xli, 413, 683; xlii, 251;
xliv, 157. Often, the commentary or the context lay the stress explicitly on the
'deliverance of the body' and on it alone: *PL*, xxxvi, 398, 899f; xxxvii, 1826;
xl, 614; xlii, 864; xliv, 425, 433, 559, 561, 844. See also xxxvii, 1490; xl, 97,
where the word *adoptionem* is not even reproduced. It is rarer for the commentary
to take up the idea of adoption, and then it is in order to distinguish it from that
in v. 15 (*PL*, xliv, 591, 849) and to interpret it as an extension to the body of
the benefit of spiritual adoption: *PL*, xxxv, 2076; xxxvii, 1532; xl, 69. In
xxxviii, 350, the text is merely quoted among others which concern adoption.
[4] According to ZAHN, *loc. cit.*, it is the witnesses of the Western text who have
suppressed (*getilgt*) υἱοθεσίαν because 'obscure and unnecessary'.

significance of the 'deliverance of the body' in Pauline theology, a reader might have thought such an objective unworthy of the passionate expectation described by the Apostle and felt that he was doing a good job if he substituted a more important object, by adding 'adoption'.

However this may be, the word *is* omitted and by witnesses of considerable authority. It is one of the benefits of modern textual criticism to have modified the almost superstitious regard of earlier generations for the Alexandrian text, and to have recognised that the so-called Western text has often preserved excellent readings. It seems to me that we have an example of this here and that the omission of υἱοθεσίαν in the old 'Western'[1] tradition of *Rm* 8:23 deserves to receive a hearing at long last from the editors and interpreters of the New Testament.

[1] The instances of P[46] and Ephraem prove that in reality it comes from the East.

3. Body, Head and *Pleroma* in the Epistles of the Captivity[*]

The 'Body of Christ' is one of the major themes of the epistles of the captivity. It appears already in the earlier epistles, *1 Co* and *Rm*. This however is only in an episodic way, whereas in *Col* and *Ep* it occupies a central place. Moreover, in these latter writings, it is related to new themes, those of the 'Head' of the Body and of the 'Pleroma', which in their turn qualify and enrich it. The study of this complex of ideas is bound to lead us deep into the teaching of the epistles of the captivity and ultimately into the whole of Paul's teaching whose final development they represent[1].

The theme of the 'Body of Christ' poses two chief problems: (1) What is its origin? (2) Is it used in *Col* and *Ep* in a different way from that of the earlier epistles?

It is usual enough to look for the origin of this Pauline theme in the well-known classical figure in which the State is compared to a gigantic body the limbs of which are the citizens. The point of this Greek, and particularly Stoic, conception is to emphasise the unity of an organised society in the diversity of the individuals who make it up[2]. Paul would have had recourse to this to express the solidarity of all Christians in Christ. In this first application of the theme, which makes its appearance in *1 Co* 12:12–30 and *Rm* 12:4–5, it does

[*] First published in *R.Bibl*, 1956, pp. 5–44.
[1] The literature on this subject is immense. I shall quote recent works as far as it is opportune. But it would be endless, and profitless, to adduce the authorities for and against each exegetical option. – I regret that I have been unable to consult three important works: T. Schmidt, *Der Leib Christi* (Σῶμα Χριστοῦ). *Eine Untersuchung zum urchristlichen Gemeindegedanken*, Leipzig, 1919; A.E.J. Rawlinson, 'Corpus Christi', in *Mysterium Christi*, ed. G. K. Bell and A. Deismann, London, 1930, pp. 225–44; J.A.T. Robinson, *The Body: a study in Pauline Theology*, Chicago-London, 1952. – The ideas set out in this article already underlie the brief commentary which I provided for the Epistles of the Captivity in the *Bible de Jérusalem*, (separate fascicule), Paris, 1951, 2nd ed. 1953.
[2] See the texts assembled by A. Wikenhauser, *Die Kirche als der mystische Leib nach dem Apostel Paulus*, Münster, 1937, pp. 130–43, or by J. Dupont, *Gnosis. La connaissance religieuse dans les épîtres de saint Paul*, Louvain, 1949, pp. 435–8.

not amount to anything more than a metaphor illustrating the moral unity of Christians with Christ and with one another: it is a question still of 'one body in Christ', not of 'the body of Christ'. This second aspect emerges only in the epistles of the captivity to express a fresh point of view whose importance is immediately obvious: no longer a moral unity 'in Christ', but the real, physical unity of a Body which has become that 'of Christ', a Body of which he is the possessor, the essential part, the Head. Schlier, who takes things in this way[1], evidently requires a new factor to account for this notable change in Paul's thought. And this he believes he has found in the Gnostic myth of the heavenly *Anthropos*, the *Urmensch*, which in this and in other ways, would have exerted a profound influence on the author of the epistles of the captivity, who in his view is not Paul. Wikenhauser (*op. cit.*) reacting against Schlier asserts that *1 Co* and *Rm* already contain the theme of the 'Body of Christ', not merely that of a Body 'in Christ', and that an opposition therefore on this point cannot be established between the earlier epistles and those of the captivity. But when it is a matter of explaining the origin of this theme in Paul – which he says is 'mysterious' (*rätselhaft*) – he too, like Schlier and Käsemann[2], shows an inclination to look for it in the myth of the *Urmensch*. In reviewing Wikenhauser's work, I took up a position which I would no longer hold today[3]. Conceding to Schlier that the theme appears in *1 Co* and *Rm* still only as a metaphor, dependent on the classical figure, expressing the union of Christians 'in Christ', I proposed to explain its evolution into the theme of the 'Body of Christ' in *Col* and *Ep*, not by the recourse had by an author, other than Paul, to the Gnostic myth, but by the fusion, in Paul's own mind, of this secular image with one of his fundamental ideas, that of the mystical union of Christians with Christ. I conceived 'the idea of the Body of Christ' as 'a particular modality, later in time, of the idea of the mystical union of Christians with Christ, issuing from the conjunction of this idea with the secular analogy of the social group/human body' (*loc. cit.*, p. 118). Now, this point of view does not seem to me any longer to be tenable, for two principal reasons. On the one hand, I doubt whether Paul ever thought of a

---

[1] H. SCHLIER, *Christus und die Kirche in Epheserbrief*, Tübingen, 1930.
[2] E. KÄSEMANN, *Leib und Leib Christi*, Tübingen, 1933, in opposition to Schlier, maintains that the 'Body of Christ' theme of *Col* and *Ep* is already to be found on *1 Co* and *Rm*: but he draws the conclusion that this Pauline conception from the great epistles is already dependent on the Gnostic myth.
[3] *RBibl.*, 1938, pp. 115–19.

'mystical union' of the Christian with Christ other than under the form of a physical (sacramental) union of the body of the Christian with the individual body of Christ[1]. On the other hand, in consequence and in confirmation of this view, I think, with Wikenhauser and Käsemann and against Schlier, that the theme of the 'Body *of Christ*' is well and truly to be found in *1 Co* and *Rm*, just as much as in *Col* and *Ep*. And in so doing, I am of the opinion that this theme of the earlier epistles is substantially the same as in those of the captivity, although, in the latter, it receives a fresh modification from its fusion with new themes, which we shall study later; but I maintain that whether in its substance or in its modifications, this theme takes its origin from the most specifically Pauline ideas, without its having been necessary to have recourse to the Gnostic myth and without the classical figure of the 'social body' having added anything to it beyond mere literary presentation.

1. THE REALISM OF THE 'BODY OF CHRIST'

1. *The physical realism of our union with Christ.* – One of Paul's most fundamental ideas, as also of the primitive community in general, is certainly that of the union of Christians with Christ. It is by linking himself to Christ and his work of redemption that the sinner is justified, that he received salvation from God. One of the formulas most dear to Paul to express this primary conviction is ἐν Χριστῷ[2]. How does this union by which we live 'in Christ' come about? By faith in the first place, certainly, but also by baptism. The two things are inseparable, just as the spirit and the body are inseparable in man.

[1] In his article 'L'Église, Corps du Christ. Sens et provenance de l'expression chez saint Paul', *Science Religieuse, Travaux et Recherches* = *RSR*, XXXII, 1944, pp. 27–94), L. Malevez, S.J., kindly accepted my way of regarding it, while at the same time adding an important complement to provide a better explanation of the fate I assigned to the hellenistic metaphor of the 'body' in the evolution of the Pauline expressions (pp. 83ff.). My present position does justice to his criticism and takes it even further, by emphasising more strongly the physical realism of the 'body' and attributing less importance to the influence of the hellenistic figure. On my part, I would no longer speak of a 'fundamental Pauline intuition, perhaps anterior to the image of the body, and surely independent of it in its deepest sense; I mean that intuition in which Paul sees the faithful united to Christ and participating in his life' (p. 33), nor would I write: 'Without doubt, I repeat, Paul would never have thought of describing our identification with the Lord in terms of the body of Christ if he had not already known the hellenistic figure' (p. 92).
[2] E.PERCY, *Der Leib Christi* (Σῶμα Χριστοῦ) *in den paulinishen Homologoumena und Antilegomena*, Lund, 1942, sees clearly that the 'Body of Christ' theme has to be explained starting from the fundamental theme of Christians 'in Christ', conceived by the Apostle in an objective and very realistic way.

What Peter demands above all from the newly converted is to believe in Jesus and to be baptised in his name. This primary demand is common to all primitive Christianity, as the indispensable condition of participation in the salvation brought by the Cross. There can be no doubt that it was as essential for Paul as for all the Apostles (cf. Ac 19:1–6), even if he did refuse to give baptism himself *1 Co* 1:14–17); and his epistles, which represent his Catechesis and his Didaskalia, not his Kerygma, allow us on occasion to glimpse what a profound and realistic conception he had of Baptism as a means of attachment to Christ. In *Rm* 6:1–11, in particular, he describes how this rite plunges us into the death of Christ in order to make us share in the risen life. At the basis of this cardinal passage, there is a conception of salvation which has a physical realism that our modern way of thinking is too prone to soften down[1]. Sin cast us into death, not only of the soul, but also of the body, according to the anthropological monism which is of the essence of semitic and Biblical thought[2]. The return to the life of salvation cannot then consist in the freeing of the soul, liberated from the evil, tangible matter of the body, as Greek dualism, taken up later by the Gnostics, would have it; it demands on the contrary the re-establishment of human integrity

---

[1] This way of thinking is Greek in origin, stemming in particular from Platonism; it gives all its attention to the soul, to the detriment of the body, which it regards as the soul's instrument, or even prison, from which it would be much better if it were freed. This intellectualist attitude is clearly to be seen in the Lutheran conception of salvation which held sway among Protestants until quite recently; it has crept into the thought even of certain Catholic theologians or exegetes, in a more or less conscious fashion. Applied to the problem of the 'Body of Christ', it leads to the 'body' being regarded as a metaphor for the Church as an organised society; it is 'of Christ' in this sense that it is created and animated by the Spirit of Christ, without their being any reference to the physical body of the dead and risen Lord which is the channel through which the Spirit comes. This conception, strongly influenced by Deissmann's fluid 'pneumatic' Christ, is too much present in the work of Wikenhauser quoted above. Cf. PERCY, *op. cit.*, pp. 9–11.

[2] Our age has become aware again of this biblical anthropology, according to which the body is not a part of man opposed to the soul (Platonic dualism), but itself also signifies the whole man in his concrete reality as a living person. This anthropology is ordinarily Paul's; cf. KÄSEMANN, *op. cit.*, p. 118ff; W. GUTBROD, *Die Paulinische Anthropologie*, Stuttgart, 1934, p. 32ff; E. PERCY, *op. cit.*, pp. 11ff; R. BULTMANN, *Theologie des Neuen Testaments*, Tübingen, I (1948), pp. 189ff; L. MALEVEZ, *art. cit.*, pp. 84–6; H. MEHL–KOEHLEIN, *L'homme selon l'apôtre Paul*, Neuch9tel, 1951, p. 9ff; L. CERFAUX, *Le Christ dans la théologie de saint Paul*, Paris, 1951, p. 212ff; K. GROBEL, 'Σῶμα as "Self Person" in the Septuagin', in *Neutestamentliche Studien für Rudolf Bultmann* (Beih. z. *ZNW*, 21), Berlin, 1954, pp. 52–9. It will always be this biblical and Pauline sense that we shall be using in what follows when we speak of the personal 'body' of Christ and of the 'body' of the Christian, though it must always be understood that this body/person has as its basis the physical body and even emphasises this sensual (in the strict sense) aspect of man.

by the return of the body itself to life. In the progress of revelation, belief in a real immortality (the miserable survival in Sheol cannot deserve the name) was asserted only by the inclination towards belief in the resurrection of bodies[1]. Jesus, first, according to Paul, re-opened the way to salvation only by putting to death in his own person the 'body of Sin' which he had deigned to assume in obedience to the Father (*2 C.* 5:21; *Rm* 8:3), undergoing the just condemnation of the Law[2], and by giving it back life through the gift of the Spirit at the moment of this Resurrection (*Rm* 1:4). This 'spiritual', 'life-giving' body *1 Co* 15:44f) of the risen Christ is the vehicle of the regenerated life of salvation. It is by uniting himself to Christ, even to Christ's body, that the Christian 'will be modelled on the heavenly man' who is the risen Christ (*1 Co* 15:49)[3]. And it is through the rite of baptism, enlightened by faith, that this union of the body of the Christian to the body of Christ, through death and resurrection, is accomplished.

All this must be understood very realistically. In the same way that Paul does not for a moment dream of a merely 'spiritual' resurrection of Christ, but regards his 'spiritual' body as very real, with a reality which is still physical but transformed[4], so too it is of a real, physical union of the body of the Christian with the body of Christ that he is thinking as an essential condition of salvation. Certainly this 'physical' reality is of a very special, wholly new kind, belonging to an eschatological era which has already begun . . . while the former age still continues. Here we stumble against the 'paradox' which underlies the whole Christian message and which is so particularly striking in Paul. This paradox is expressed by the 'dialectical tension' between the indicative and the imperative: you are dead . . . die then! (*Col* 2:20 and 3:5); for me, life is Christ . . . may I come to the resurrection! (*Ph* 1:21 and 3:11). Truth to tell, the literary expression of this paradox varies from epistle to epistle. In *Rm* 6:1-11, we are indeed already dead (aorists in vv. 2, 3, 5, 6, 8), but the giving of life and especially the resurrection are benefits to come (futures in vv. 2, 5, 8)[5].

[1] Cf. *RBibl*, 1949, p. 177ff.   [2] Cf. *RBibl*, 1938, p. 492ff; see above, pp. 22ff.
[3] Cf. *2 Co* 5:1ff, where the eternal home, built by God and not made by the hand of man, which is in heaven and which it is a question of putting on (at the end of time), could very well refer to the risen body of Christ rather than to the glorious body of the individual Christian, conceived as in some manner pre-existing; cf. *Ph* 3:20-1 and *Col* 3:1-4. I owe this suggestion to M. l'Abbé Feuillet. The remarks of J. DUPONT, ΣΥΝ ΧΡΙΣΤΩ. *L'union avec le Christ suivant saint Paul*, Bruges, I (1952), p. 150, could perhaps be elaborated in this sense.
[4] Cf. *RBibl*, 1949, p. 180f.
[5] It does not seem correct with PERCY (*Der Leib Christi*, p. 26, n. 62, p. 31f;

In *Col* on the contrary (2:12f; 3:1) and in *Ep* (2:5f) this life and even this resurrection are accomplished facts (aorists). There is no contradiction here, simply divergent expressions of a thought which is at the bottom identical but governed by different circumstances[1]: in *Col* and *Ep* the struggle against the Colossian heresy has led Paul to lay the stress on the heavenly existence of Christ, above the cosmic Powers, in his final triumph, and the Christians who are united to him are *ipso facto* transported to heaven with him and find themselves even now risen from the dead, even now seated with him in heaven (*Ep* 2:6) and sharing his triumph over the Powers, whom they no longer have to serve. In brief, all we have here is a bolder expression of the Pauline paradox, which only pushes it to the limits of its own internal logic and whose authenticity as Paul's cannot be denied as long as we are willing to admit that the crisis at Colossae could have fertilised his thought and his language[2].

But there is indeed a paradox here. On the plane of the eschatological world, which has already begun in the person of Christ, our death to Sin, our life in Christ, have a sovereign reality; but the former world is to continue to the Parousia, and on that level a very different reality is only too perceptible – it is still necessary to die and the fullness of life is still only an object of hope! Now our human language is adapted to our world and becomes confused when it has to express things of an eschatological order. How is it to describe this 'hidden' (*Col* 3:3) reality, which is certain for faith, more certain than the reality of the reason, and which yet escapes us? It is here that the term 'mystical' has had a great success. And yet it is never used by St Paul. The expression 'Mystical Body', in particular, appears only at a late stage in theology, applied at first to the Eucharistic body and only later still, by a transposition which itself did not take place without divergencies, to the Church[3]. Today, when the word 'mystical' readily suggests religious phenomena of a different kind, it is possible to prefer a formulation which lends itself less to a mini-

---

Die Probleme der Kolosser- und Epheserbriefe, Lund, 1946, p. 110ff) to consider these futures as merely 'logical'.
[1] See the slightly different but analogous explanations in W.T. HAHN, *Das Mitsterben und Mitauferstehen mit Christus bei Paulus*, Gütersloh, 1937, pp. 38–42; P. LUNDBERG, *La typologie baptismale dans l'ancienne Église*, Uppsala, 1942, p. 212f; R. SCHNACKENBURG, *Das Heilsgeschehen bei der Taufe nach dem Apostel Paulus*, Munich, 1950, p. 66f., p. 198f.
[2] Cf. *RBibl*, 1937, p. 512f.
[3] Cf. H. DE LUBAC, 'Corpus Mysticum Étude sur l'origine et les premiers sens de l'expression', in *RSR*, XXIX, 1939, pp. 257–302; 429–80; XXX, 1940, pp. 4,–80; 191–226; *Corpus Mysticum. L'Eucharistie et "Église au Moyen Age*, Paris, 1944.

mising of the highly concrete reality which is at the foundations of our union with Christ. Certain writers would be willing to substitute 'Ecclesial Body'[1]. We must, however, recognise that ecclesiastical tradition has given the term 'Mystical Body' an exact and expressive power which has been sanctioned by a solemn document of the Magisterium[2].

In any case, it will be understood why it no longer appears to me to be legitimate to talk about a 'mystical union' of Christians with Christ, the idea of which would have been fertilised in Paul by the secular metaphor of the social body to give birth afterwards to the idea of the 'Body of Christ', It is the contrary which is true. Paul began with this conviction that salvation was brought about by the union of the body of the Christian with the dead and risen body of Christ, a union which is realised in the rite of baptism, and after that in the rite of the Eucharist, in the light of faith. Starting from this, the current metaphor of the social body, a unity yet multiple, appeared useful to illustrate the unity of Christians with one another which resulted from their common union with the same body of Christ, this being understood with a profundity and a realism quite different from any implications of the simple Stoic metaphor.

These remarks will permit us now to get a better perception of the genesis and of the deep and wholly original meaning of the expression 'Body of Christ' in St Paul. I believe that this expression always preserves a basic reference to the personal body of Jesus, that body which died and rose again and to which the Christian must be united in order to participate in salvation[3]. This individual glorified body

[1] Cf. Yves CONGAR, in *RSPT*, XXXI, 1947, p. 83, n. 2.
[2] The Encyclical *Mystici Corporis Christi* (*Acta Apostolicae Sedis*, XXXV, 1943, p. 221f.) emphasises the traditional force of the term 'Mystical Body' and the opportunity it gives to avoid erroneous conceptions which would make the Church either a merely 'physical' or a purely 'moral' body.
[3] The merit of throwing this into strong relief belongs to Percy, *op. cit.*: 'The community as a σῶμα ἄντον is therefore ultimately identical with Christ himself... The body of Christ, identified with the community, is therefore basically the body which died on the cross and rose on the third day' (p. 44). See also L.S. THORNTON, *The Common Life in the Body of Christ*, Westminster, 1944, pp. 298–303; L. CERFAUX, *La Théologie de l'Église suivant saint Paul*, 1948, pp. 204–15; 255–9; id., *Le Christ dans la théologie de saint Paul*, Paris, 1951, pp. 212–15; 253–5; 264–6; W. GOOSSEN, *L'Église Corps du Christ d'après saint Paul*, Paris, 1949, pp. 64–70. In their common work *Die Kirche im Epheserbriefe*, Münster, 1949, V. Warnach writes: 'The Church... is the body of Christ τὸ σῶμα αὐτοῦ in a real and concrete sense. It is the body of Christ which is pneumatically transfigured by the crucifixion and resurrection and which has attained the breadth and fullness to be able to include all believers as its members because of its pneumatic mode of being which is above time and space. This enables the members of that body to share with Christ in a personal, living community... The physical

in Paul's eyes represents the first fruits of the world of the resurrected (*1 Co* 15:20), and ultimately of the whole new Cosmos. In it is the καινὴ κτίσις (2 Co 5:17; Ga 6:15), the καινὸς ἄνθρωπος (Ep 4:24; cf. *Col* 3:10) who has replaced the 'old man' with his subjection to Sin (*Rm* 6:6; *Col* 3:9; *Ep* 4:2) and all the conflicts which tore him in two (*Ga* 3:28; 6:15; *Col* 3:11; *Ep* 2:15). From now on there is nothing but 'Christ, all in all' (*Col* 3:11). In place of all the 'shadows' of the former dispensation, there is now only one reality: the Body of Christ (*Col* 2:17)[1]. But, even if it never ceases to be the individual body which suffered on the Cross and emerged glorious from the Tomb, this 'Body of Christ' does not remain limited to the one historical individuality. From now on it gathers to itself all those who are united to it, by their very bodies, in the rite of baptism, and become its 'members'. It is extended, built up and developed to the point at which it embraces the whole Church and ultimately, in an indirect way, the whole Cosmos. We are going to see this become more and more explicit in the epistles of the captivity, one of whose most essential sources this doctrine represents. For the moment what matters is to have a clear perception of the powerful realism of this theme and the roots which it plunges into the most substantial soil in the Christian message as understood by St Paul.

We should also produce confirmation of these views. If they are correct, the theme of the 'Body of Christ' ought already to have all this fundamental richness in the first Pauline texts in which it appears. Is this the case? It seems so.

'body of flesh' was laid aside on the cross, or rather transformed into the pneumatic 'glorious body' (see *Col* 1:22; 2:11; *Phil* 3:21; *1 Cor* 15:44f.) and *the Church is now one (in Eph) with this body of the Redeemer which was sacrificed on the Cross and transfigured in heaven'* (p. 11f; cf. p. 37), and H. Schlier: 'The body of Christ on the cross and in heaven is different from the body of Christ in the Church only with regard to its mode of being. With regard to the being of its being, that body is the Church, which is the body of Christ on the cross and in heaven presenting itself through the Spirit'. (p. 88). It will be noticed that this thoroughgoing identification of the Mystical Body of Christ with his physical body is not the same as that identification of the Christian with Christ justly condemned by the Encyclical *Mystici Corporis Christi*.
[1] Paul here is playing on two meanings of the word σῶμα: (1) the metaphorical sense of 'reality' as opposed to 'appearances' (shadow), cf. PHILO, *De conf. ling.*, CW, par. 190; JOSEPHUS, *Jew. War*, II, par. 28; and (2) the Christian and Pauline sense of the risen body of Christ. The 'reality' of the new world which is opposed to the 'shadows' of the old one is 'The Body of Christ'. If Paul had had only the metaphorical sense of 'reality' he would have written τὸ δὲ σῶμα ὁ Χριστός. His way of expressing himself is elliptical and pregnant; it is equivalent to τὸ δὲ σῶμά εστιν τὸ σῶμα τοῦ Χριστοῦ. Cf. CERFAUX, *Théologie de l'Église*...2nd ed., p. 248, which quotes the translation of T. Schmidt: 'The body (the essential element) is the body of Christ'. (*Der Leib Christi*, p. 191ff.)

2. *The body of Christ in 1 Co and Rm.* The principal texts as we have
said are *1 Co* 12:12–30 and *Rm* 12:4–5. But the theme is already
touched on and presupposed in two earlier passages of *1 Co*, which
are all the more valuable in that they do not develop it for its own
sake, but allude to it in passing as a well-known idea.

In *1 Co* 6:12–20, Paul is giving a warning against profaning the
body with fornication. To do this, he reminds the Christian that his
body has been made sacred by the work of Christ. This body, formerly the slave of sin, has been 'bought and paid for'[1] by a new master,
Christ (v. 20); from that moment it is devoted to the Lord, not to
fornication (v. 13); it will be raised by God like the Lord's (v. 14); it
is the temple of the Holy Spirit now (v. 19); it is a 'member of Christ'
(v. 15). This last expression clearly suggests the theme of the 'Body
of Christ' (cf. 12:12 *infra*) and proves that it is already present in
Paul's mind although it appears here for the first time. The context
in which it appears throws a remarkable light on its origin and its
realism. Its origin – if Christians are 'members' of Christ, it is because
their body[2] is united to his by communion with his death, which has
redemmed them (cf. 7:23; *Ga* 3:13; 4:5), and with his resurrection,
a sure pledge of which they have in the presence of the Spirit who
already sanctifies them (*Rm* 8:11, 23)[3]. Its realism – it is certainly a
very real, physical union, since it can be compared and contrasted
with the sexual union which fuses two bodies in one flesh! Of course
Paul emphasises the difference by saying that the Christian makes
'one spirit' with the Lord (v. 17); but this opposition of the Spirit,
the life-principle of the new world, to the Flesh, the sin-principle of
the old world, takes nothing away from the physical realism of the
Body ($\sigma\tilde{\omega}\mu\alpha$) which is with the $\nu o \tilde{\upsilon} \varsigma$ the neutral terrain on which these
two principles fight it out[4]. This Spirit is not disincarnate, it is the

---

[1] Osty's translation: i.e. 'cash down', for ready money, and not as in the Vulgate
'for a high price'.

[2] If Paul uses the word 'bodies' here to describe Christians, this could be 'for
the needs of the argument' (Cerfaux, *Théol. de l'Église*, 2nd ed., p. 213) as long
as by that we understand that this way of speaking, far from being abusive,
expresses the very basis of the union of Christians with Christ, in all its physical,
sacramental realism.

[3] Cf. the excellent article of O. CULLMANN, 'La délivrance anticipée du corps
humain d'après le Nouveau Testament', in *Hommage et Reconnaissance. Receuil
de travaux publiés à l'occasion du soixantième anniversaire de Karl Barth*, II,
Neuchâtel, 1946, pp. 31–40; and also that of J. MOUROUX, 'Le corps et le Christ',
in *Science Religieuse* (= *RSR*, XXXI), 1943, pp. 140–69, reprinted in *Sens chrétien
de l'homme*, Paris, 1948 ch. 5.

[4] Cf. R. BULTMANN, *Théol. de N. T.*, Tübingen, 1948–53, p. 192ff; *Glauben und
Verstehen,*, 1952, p. 45f.

Spirit which gives life to the 'Spiritual' body of the risen Christ, and through that to the body of the regenerated Christians (*1* Co 15 :44–49 ; see above p. 55)[1]. It can be seen then from these few verses in what a real, corporeal fashion Paul conceives this union with Christ which others elsewhere call 'mystical' and how it is this fundamental conception which gives rise to the theme of the 'Body of Christ' of which Christians are the 'members'.

1 Co 10:17, presents us with another glimpse, also in passing, of this familiar theme of Paul's. He is talking about the Eucharist (v. 16) and comments thus on its effect of communion: 'The fact that there is only one loaf means that, though there are many of us, we form a single body because we all have a share in this one loaf' *:Jerusalem Bible*). The context prohibits us from seeing in this unique body made up of Christians nothing more than a metaphor of their collective unity in Christ. It is too clear that this body, in the first place, is the individual body of the dead and risen Lord, with which they communicate by receiving the Eucharistic bread. The word σῶμα must have the same meaning in vv. 16 and 17. The inference implicit in the relationship between the two verses is striking: by receiving into their body, through the sacramental rite, the Body of Christ, they *are*, all together, a single body, individual in the first place, but assuming into itself the bodies of all those whom it unites to itself. We have here again the same genesis and the same realism, in the sphere of the sacraments, of the theme of the 'Body of Christ', with this interesting slant that here the context of the thought is no longer Baptism but the Eucharist[2].

When we come next to the development in *1 Co* 12:12-27, we are no longer tempted to see it as the first appearance of the idea of the 'Body of Christ' and to explain it with the help of the classical analogy between the individuals composing a single society and the members of the human body. This analogy is of course used by the Apostle, but only as an illustration of a doctrine he held already, not

---

[1] It is in opposition to the σῶμα united to the prostitute under its aspect of σάρξ that Paul here writes πνεῦμα; in reality he is thinking of the σῶμα πνευμάτικον of the risen Christ, of which the Christian is a member. Cf. PERCY, *Der Leib Christi*, p. 14f.

[2] Some exegetes go so far as to see in communion with the Eucharistic body of Christ the experience which has contributed most to revealing to St Paul the identification of the Christian community, i.e. the Church, with the individual risen body of Christ. Cf. A.E.J. RAWLINSON, 'Corpus Christi', in BELL-DEISSMANN, *Mysterium Christi*, Berlin, 1931, pp. 275–96 (a work to which I have not had direct access); CULLMANN, *art. cit.*, p. 37; CERFAUX, *Théol. de l'Égl.*, 2nd ed., p. 202f; *Le Christ . . .*, p. 214.

as the source from which it sprang[1]. He knows, and has already said, that Christians are all united to the risen body of Christ and make up a single body with him. This is a basic conviction of his faith and his theology. But it suggests spontaneously the secular metaphor of the 'social body' of which he is already aware anyhow as he is of so many other themes of popular philosophy which are Stoic in origin; and this metaphor he finds very appropriate to illustrate a conse-quence of his Christian convictions, namely the union of Christians, not only with Christ, but *with one another*. He uses it therefore in the service of his own thought. The development which results allows us to see clearly the combination of the two elements, the Christian idea and the secular image, as well as their relationship.

The point of departure is provided by the problem of charismas (vv. 4–11). It is a question of showing that their diversity must not become a principle of division, since it is the same Spirit who is their common source. To emphasise this unity in diversity, Paul introduces the image of the body which remains one though made up of different members (v. 12), but he calls on this well-known metaphor only because he has in mind his conception of the Body of Christ, where the metaphor finds a fresh and outstanding application: the words with which v. 12 concludes suggest this Christian application. They are elliptical, and differing ways of completing them have been put for-ward; I think that we have to understand, 'In the same way Christ too . . . is one body whose different members (who are the Christians, cf. 6:15) compose its unity'[2]. This primordial theme of the body of Christ is, besides, immediately elaborated with that sacramental realism in which we have already discovered its origin (v. 13). Baptism has immersed all Christians in one and the same body (13a) which can only be the individual, eschatological body of Christ: compare *Rm* 6:3[3]. This union takes place in 'a single Spirit', the Spirit which gives life to the body of the risen Christ, the second Adam, (*1 Co* 15:45) and through it to the bodies of all Christians. Following

---

[1] Cf. Wikenhauser, *op. cit.*, p. 99.

[2] Cf. PERCY, *Der Leib Christi*, p. 5; CERFAUX, *Théol. de l'Éng.*, 2nd ed., p. 206, n. 2.

[3] Cf. HANSON, *The Unity of the Church in the New Testament*, Uppsala, 1946, p. 81. Even if it is impossible to see here in βαπτίζειν εἰς the precise image of 'plunging' (cf. OEPKE, *TWNT*, I, p. 537), we must at least preserve for this expression the idea of baptism's uniting to a person, here to the dead and risen body of Christ (cf. PERCY, *Der Leib Christi*, p. 16; CERFAUX, *Théol. de l'Égl.*, p. 207f; *Le Christ* . . ., p. 252) and not translate it 'to form only a single body' (OSTY in *Bible de Jérusalem*; cf. ALLO, commentary *ad. loc*; WIKENHAUSER, *op. cit.*, p. 102; SCHNACKENBURG, *op. cit.*, p. 23) which would then be the meta-phorical body of the 'mystical Christ', distinct from the personal Christ.

on this baptismal incorporation, there are among them no longer
Jews and Greeks, slaves and masters (v. 13b), because they have put
on the 'new creature', the 'new man' which is the risen Christ: compare *Ga* 3:27f; 6:15; *Col* 3:11; *Ep* 2:15. The 'one spirit' of which
they have all been given to drink (v. 13c) could still be an allusion to
the rite of Baptism[1]; but I think it is more likely that the image of
'drinking' suggests the other great rite by which we are incorporated
into Christ, the Eucharist[2]; compare *1 Co* 10:3f where the Old
Testament types of baptism and spiritual nourishment (food and
drink) follow one on the other as they do here. Having thus recalled
his master idea that Christians belong really and sacramentally to
the Body of Christ, and thus laid the foundation for his application
to this theme of the secular metaphor of the members in one body,
Paul elaborates this metaphor in detail (vv. 14–26): different members
are enumerated for the conclusion to be drawn that none of them is
the entire body and none can act independently, but that the body
needs them all and requires their concerted action. It will be noticed
that the head appears in this list only as one member among the rest
(v. 21), a fact which will be of use to us presently. Having set out the
classical metaphor, with its obvious application to the harmony
required in the exercise of 'charismas', Paul returns with a concluding
phrase to the major and properly Christian theme which in his eyes
legitimises this application. The categorical force of this concluding
phrase will be appreciated. Paul does not say :'You are one body in
Christ', as if remaining on the level of the classical metaphor, which
would certainly not authorise any further development; he says:
'You are the Body of Christ'[3], which is much stronger and can only
be asserted in virtue of a quite different conception, one which is

---

[1] Thus PERCY, *Der Leib Christi*, p. 17; similarly SCHNACKENBURG, *op. cit.*, pp. 78–
80, who sets out the different interpretations (baptism, Eucharist, confirmation)
and himself prefers baptism.
[2] KÄSEMANN, *op. cit.*, p. 176; CERFAUX, *Théol. de l'Égl.*, 2nd ed., pp. 183 and 207.
[3] Schlier, *Christus und Kirche* . . ., p. 41, translates this: 'You are one body which
belongs to Christ' and opposes this idea, which would express merely the unity
of Christians with one another by reason of their belonging to Christ, to that
of the Epistles of the Captivity, where the body becomes properly that 'of Christ'.
Against this see WIKENHAUSER, *op. cit.*, p. 100; PERCY, *Der Leib Christi*, p. 4f.
Without drawing the same conclusions, Cerfaux (*Théol. de l'Égl.*, p. 211) too
prefers to translate it, 'You are one body which is that of Christ', in order to
respect the absence of articles. This may be a legitimate shade of meaning.
However the omission of the article in front of a noun followed by a genitive,
especially if it is a proper name, is a Semitic usage which is not rare in the N.T.;
cf. BLASS-DEBRUNNER, *Gramm.*, par.[8] 259, 2; ABEL, *Grammaire* . . ., par. 30.
Compare in particular in St Paul: *1 Co* 10:21 ποτήριον κυρίου and 11:27 τὸ
ποτήριον τοῦ κυρίου; *1 Th* 5:2 ἡμέρα κυρίου and *2 Th* 2:2 ἡ ἡμέρα τοῦ κυρίου.

theological and Pauline, that of the real union of Christians with the risen Body of Christ.

If from here we pass on to *Rm* 12:4-5, it may seem at first sight as though the specifically Pauline theme of the 'Body of Christ' does not come into play. Paul only says: 'So all of us are only one body *in Christ*'. If we confined our attention to this passage by itself, it would be possible to believe that Paul was not transcending the level of the secular metaphor, which he recalls in v. 4 and from which in this case he would be taking the image of the Christians forming a unified collectivity with Christ as its moral bond. But it is not legitimate to isolate the text in this way. It was written shortly after that of *1 Co* 12:12-28, which it obviously takes up again. The context of thought is the same, the diversity of charisms. And the swift reminder of the classical analogy (v. 4) is only a brief summary of the elaborate development in *1 Co*. It is allowable, then, and even necessary, to understand *Rm* in the light of *1 Co*; Paul has not forgotten here what he said so clearly there. Besides it would be wrong to see in ἐν Χριστῷ the expression of a simple 'moral' bond. This formula, though of itself vague, carries a powerful meaning in Paul: it is as it were the slogan which for him encapsulates the whole system of our union with Christ, of the recreation of all things 'in Christ', with all the realism which he attributes to this renewal. This one body that Christians are 'in Christ' – after the previous assertions we can have no doubt – is for Paul the 'Body of Christ'[1].

If the origin of the 'Body of Christ' theme put forward here is correct, there is no need to have recourse to the Gnostic myth of the *Urmensch*. Certainly this recourse cannot be rejected *a priori* for dogmatic reasons. Paul, like many other vehicles of Biblical revelation, gets inspiration from the thought of the surrounding, contemporary world and could have profited by this myth, even while Christianising it. But from a historical and exegetical point of view this borrowing seems very unlikely. In the first place, this Gnostic concept is known to us only from texts later than Paul, so that it is far from proved that he could have known them and been dependent on them[2].

---

[1] Wikenhauser (*op. cit.*, p. 101), followed by Percy (*op. cit.*, p. 6), observes quite correctly that it was grammatically impossible to write 'a body of Christ'. Holding on to ἐν, which for him is essential, Paul resolves this difficulty by writing ἐν Χριστῷ in place of the genitive Χριστοῦ. 'In Paul's language, the genitive and formulas formed with prepositions are very often equivalent', Cerfaux says in this regard (*Théol. de l'Égl.*, p. 212, n.l.).

[2] Käsemann (*op. cit.*, p. 155) admits that the texts he adduces are late, but maintains that the Gnostic myth they presuppose *must* be earlier than the *Deuteropaulinen*,

Secondly, the myth normally connotes the idea of the Heavenly Man, Head of the Body which he comes to deliver on earth[1] an idea which is not brought into play at the first appearance the theme makes in Paul. I admit that it appears further on in the epistles of the captivity, but we shall see that the situation of Christ in heaven and his role as Head are asserted in these epistles in reaction against the errors of the Colossians, not under the influence of the Gnostic myth, and that far from constituting one of the essential components of the 'Body of Christ' theme these conceptions survive rather as elements foreign to this theme, and are integrated into it only later and by way of combination. In any case these elements which are characteristic of the Gnostic myth are not yet to be found in the 'Body of Christ' theme as we have just seen it making its appearance in the earlier epistles, and that ought to be enough to deter us from looking for the explanation of the theme in the myth[2].

Nor indeed is recourse to the myth at all necessary since the theme, understood as we have proposed, is not as 'enigmatic' as Wikenhauser would like. We have found it sufficient to take seriously, on the one hand, Paul's faith in the Death and Resurrection of Christ, the source of salvation for all those who are united to it through faith and baptism, and on the other the physical realism which he attributes to the eschatological renewal, to see the idea of the sacramental union of Christians with Christ spontaneously throw up that of the Body of Christ who gathers into his risen being all those who die and rise with him.

In sum, it is in the Old Testament and in Judaism that it is most fitting to look for the principal source of these categories of Paul's thought. The two components we have just singled out are to be found there. On the one hand, there is the idea of an individual who

because it alone is capable of explaining them. This is the whole question. And it can only be resolved in this way if every explanation through Jewish or Pauline conceptions is proved impossible. But this is not the case, whatever Wikenhauser too (*op. cit.*, pp. 225–31) may think. In fact, the Gnostic explanations of Schlier and Käsemann, which are too dependent on the reconstructions of Reitzeinstein, have not found much of a hearing; cf. PERCY, *op. cit.*, p. 39ff; 'Zu den Problemen des Kolosser- und Epheserbriefe', *ZNW*, XLIII, 1950–51, p. 194; CERFAUX, *Théol. de l'Égl.*, pp. 280–2; L. MALEVEZ, *art. cit.*, pp. 79–82; GOOSSENS, *op. cit.*, pp. 90–8.

[1] Thus Schlier, but Käsemann (*op. cit.*, p. 74f) believes that he can discern a form of the myth in which the head plays no part.
[2] It cannot be denied that there are analogies of expression between the Pauline epistles and the alleged texts of the Gnostic myth, but they are explicable enough, either from ideas which were widespread in the ancient Oriental and Hellenistic worlds, including late Judaism which had undergone their influence, of from the borrowings which the second-century Gnostics (who are most often quoted at us) made from Paul himself.

'represents' the group in a kind of 'corporate personality'[1], an idea which is found again in Paul particularly under the form of Christ as 'Second Adam'[2]; and on the other, the physical realism which never thinks of man without his body and associates the latter strictly with the whole work of eschatological salvation[3]. It is also possible that the ideas of Judaism at the beginning of our era had been influenced on this point by Graeco-Oriental syncretism; in which case Paul would be dependent on the latter only by way of the former, indirectly. To pursue these lines of thought would require a whole study which I cannot undertake here.

3. *The Body of Christ in Col and Ep*. If it is true that the theme of the 'Body of Christ' is already to be found in *1 Co* and *Rm*, with its essential components, it remains true nevertheless that in the epistles of the captivity it receives a wholly fresh emphasis which we must now describe.

We are struck first of all by the frequency with which it appears. It is no longer alluded to in passing, in connection with some other subject like fornication, or the Eucharist, or even the division of charismas; instead, it occupies a central position and serves to denote the very object of redemption, the assembly of the saved. Christ is the saviour of the Body (*Ep* 5:23), the body which is his own and of which we are members (v. 30). It is as parts of this one Body that we have been called (*Col* 3:15), that Jews and Gentiles have been reconciled (*Ep* 2:16). This Body is a living, coherent, hierarchic organism, which gathers all Christians into itself and which increases 'with a growth in God' (*Col* 2:19; *Ep* 1:16). In a word, it is the Church (*Col* 1:18,24; *Ep* 1:23; 5:23ff) and it has Christ for Head (*Col* 1:18; 2:19; *Ep* 1:22; 4:15f; 5:23). Finally it is associated with the idea of 'Fullness' (*Col* 1:18f; 2:9; *Ep* 1:23; 4:13ff).

Before analysing everything which is fresh in these texts, we must note how closely they are linked to the preceding ones in what concerns the fundamental idea we have discerned at the basis of the

---

[1] Cf. T.W. MANSON, *The Servant-Messiah*, Cambridge, 1953, p. 74, with bibliographical notes.
[2] Cf. in particular S. HANSON, *op. cit.*, *passim* and especially pp. 65ff, 116; L.S. THORNTON, *op. cit.*, especially ch. 9 and 10. See also PERCY, *Der Leib Christi*, pp. 38–43; Id., *ZNW*, XLIII, 1950–51, p. 192, nn. 47 and 49; L. MALEVEZ, *art. cit.*, pp. 40–50; H.J. SCHOEPS, *Theologie und Geschichte des Judenchristentums*, Tübingen, 1949, p. 99ff; SCHNACKENBURG, *op. cit.*, p. 110ff.
[3] On all this, see A. SCHWEITZER, *Die Mystik des Apostels Paulus*, Tübingen, 1930, pp. 110–40.

'Body of Christ' theme, that is, the physical, sacramental union of Christians with the dead and risen body of Christ. We found this union expressed in *Rm* 6:3ff and we find a striking echo of it in *Col* 2:11-13. Here too it is a question of baptism (v. 12) which is called 'circumcision according to Christ' (v. 11) and this circumcision which is 'not performed by human hand' consists in 'the complete stripping' of the 'body of flesh' (ἀπέκδυσις), this same 'body of flesh' through the death of which Christ has brought reconciliation (1:22). This unusual expression does not refer simply, in this latter text, to the individual body of Christ as opposed to his 'mystical' body[1]; nor simply to his 'incarnation' body[2]. According to a characteristically Pauline usage[3], this expression describes the body submitted to the tyranny of the Flesh, that is of Sin with all its consequences; and this is the meaning it has (as one would expect *a priori*) in 1:22 and 2:11. With his vigorous realism, Paul is not afraid to say that God made Christ Sin (*2 Co* 5:21), that he sent him with a flesh like to that of Sin (*Rm* 8:3), similarly that he made him subject to the Law (*Ga* 4:4), the minister of the circumcision (*Rm* 15:8), a slave (*Ph* 2:7), accursed (*Ga* 3:13); not that he had committed sin himself (2 Co 5:21 τὸν μὴ γνόντα ἁμαρτίαν; *Rm* 8:3 ἐν ὁμοιώματι), but he really did assume human nature in the pitiable state which resulted from it, taking on the sinful and condemned Flesh of the Old Man to destroy it in himself by the just death of the Cross (*Rm* 6:6, 8:3) and to substitute for it the recreated nature, with its body regenerated by the Spirit (*Rm* 8:4-11). It is this very familiar doctrine of St Paul which is to be found in *Col* 1:22 and 2:11, and it is indeed in the baptismal union with Christ that the Christian is completely stripped of his body of flesh (2:11), is buried with him and raised with him through the faith which gives the physical rite its salvific power (v. 12), and in a word is stripped of the old man and puts on the new, recreated in the Image, in Christ, who from now on is all in all (*Col* 3:9-11).

We do indeed find again in the Epistles of the Captivity the very Pauline conception of the physical incorporation of the saved in the Death and Resurrection of Christ, and there too, in *Col* 3:15 and *Ep*

[1] LIGHTFOOT, *Comm. ad loc.*
[2] Cf. A. DUPONT-SOMMER, *Aperçus préliminaires sur les manuscripts de la Mer Morte*, Paris, 1950, p. 46; Id., *RHR*, CXXXVII, 1950, p. 164; and the remarks of R. de Vaux in *La Vie Intellectuelle*, Apr. 1951, p. 66f.
[3] The expression is found elsewhere only in *Enoch*, cii, 5 where it means the mortal perishable body (cf. JEREMIAS, *ZNW*, XXXVIII, 1939, p. 122f) and in *Si* 23:16 (23) ἄνθρωπος πόρνος ἐν σώματι σαρκὸς αὐτοῦ. In this latter text σάρξ suggests the aspect of the body submitted to sin as in Paul.

2:16, we see how the theme of the 'Body of Christ' flows immediately from this conception. For this 'one body' into which the faithful have been called (*Col* 3:15) and in which Jew and Gentile have been reconciled (*Ep* 2:16) is not only a moral or social body in the sense of the classical metaphor, it is first and above all the personal body of Christ which died on the Cross[1], in which Hatred was destroyed (*Ep* 2:16), that Flesh in which the Law was annulled (*v.* 14f; cf. the cancelling of the χειρόγραφον Col 3:15), in brief the Old Man whom he had deigned to put on, with all his conflicts, and for which in a kind of re-creation he had substituted the one New Man, in whom peace, within himself and with God, reigns (vv. 15–18). This dead and risen body, this Man re-created in a new state, is first and foremost Christ himself; but it is also all those he contains within himself in his role of Second Adam, acting, dying and rising on behalf of the whole human race. All men act out their destiny in him, in virtue of this not merely moral but ontological union, which binds them to him as their principal; for they are all contained in him as the creative and re-creative 'Εικών (*Col* 1:15–20), whose actions are valid for all. This *de jure* union becomes *de facto* if they realise it freely through Faith and Baptism. Christ is the New Man, and in putting on Christ (*Ga* 3:27), they put on the new Man (*Col* 3:10; *Ep* 4:24). He is the risen Body, the first-fruits (*1 Co* 15:20–23) and sole reality of the eschatological world (*Col* 2:17); by uniting themselves to him, they all become the 'one body' (*Col* 3:15; *Ep* 2:16), the 'Body of Christ'. The 'one spirit' which animates this Body is the Holy Spirit which gave life to his risen body on Easter morning and which then fills also those who are united to him, helping them to advance together towards the Father (*Ep* 2:18). These major themes are taken up again in *Ep* 4:4–6, in a rich formula whose strongly baptismal character is very noticeable[2]; just as there is, at the end of everything, only one God and Father of all, who is above all, through all and in all, and just as there is, by way of access, only one Lord (Christ) to whom the Christian is united by one same Faith and one same Baptism, in exactly the same fashion, in order to advance towards this end along this way, in the same calling and in the same hope, there is only one Body and only one Spirit. Here again it would be useless,

---

[1] Cf. PERCY, *Der Leib Christi*, pp. 29, 39, 44; *Die Probleme . . .*, pp. 281, 284, 288f, 317; *ZNW*, XLIII, 1950–51, pp. 191–3.

[2] Cf. O. CULLMANN, *Les premières Confessions de foi chrétiennes*, Paris, 1943, pp. 15, 34f; P. BENOIT, 'Les origines du Symbole des Apôtres dans le Nouveau Testament', in *Lumière et Vie*, 2 (Feb. 1952) p. 51; see below, p. 113.

and even wrong, to recognise under these expressions only the individual body of Christ and his Spirit, or only his 'mystical' Body and the Spirit communicated to Christians. It means the two taken together, indissolubly linked: the individual body of Christ increased by all the Christians who are united to him, even in the body, by faith and baptism; the Spirit filling this individual body of Christ, and through it all the members of his greater Body.

If then we find the same fundamental doctrine of the 'Body of Christ' in *Col* and *Ep*, clarified perhaps by certain new expressions, but substantially the same as in the earlier epistles, we must also recognise that it shows some quite fresh elements which develop and modify it. These can be resumed under two chief heads. On the one side, the Body of Christ seems to be further personified and to be better distinguished from the individual Christ, a fact expressed in literary terms by the combination of Σῶμα with Ἐκκλησία and Κεφαλή. On the other, it is set in a more cosmic perspective of salvation, and this is shown by its association with the word Πλήρωμα. We have therefore to examine these new themes, their origin and their significance, to see what they add to the Pauline theme of the 'Body of Christ' and to ask whether they too can claim parentage of the Apostle's thought.

This use of the word Ἐκκλησία in the singular to denote the whole assembly of Christians is not absolutely new in St Paul. It is found already in *1 Co* 15:9; *Ga* 1:13; *Ph* 3:6, where the Apostle says that he persecuted the Church of God; it is especially to be noticed in *1 Co* 12:28[1], where the context links it clearly with the theme of the 'Body of Christ', since this 'Church' in which God has established apostles, prophets, doctors, etc., is evidently that 'Body of Christ' whose unity Paul has just been proving despite the diversity of charismas (vv. 4–27). There is in this passage a very close association of the terms σῶμα Χριστοῦ (v. 27) and ἐκκλησία (v. 28) which completely prepares us for the equating of them in *Col* and *Ep*. We have however to recognise that this 'world-wide' use of the word seems very weak in the earlier epistles in comparison with the very numerous texts in which it is used to designate local communities, whether in the singular *1 Th* 1:1; *2 Th* 1:1; *1 Co* 1:2; 4:17; 6:4; 10:32; 11:18, 22; 14:4, 5, 12, 19, 23, 28, 35; *2 Co* 1:1; *Rm* 16:1, 5, 23; *Ph* 4:15; *Phm* 2) or in the plural (*1Th* 2:14; *2 Th* 1:4; *1 Co* 7:17; 11:16; 14:33, 34; 16:1, 19; *2 Co* 8:1, 18, 19, 23, 24; 11:8, 28; 12:13; *Ga* 1:2, 22; *Rm* 16:4, 16). This

[1] See however the reservations of CERFAUX, *Théol. de l'Égl.*, pp. 147–51.

meaning of local assembly is found again in *Col* 4:15, 16, but the worldwide sense is far more salient, even ordinary, in *Col* and *Ep*, and the identification of the word used in this way with the expression 'Body of Christ', already prepared for in *1 Co*, becomes completely explicit in them: *Col* 1:18 (epexegetic genitive), 24; *Ep* 1:22f; 5:23–30. This literary fact expresses a personification of the Body of Christ which is really remarkable. By calling it the 'Church', he emphasises the collective existence of this assembly of the saved as that of an organised and unified society, and as that of a living person distinguished from the personal Christ, though living only through him. It would be too strong to call it autonomous, since its whole being comes from Christ and it subsists only ἐν Χριστῷ. Nevertheless it is not identical with him; it is rather the object of his redemptive work, of his love and of his life-giving influence. This can be seen clearly in the beautiful passage in *Ep* 5:23–32, where it appears face to face with Christ as his bride, closely united to him certainly, but in the end distinct from him, whom he loves, for whom he delivers himself, and whom he purifies and sanctifies.

II. CHRIST HEAD OF THE POWERS AND HEAD OF THE BODY

This clearer distinction between Christ and his quasi-personified Body is particularly apparent in the theme Christ Head of the Body, Head of the Church. For even if the body is united to the head by a indissoluble bond, it is nevertheless not identical with it; the head is its captain; its vital principle; the body must obey it, receive its influx of life, grow under its propulsion and in a way towards it. Thus it is that Paul exploits this image and the way he does so expresses very well the distinction and at the same time the close unity it does not prevent. In *Col* 1:18, Christ, who has just been called the first-born of all creation, in whom, through whom and for whom all things were created, is also the Head of the Body, the Church. We realise that he has become this in a second stage of the divine plan, that of re-creation; he existed in himself before taking on this role. This is clearly indicated also in *Ep* 1:22, which first describes the heavenly triumph of Christ (vv. 20–1) and then says that God '*made him* ... the head of the Church'. Similarly again in *Ep* 5:23, the parallelism of the two expressions κεφαλὴ τῆς ἐκκλησίας and σωτὴρ τοῦ σώματος suggests that the Church is distinct from its Head as the Body is from Him who saves it. Lastly in *Col* 2:19 and *Ep* 4:15f, it is possible to see Christ the Head established in his place in heaven (cf. *Col* 3:1–2; *Ep* 1:20–1; 4:10) and the Boey of the Chirch being built up on earth by the energy it receives from him and growing towards him. I have already set out[1] my proposal to explain this clearer distinction between Christ the Head and the Church his Body by the fresh horizons opened up for Paul in the dispute with the Colossians: led by circumstances to insist more strongly on the place of the glorified Christ in heaven above all the cosmic and heavenly Powers to which the Colossian teachers wanted to attribute too great an importance, Paul envisages his relation with Christians in a slightly different perspective. Sometimes, pushing the paradox of his realised eschatology to its full length, he sees them as already risen and seated in heaven with Christ (*Col* 2:12; *Ep* 2:6; cf. above p. 56); sometimes, returning to the reality of the earthly existence which continues, he feels more strongly the distance which remains provisionally between the leader who is already glorified and the followers who are struggling on earth to rejoin him, a distance which necessarily implies a certain distinction between the Head and his Body, and a stress on the personification of the latter. This explanation still seems to me to be valid; but I think it is possible to make it still more precise by a closer examination of the genesis of the image of the Head.

It is quite certain that, through its combination with the theme of the Body, it represents a new element, proper to the epistles of the captivity. In the previous passages which touch on this theme nothing of this sort was to be found. Certainly the head appears in the development in *1 Co* 12:12–27, at v. 21, but it does so with a totally different significance; it is *not* Christ, who is the totality of the σῶμα, it is only one of the members, a worthier one no doubt but still on the same level as the rest and one which can engage the feet in a discussion of the usefulness of their respective functions; if we wanted to turn this text into an allegory, we could say in the life of the Church the head represented a governor, a leader of the community, even, with a slight anachronism, the bishop. The idea of Christ the Head of the Body-Church is therefore quite new in *Col* and *Ep*. How then are we to explain its appearance? Some exegetes see it only as a very natural development of the idea of the Body itself[1]. Since every body has a head, and since the Church is the Body of

---

[1] 'L'horizon paulinien de l'épître aux Ephésiens', *RBibl*, 1937, pp. 342–61, 506–25.
[2] Percy, for example, (*Die Leib Christi*, p. 52f) is too much inclined to see things in this way.

Christ, anyone who wanted to emphasise the directing and life-giving role of Christ would surely spontaneously render the image more precise by making him the Head of this Body the Church. On reflection, however, this explanation does not appear so satisfactory. It is already far from satisfactory for those who derive the 'Body of Christ' theme from the secular metaphor of the 'social Body', since the latter could very well talk of the head as an outstanding member in the manner of *1 Co* 12:21, but not as a principle of the whole body, distinct from the body, in the manner of *Col* and *Ep*[1]. It is still less so for those who see the origin of this theme in Paul's fundamental conviction about the physical union of the Christian with the individual body of Christ, since, in a context of thought where the stress is laid so heavily on the closeness of the unity established between the risen Christ and those who have 'put on' Christ, the image of the Head, with the distinction which it implies, introduces a disturbing element. It can, if it is really necessary, be adapted to this theme by making certain adjustments, as we shall see; but it cannot derive spontaneously from it.

Others, here again, look to the myth of the heavenly Anthropos[2]. But before having recourse to this dubious source it is necessary to be certain that a simpler explanation is not to be found in the internal development of Paul's own thought. This I believe to be the case and that the origin of this new datum of Christ the Head and its combination with the earlier theme of the Body of Christ can be discovered in the texts themselves. To put it in a nutshell before explaining it, I think that the image of Christ the Head appears first, not in relation to the Body/Church, but in relation to the heavenly Powers, to mark his supremacy over them[1]: he is their Head in the sense of 'captain',

---

[1] In the Greek-speaking world to which Paul belonged, κεφαλή was not applied to the leader of a social group (differing from the use of *Caput* in Latin); cf. DUPONT, *Gnosis*, pp. 440–5; SCHLIER, art. κεφαλή, *TWNT*, III, p. 673, 61f. But see W. L. KNOX, 'Parallels to the N.T. Use of σῶμα', *JThSt*, xxxix, 1938, pp. 243–246; *Id.*, *St Paul and the Church of the Gentiles*, Cambridge, 1939, p. 161f.

[2] SCHLIER, art. κεφαλή, *TWNT*, III, pp. 675–7, 679ff; KÄSEMANN, *op. cit.*, pp. 71–4, 156f.

[1] Cf. my article in *RBibl*, 1937, p. 523f. This relation of Christ the Head to the heavenly Powers is not even mentioned in E. MERSCH, *Le Corps Mystique du Christ*, Paris, 2nd ed., 1936, I, pp. 161–5. Wikenhauser (*op. cit.*, p. 209ff) does not ignore it, but the fact that he deals with it *after* the relation of Christ the Head to the Body/Church (p. 197ff) indicates that he does not perceive its importance as a source in Paul's thought. The same reproach can be made against T. SOIRON, *Die Kirche als der Leib Christi*, Düsseldorf, 1951 (cf. my review in *RBibl*, 1954, p. 287f) and against J.M. GONZALEZ RUIZ, 'Sentido soteriológico de κεφαλή en la cristologia de san Pablo', in *Anthologica Annua*, Rome, I, 1953, pp. 185–224. P. PRAT (*La Théologie de Saint Paul*, I, pp. 359–69; II, pp. 341ff) already sets

of authority, which is the biblical sense of this metaphor. It is only after this, in a second stage, that the datum introduced in this way is combined with the theme of the Body, thanks to another significance, Hellenistic this time, of the metaphor: Christ then becomes the Head of the Body, as its vital principle, though this does not exclude his also playing a role of authority in its regard. Let us see how this evolution is revealed in the texts. It was already complete by the time *Col* and *Ep* were written. We must therefore expect that more than one passage will reflect the second stage, with the combination already made; but I think that there are passages where the first stage is to be found and where one can see the transition from the first to the second taking place.

The first question to ask concerns the moral metaphorical value of κεφαλή for St Paul. We have seen that this notion does not appear in his earlier passages on the 'Body of Christ', except in *1 Co* 12:21, where it is simply one of the members of the body. But it is found in *1 Co* 11:3ff in regard to the veiling of women, and here it clearly has the sense of 'chief', of a principle of authority: 'Christ is the head of every man, man is the head of woman, and God is the head of Christ'. The idea is certainly not that Christ is the life-giving principle from which the life of the Christian flows, but simply that man has authority over woman, just as Christ has authority over man and is himself under the authority of God. Paul is establishing a hierarchy of dignity and command[1]. And this is indeed the normal metaphorical sense of 'head' in the Semitic, and particularly the Biblical, world, as Dom J. Dupont has shown[2]. It is therefore likely *a priori* that the word will be taken first in this sense when it appears in the epistles of the captivity, and this we find to be the case[3]. *Col* 2:10 is very clear; Christ 'is the head of Sovereignty and Power'. He is certainly not their head by way of life-giving principle, but as chief or sovereign. For it is going to be said a little further on that these Sovereignties and Powers have been stripped of the authority which they used to wield over the men of the old dispensation, by means of the Law and

out the thought of St Paul in a systematic way, which is open to discussion on more than one point, without troubling himself enough about its sources. On the other hand see the excellent remarks of L. Malevez (*art. cit.*, pp. 89–92), followed by W. Goossens (*op. cit.*, p. 88f).

[1] J.M. Gonzalez Ruiz (*art. cit.*) is exaggerating when he claims that, not only in Paul but even in the biblical and Hellenistic sources, the image of 'head' always implies the idea of 'salvation'.

[2] *Gnosis*, p. 446f. Cf. SCHLIER, art. κεφαλή, *TWNT*, III, p. 674f.

[3] DUPONT, *Gnosis*, p. 447ff.

its Record, and now have to follow behind Christ like the conquered in the triumphal procession of their conqueror (v. 15). The same thought is expressed in *Ep* 1:20–2; the resurrection and the enthronement of Christ in heaven have placed him above every Sovereignty, Authority, Power or Domination . . . God has put all things under his feet and has made him Head over all things . . . The mention of the Church which follows results from the combination of the theme of the Head with that of the Body, and we shall return to it later; but it does not contradict the fact that here too the image of the Head appears first in relation to the heavenly Powers to indicate Christ's supremacy over them. *Col* 2:18–19 again reveals the same primary acceptance of the term, followed by the same combination: to cling to worn-out observances, to the 'shadows' of the old dispensation, is in Paul's eyes to worship angels and not to grasp the Head, in other words to have regard for inferior Powers and to neglect their Chief, Christ. What follows, in the remainder of v. 19, results from the combination with the Body of Christ[1] theme, but it must not lead us to overlook the fact that here again the term Head appears first in opposition to the Angels, to indicate that Christ is superior to them and alone deserves obedience and worship.

The image of Christ 'the Head' does not then appear in *Col* and *Ep* as a deduction from the 'Body of Christ' theme, but from a quite different angle which is to express his authority as Chief over the angelic Powers: this idea is at the basis of the epistle to the Colossians, as a fundamental reaction against the speculations of their teachers, and it brings into play a metaphorical use of the word 'head' which is well established in the Language of the Bible and already represented in Paul himself.

But it was plainly fated that this new notion of Christ the Head should get combined with the earlier theme of the Body of Christ, since head and body are of themselves such closely allied images. And this combination could very well have taken place first by using the sense of authority for which the image of the head had been chosen. After all the head has a function of command, of government over the whole body. This is in fact the way the combination makes its first appearance in these two epistles. After saying that God has established Christ the Head over all things, *Ep* 1:22–3 adds τῇ ἐκκλησίᾳ: Christ is not only Chief of the heavenly Powers, a fact which

---

[1] It is because he has failed to understand this that Dibelius (*Comm. ad loc.*) gives σῶμα here the sense of cosmos.

is of less importance for *Ep* than it is for *Col*, but he is also and especially Chief of the Church which is his Body, that Church which
occupies a central place in the thought of *Ep*. Similarly in *Col* 1:18,
in a context of supremacy and primacy, Christ is called 'Head of the
Body, the Church', in the sense of Chief or Principal, as the terms
which follow indicate: ἀρχή, πρωτότοκος ἐκ τῶν νεκρῶν, ἐν πᾶσιν
πρωτεύων.

However the combination once made could be developed and
enriched thanks to another significance of the idea of the head, that
of vital principle, source of movement and life[1]. This physiological
force is no longer to be sought for in the world of Semitic thought, for
which the heart was the seat of life, but in Hellenistic philosophy and
science. Here too however there was discussion. Aristotle for example
stood out for the heart as the centre of sensation. But Plato had made
the head the seat of reason, of νοῦς, and the Stoics said the same: τὸ
ἡγεμονικὸν ἐν τῇ κεφαλῇ. More precisely, physicians like Hippocrates
and Galen sought in the ἐγκέφαλον for the nerve-centre which directs
all the members[2]. It is difficult not to hear in *Col* 2:19 and *Ep* 4:16
an echo of this physiology on which St Paul seems to have been
informed,[3] perhaps by the 'beloved physician' (*Col* 4:14): they make
use of technical terms such as ἀφαί and σύνδεσμοι in a way which
is fundamentally correct. These are the very texts in which we see
Christ the Head perform a new function in regard to the body, a
function which is not merely authoritative but life-giving: from him
there flows through joint and ligament the vital influence which feeds
the body with energy, assures its cohesion and produces harmonious
growth. In this way, the combination of the theme of the Head (over
the Powers) with that of the Body of Christ is effected, and by a very
happy adaptation: the introduction of the notion of the Chief established in heaven could, as we have seen, have implied a separation
between Christ and his Body that would have been damaging to
their close union; but through the connotations of the physiological
bond which unites the Body to the Head, this union is reaffirmed and
in a way made richer and more exact. On the one hand, we avoid

[1] Cf. CERFAUX, *Théol. de l'Égl.*, p. 252.
[2] Cf. LIGHTFOOT, *Comm. ad loc.*; DUPONT, *op. cit.*, pp. 442f, 447.
[3] This is contested by S. BEDALE, 'The Meaning of κεφαλή in the Pauline Epistles',
in *JThSt*, New series, V, 1954, pp. 211–15, who wants to make the use of κεφαλή
in Paul dependent only on the meaning of the Biblical word *rôš*; here the sense
of 'first', 'beginning' = ἀρχή: the Church/Body grows towards Him who is
its archetype. He does not however completely reject a secondary reference to
the physiological side. . . .

that absolute identity between the individual Christ and the Christians united to him which would be incorrect[1]; he is their Chief, already established in heaven, where they will have to go to rejoin him. On the other, a very intimate union is set up between him and them by means of this vital influence, in which is it possible to see, applying the image but not straining it, the contact of the sacraments and the communication of the πνεῦμα[2] (compare ἐπιχορηγούμενον in *Col* 2:19 and ἐπιχορηγία in *Ep* 4:16 with ἐπιχορηγία τοῦ πνεύματος Ἰησοῦ Χειστοῦ in *Ph* 1:19).

The admirable text of *Ep* 5:22–32 on marriage gives us a kind of synthesis resulting from this fusion of themes we have just been studying. In it we find first of all the fundamental idea of the 'Body of Christ' of which Christians are the 'members' (v. 30), incorporated by Christ into himself through the purifying and sanctifying action of baptism (v. 26). But this baptismal action and salvation are presented in a collective manner which personifies the assembly of Christians: it is the 'Body' which Christ has saved (v. 23) and the 'Church' that he has baptised (v. 26). And yet, however closely united to Christ as his Body the Church may be, it is not identical with him. He is distinguished from it as its Head, first in the sense of Chief; the Church is under his authority, thus becoming the model of the obedience that every wife owes her husband (vv. 23–4). But this image of Head or Chief still has something of separation about it and Paul does not want to preserve this, since this Chief is also the 'Saviour' who 'loved the Church and gave himself for her', substituting himself for sinners to die and then sharing with them the purification and sanctification wrought by his sacrifice. To emphasise this union in the gift of his suffering and his life, Paul does not use the other significance, the vital principle, here, though the image of the 'head' offered it to him. Instead he prefers a much more striking one, which fits in very easily and which he found in the Old Testament:

[1] The Encyclical 'Mystici Corporis Christi' utters a warning against the excesses which could be committed in this regard; cf. the commentary of L. MALEVEZ, 'Quelques enseignements de l'Encyclique "Mystici Corporis Christi" ', *NRTh*, LXVII, 1945, p. 996f; L BOUYER, 'Où en est la théologie du corps mystique?', in *RSR*, XXII, 1948, pp. 317, 327.

[2] 'Huic autem Christi Spiritui tamquam non adspectabili principio id quoque attribuendum est, ut omnes Corporis partes tam inter sese, quam cum excelso Capite suo coniungantur, totus in Capite cum sit, totus in Corpore, totus in singulis membris; quibus pro diversis eorum muneribus atque officiis, pro maiore vel minore, quo fruuntur spiritualis sanitatis gradu, diversis rationibus praesens est atque adsistit. Ille est, qui caelesti vitae halitu in omnibus corporis partibus cuiusvis est habendus actionis vitalis ac reapse salutaris principium' (Encyclical *'Mystici Corporis Christi'*, *ASS*, XXXV, 1943, p. 219).

the husband is not only the Chief whom the wife must obey, he is also and especially the intimate associate who loves his wife as his own flesh and sacrifices himself for her: this is what Christ did for the Church, his Bride (vv. 25–9). In this union which is the model for human marriage and of a comparable physical realism, the 'mystery' of Genesis (vv. 31–2) is fully realised and finally clarified. These lines have a unique richness and we may be allowed to see in them the ultimate flowering of Paul's thought on the Church as the Body of Christ.

A question presents itself spontaneously here. Does it not follow from the fusion of the 'Head of the Powers' theme with the theme of the 'Body of Christ', that those Powers become an integral part of the Body? In no way, and nothing shows more clearly that the 'Head' and the 'Body' themes are different in origin, as well as the fact that the Pauline idea of the 'Body of Christ' does not derive in the first place from the Stoic metaphor. For the latter did not limit itself to comparing the socio-political set-up to a body; it went as far as to characterise the entire Cosmos as a great 'body', and the cosmic extension of the expression is in fact its first application[1]. It was to describe the Cosmos as a great Whole whose different parts are bound to one another and unified by the divine spirit circulating through them that Stoic philosophy first had recourse to the image of a body unified in its diverse members; the use made of this image to describe socio-political unity is only a restricted application of it. Given this, if Paul had drawn the idea of describing the assembly of the saved first as a 'Body in Christ' and then as a 'Body of Christ' from these literary circles, he would have been able to keep this same 'body' image when, in *Col* and *Ep*, he had to give a cosmic extension to Christian salvation: he only had to utilise the cosmic extension which this image carried already in Stoic thinking. But he did nothing of the kind. For him, the 'Body of Christ' is always limited to the *human* assembly of the saved, the Church[2]; he uses a different word, Pleroma, when he wants to refer to this extension of Christ's work. We shall return shortly to this ultimate development. At the moment, our interest lies in asserting that the 'Body of Christ' does not go beyond the bounds of humanity[3]. And after what we have said above the

---

[1] Cf. DUPONT, *op. cit.*, pp. 431–5; W.L. KNOX, 'Parallels to the N.T. Use of σῶμα', *JThSt*, XXXIX, 1938, p. 243ff.
[2] Dibelius (*Comm.*) is wrong in wanting to give σῶμα in *Col* 2:19 a cosmic significance; against this cf. J. SCHMID, *Der Epheserbriefe des Apostels Paulus*, Freiburg, 1928, p. 180, n. 1; PERCY, *Der Leib Christi*, note 89; *Die Probleme . . .*, pp. 382–4.
[3] Cf. WIKENHAUSER, *op. cit.*, p. 221ff; CERFAUX, *Théol. de l'Égl.*, p. 156f.

reason for this is clear. He does not owe this expression to the Stoic metaphor, which would of itself have allowed a cosmic enlargement; he owes it to his properly Christian conception of the physical union of the body of the Christian to the dead and risen body of Christ by means of the sacraments. In this perspective, there is no room in the Body of Christ for any beings other than saved mankind: It was human nature that Christ assumed, in the state to which it had been reduced by sin, in order that he might recreate it in the Spirit and restore it; it was mankind and man alone that he bore within himself on the cross and on Easter morning; it is men whom he unites to himself through Faith, Baptism and the Eucharist, and who, by putting him on, become his Body.

Thus our answer to the question raised is provided: the heavenly Powers form no part of the Body of Christ. Paul never says so, and in fact it is impossible. Does this mean that they are not interested in the salvation of mankind? or that the Angels do not share in the grace of Christ? That is quite another matter. To reply to this fresh question we should first have to determine how far Paul identifies the cosmic 'Sovereignties and Powers', in which the Colossian teachers were interested, with the 'Angels' of Biblical tradition. It is a delicate problem and cannot be dealt with here. It must suffice to say that it is not certain that either the cosmic Powers or the Angels fall outside the sphere of Christ's work in the absolutely universal extension which Paul assigns to it. Since, in the new world, there is no longer anything but Christ, who is 'all in all', the angelic and material universe, which constitutes the framework for mankind in Biblical thought, must of necessity be integrated into the re-creation as they were in the creation. On this score, the cosmic or angelic Powers certainly have an interest in Christ's redemption. But it is only indirectly. They do not form part of the Body. And the least we can say is that in these epistles Paul assigns them a rather modest role in the great renewal[1]. Submitted to Christ as to their Head (*Col* 2:10), they have even been put under his feet (*Ep* 1:21f; cf. 1 *Co* 15:24f). Stripped of their authority over men, who no longer have to render them worship (*Col* 2:18), they are publicly exposed for what they are (intermediaries whose reign has come to an end) and must follow in the triumph of Christ (*Col* 2:15). Once they were associated with the

---

[1] J. Gonzalez Ruiz's interesting but too systematic study (*art. cit.*) would have gained if he had distinguished more clearly between the different modes by which the Church and the heavenly Powers participate in the 'salvation' of Christ.

divine plan of salvation through the adminstration of the Law which was confided to them, but they did not know the 'mystery' with this plan which was reserved for the end of 'this age' (1 *Co* 2:7f), now they have to learn about this mystery as it were from outside by watching the Church (*Ep* 3:10)[1]. For the remainder, Paul has not left us any very clear teaching on this subject and in reading it we may well wonder what their moral standing is and in what way, voluntarily or compulsorily, they have been integrated into the eschatological world. For even if according to more than one text they can pass for neutral, even good (*Col*, for example), the fault lying with the men who attach themselves unduly to their superseded authority, there are other texts in which they appear as frankly evil, enemies of Christ and Christians (*Ep* 6:12 and 2:2; cf. *1 Co* 15:24f; *Rm* 8:38). They are included in the universal 'reconciliation' of *Col* 1:20, but it is permissible to believe that this term has the salvation of humanity principally in view (cf. v. 22 and *2 Co* 5:18–20; *Rm* 5:10f; 11:15) and applies to the cosmic framework only in a wide sense which would imply the return to order and would not exclude the reduction of hostile elements to impotence[2]. In this regard, the parallel in *Ep* 1:10, with its ἀνακεφαλαιώσασθαι, is more expressive and more correct: everything has to be brought back under Christ as under a single Head,[3] acknowledged and even life-giving for some, imposed by force on others.

III. THE PLEROMA

Paul is interested above all in the salvation of mankind. According to a thoroughly Biblical tradition, affirmed from the opening pages of Genesis, the Cosmos is for him only the frame of mankind, and when he mentions it, which is rarely enough, it is only from the point of view of man and his salvation. He does not speculate about the 'new heavens' and the 'new earth' of the eschatological era, in the manner of *2 P* 3:13 and *Rv* 21:1. The only passage in his great epistles in which he envisages the effects of Christian salvation on the material universe is *Rm* 8:19–22. If he mentions the angelic powers, good or

[1] Cf. PERCY, *Die Probleme* . . ., p. 94ff; *Id., ZNW*, XLIII, 1950–51, p. 185f. See also J. GEWIESS, *Christus und das Heil nach dem Kolosserbriefe*, Diss. Breslau, 1932, pp. 1–13.
[2] On the contrary assertion of W. MICHAELIS, *Versöhnung des Alls*, Bern, 1950, see my review, *RBibl*, 1952, pp. 100–3.
[3] Although ἀνακεφαλαιώσασθαι derives properly from κεφάλαιον, it can be admitted that Paul in using it was thinking of the related word κεφαλή; cf. V. WARNACH, *op. cit.*, p. 8, and the authors quoted by him in note 11.

evil, a little more often, it is only in so far as they act for or against the kingdom of Christ over his brothers, mankind.

It is the same preoccupation which makes him react against the speculations he encounters at Colossae. These are, however, of a nature to oblige him to confront more clearly than before the problem of the new Cosmos and to define the sovereign position of Christ in it. At Colossae, so great an interest was taken in the cosmic Powers that there was a risk of Christ's being neglected in their favour, either by being ranged among them or even by being relegated beneath them. Paul's response is a categorical assertion of Christ's absolute supremacy over these Powers, and through them over the whole of the former Cosmos which they governed. His kingdom has been substituted for that of these στοιχεῖα τοῦ κόσμου. This supremacy Paul illustrates by the cosmic trajectory which has taken Christ from the kingdom of the dead to the highest heaven, putting him in possession of the entire universe (*Ep* 4:8–10), and this is expressed, as we have seen, by saying that the glorified Christ is the Head of the Powers. But since he reserves the word σῶμα for the central part of this new world, that is, regenerated humanity, the Church, he needs another word to designate the cosmic frame of this humanity, which, without being directly linked like humanity to Christ, nevertheless participates in an indirect way in his work of salvation. And this, I believe, is to be found in the word πλήρωμα.

The word is to be met with already in earlier epistles, in different constructions: the 'fullness' of the earth (*1 Co* 10:26), of time (*Ga* 4:4), of the Jews or the converted Gentiles (*Rm* 11:12, 25), of the Law (*Rm* 13:10), of the blessing of Christ (*Rm* 15:29). But it appears often enough (six times) in the Epistles of the Captivity by themselves, and, except in *Ep* 1:10 (fullness of time; cf. *Ga* 4:4), with a special accent which makes it sound like a technical term. After being introduced standing by itself in an absolute construction (*Col* 1:19), it is qualified afterwards sometimes as the fullness of divinity (*Col* 2:9) or of God (*Ep* 3:19), sometimes as the fullness of Christ (*Ep* 1:23; 4:13). Lastly it appears in close literary contact with the term σῶμα: *Col* 1:18 and 19; 2:9 σωματικῶς; *Ep* 1:23; 4:13 and 16. This suggests that it adds a useful complement to the theme of the 'Body of Christ' and for this reason deserves to be examined. We shall begin by establishing its meaning in *Col* 1:19, and we shall then discover that this meaning is to be found in other passages, though it receives certain modifications and enrichments in them.

It is a difficult word and has been the subject of diverse interpretations as we discover when we begin to study *Col* 1:19. One interpretation sees the πλήρωμα as the Church, which 'completes' Christ as the Body completes the Head[1]. This way of looking at it, which relies on the parallel text in *Ep* 1:23, is not wholly incorrect, in this sense that Paul reaches a point, at the end of a certain evolution which is expressed in the epistle to the Ephesians, where in practice he identifies the Pleroma with the Church, which is the only reality to interest him in this epistle. But this does not apply to *Col* 1:19, where this evolution has not yet taken place. Here the context makes it difficult to see it already as the Church. Not only is it hard to understand the appearance of a new term, if it is a question merely of the Church, but the 'dwelling' (κατοικῆσαι) of the Pleroma in Christ suggests that it is firmly acquired and established and this scarcely corresponds to the state of growth and becoming of the Body of Christ (2:19). This 'dwelling' seems to represent an earlier stage of the divine plan than that of the ἀποκαταλλάξαις . . . ἐιρηνοποιήσαs: God causes the Pleroma to dwell in Christ so that he can afterwards (the καί is consecutive) reconcile and bring peace to all things in him. The Church is the end of this work of redemption, it cannot be its beginning.

Thus the majority of exegetes, ancient and modern, see something quite different in the πλήρωμα, viz. the Fullness of the Divinity or of the divine life[2]. They rely in particular on the technical sense of this term in the Gnostics of the second century. These latter used it to denote, in opposition to the Kenoma, the spiritual world of the divine Aeons which proceeded from the first divinity in successive emanations and in a way shared out among themselves in hierarchical pairs the attributes and energies of the divinity. It is thought that the teachers of Colossae must already have had a doctrine of this kind and have assigned Christ only a partial and subordinate rank in this diffusion of the divine essence. To which Paul would be

---

[1] Cf. THEODORET, *PG*, LXXXII, 601 ; SEVERAIN OF GABALA (K. STAAB, 'Pauluskommentare aus der griechischen Kirche', in *N.T. Abhdl.*, XV, Munster, 1933, p. 320); J.A. ROBINSON, *St Paul's Epistle to the Ephesians*, London, 1903, pp. 42f, 87f, 100.
[2] This exegesis is so general that there is little use in listing names. Besides the general run of Commentaries, I will mention by way of example: J. SCHMID *op. cit.*, p. 184: 'Die gesamte Wesenfülle der Gottheit mit allen göttlichen Kräften und Vollkommenheiten'; J. GEWIESS, *op. cit.*, p. 24ff; WIKENHAUSER, *op. cit.*, p. 188f; PERCY, *Der Leib Christi*, p. 51; *Die Probleme* . . ., p. 76, etc.: 'die Wesenfülle Gottes'; L.S. THORNTON, *op. cit.*, p. 289; S. HANSON, *op. cit.*, p. 128ff; L. CERFAUX, *Théol. de l'Égl.*, p. 245ff; *Le Christ* . . ., pp. 320–2: 'The concentration of divine sanctifying power'.

replying that the *whole* Pleroma dwells permanently in Christ,[1] that is to say that he possesses the whole divine essence, to the detriment of the heavenly Powers who are relegated beneath his feet. This interpretation raises a first difficulty: it is by no means proved that these Gnostic speculations of the second century were to be met with at Colossae in the time of St Paul. It is not even certain that the latter has taken over the term πλήρωμα from his opponents though this is commonly accepted; he could very well have drawn it himself from another literary circle and with another meaning, as we are going to see. Another difficulty rises from the immediate context. If πλήρωμα here means the fullness of the divine essence, the idea that God 'was pleased'[2] to 'cause' it 'to dwell' in Christ surely smacks somewhat of Nestorianism. For in the last resort the divinity of Christ cannot be the effect of a 'dwelling' of the divine essence in him, nor the result of the 'good pleasure' of God. According to the whole teaching of Paul, Jesus is divine by nature; in so far as he is the Son of God, he does not become divine. Here too we know from verse 15 onwards that he is the 'Εἰκών in whom, through whom and for whom all things have been created. His divinity is for the reader an acquired fact, a necessity of nature, the point of departure for the whole development of Paul's thought on his role as creator and re-creator. What need was there to go back over this already given fact in v. 19, especially to say that it was a matter of 'dwelling' resulting from 'good pleasure'? It may perhaps be replied that ἐν αὐτῷ refers to the human nature of Jesus and that v. 19 enters on a new stage of the divine plan, that of the Incarnation. But this would be incorrect. No more here than elsewhere does Paul distinguish between the divine and the human natures in Christ. His thought is always focused on the person of Jesus, the Son of God made man, and the pronoun αὐτός which is repeated again and again and in all its forms in this passage refers throughout to this concrete person[3]. Already as the Son of God

---

[1] This is the way Lightfoot interprets κατοικῆσαι in opposition to παροικῆσαι.
[2] Exegetes disagree over εὐδόκησεν. The grammar authorises two constructions each of which has its parallels. (1) πλήρωμα can be the subject of both εὐδόκησεν and κατουκῆσαι; cf. *Rm* 15:26; *1 Co* 1:21; *Ga* 1:15f; *1 Th* 2:8; 3:1; but in this case it must also be the subject of ἀποκαταλλάξαι and εἰρηνοποιήσας, this participle being masculine by a construction *ad sensum* (thus Ewald, Abbott, Dibelius, Percy, Masson, etc.). Or (2) the subject of (εὐδόκησεν is ὁ Θεός understood, πλήρωμα then being the subject only of the infinitive phrase which is the object of εὐδόκησεν (thus Haupt, Lohmeyer, etc.). This second construction is equally plausible (cf. *2 M* 14:35; POLYBIUS, I, 8:4) and seems to me to be preferable, both for the grammatical agreement (εἰρηνοποιήσας) and for thought.
[3] Cf. HUBY, *Comm.* (*Verbum Salutis*, VIII), Paris, 1935, p. 42f.

incarnate he is the (visible) Image of the invisible God; and it is on this account that he can be called the 'first-born of all creation', created himself in so far as he is man, while at the same time being the first cause as Son of God. Vv. 18–20 do indeed describe a new stage in the historical unfolding of the divine plan, but it concerns a new role and a new activity of Christ, taking up and re-creating the old creation, not the Incarnation which has been presupposed since vv. 13–15. The dwelling of the Pleroma in Christ, which is the object of a gratuitous decision (εὐδόκησεν) of God, comes as a comment on and explanation of (ὅτι) the new primacy which is added to his primacy as creative Image (ἵνα γένηται ἐν πᾶσιν αὐτὸς πρωτεύων), when he becomes the πρωτότοκος ἐκ τῶν νεκρῶν after having been the πρωτότοκος πάσης κτίσεως. It cannot be merely the result of the resurrection, since it appears in v. 19f at least logically prior to the reconciliation through the Cross, but it is set in a close relationship to the work of redemption.

If the Pleroma which comes in this way to dwell in Christ is neither the Church nor the divine essence, what is it? Is it the Cosmos? This is what Theodore of Mopsuestia thought[1] and it seems the best interpretation to me, though it needs to be filled out and made more precise. In any case it has the great advantage of introducing a meaning of πλήρωμα which was well established in literary circles known to St Paul and from which he could have borrowed it[2].

One of the key-concepts of Stoic philosophy consists in regarding the Cosmos as a great Whole where the divine Principle, Νοῦς or Πνεῦμα, penetrates to every corner of the material universe. This is a monist, immanentist and materialist conception and it is opposed to the dualistic one where Spirit and Matter, the world of ideas and and the world of tangible things, are ontologically divided and even hostile to one another. For the Stoics, faithful in this earliest Greek science, the divine Breath is itself material, though infinitely subtle,

[1] *Theodori Episcopi Mopsuesteni in Epistolas B. Pauli Commentarii*, ed. H.B. SWETE, Cambridge, 1880, I, p. 275f: 'plenitudinem Dei' et ecclesiam vocat, necnon et omnia, quasi quia et in omnibus sit et omnia impleat . . . omnem creaturam, quae ab eo repleta est provabit illi coniungere; *ibid.*, p. 286 (on 2:9): omnem plenitudinem deitatis hoc in loco iterum dicit universam creaturam repletam ab eo . . .
[2] For what follows, see the admirable pages of J. DUPONT, *op. cit.*, pp. 453–76, who seems to me to have understood perfectly, with all due deference to J. GEWIESS, 'Die Begreffe πληροῦν und πλήρωμα im Kolosser- und Epheserbrief' (in *Vom Wort des Lebens*, Festschrift für Max Meinertz, Münster, 1951, pp. 128–41), p. 135, n. 29. Cf also CERFAUX, *Le Christ . . .*, p. 321.

and it fills the universe from end to end, giving being and life to all things. Πλήρωμα was the word they used to express this idea: the divine Principle 'fills' all things, and is itself 'filled' by all things. In contradistinction to the Dualism revived by the Gnostics of the second century, who opposed the 'empty' world of appearances (κήνωμα) to the 'full' world of divine realities (πλήρωμα), Stoic monism used the term πλήρωμα to encompass the whole Cosmos, unified in its diversity, where the divine Spirit compenetrated the world of tangible realities, 'filling' them with its universal presence and being filled by them. It will suffice to quote a few texts[1]. Hippolytus, *Philosophoumena* (DIELS, *Dox. Graec.*, 571, 24f): πεπληρῶσθαι πάντα καὶ μηδὲν εἶναι κενόν, ταῦτα καὶ οἱ Στωικοί. Seneca, *De Benefic.*, iv, 8, 2: Quocumque tu flexeris, ibi illum (sc. Deum) videbis occurrentem tibi; nihil ab illo vacat, opus suum ipse implet. Aristides, in his *Encomium on Serapis*, 45, 21: διὰ πάντων ἥκει, καὶ τὸ πᾶν πεπλήρωκεν, 24, πάντα αὐτὸς εἷς ὤν, ἅπασιν εἰς ταυτὸν δυνάμενος. Corp. Herm., XVI, 3: τὸν τῶν ὅλων δεσπότην καὶ ποιητὴν καὶ πατέρα καὶ περίβολον, καὶ πάντα ὄντα τὸν ἕνα, καὶ ἕνα ὄντα τὸν πάντα· τῶν πάντων γὰρ τὸ πλήρωμα ἕν ἐστι καὶ ἐν ἑνί . . .

The idea and even the word for the universe as 'Pleroma' were therefore at Paul's disposal in a literary milieu that was well known to him. Stoic philosophy was widely diffused throughout the Graeco-Roman world and had thoroughly impregnated the popular philosophy which the itinerant scholars of the 'diatribe' hawked everywhere. Paul borrowed from this more than once, idea as well as style, and there is no difficulty in accepting that he took this notion of the cosmic Pleroma from there as well[2]. This materialist and immanentist philosophy needed a certain manipulation before being put at the service of biblical thought, but it was certainly closer to the latter after all than Platonic dualism was. Biblical revelation maintains the spirituality and the transcendence of God, but it does also insist on the close union which links him to the created world, a world which has issued entirely from his hands and lives only by his breath. It makes a strong distinction between spirit and matter, but it does not oppose them one to another as two contrary principles as do Zoroastrianism and Gnosis. In many a passage of the Bible we encounter

---

[1] Other texts are to be found in W.L. KNOX, *St Paul and the Church of the Gentiles*, Cambridge, 1939, p. 163; J. DUPONT, *op. cit.*, pp. 454–68.
[2] In so doing, I no longer believe that Paul borrowed the word πλήρωμα from the Colossian teachers, as is generally admitted and for which Dom Dupont reproached me (*op. cit.*, p. 430). Cf. PERCY, *Die Probleme . . .*, p. 77, 285.

the idea that God is present in the world and even that he 'fills' it[1]. It is interesting to find the word already in use in the Septuagint in a 'cosmic' sense, in stereotyped expressions such as ἡ γῆ καὶ τὸ πλήρωμα αὐτῆς, to signify the 'fullness' of that which is encompassed by the earth (*Jr* 8:16; 29:2; *Ezk* 12:19; 19:7; 30:12; 32:15; *Ps* 23:1; cf. *1 Co* 10:26), or the sea (*Ps* 95:11; 97:7; *1 Ch.* 16:32), ir even the οἰκουμένη (*Ps* 49:12; 88:12). But it is still more significant to read that the whole earth is full (πλήρης) of the glory of God (*Is* 6:3; *Ps* 71:19) and to hear God say: μὴ οὐχὶ τὸν οὐρανὸν καὶ τὴν γῆν ἐγὼ πληρῶ; λέγει κύριος (*Jr* 23:24). Affirmations such as that in *Ps* 138:8 (*si ascendero in caelum, tu illic es; si descendero in infernum, ades*) scarcely differ at all from that of Seneca quoted above. There is in these texts a sense of the divine ubiquity which was all ready to make use of the Stoic formulas when the latter should come into contact with the biblical revelation. This has happened for example in the books of Ecclesiasticus and Wisdom. It is enough to read *Si* 43:27 (σύντέλεια λόγων· τὸ πᾶν ἐστιν αὐτός), *Ws* 8:1 (Wisdom διατείνει δὲ ἀπὸ πέρατος εἰς πέρας εὐρώστως, καὶ διοικεῖ τὰ πάντα Χρηστῶς, cf. 7:24) and especially *Si* 16:29 (κύριος εἰς τὴν γῆν ἐπέβλεψεν καὶ ἐνέπλησεν αὐτὴν τῶν ἀγαθῶν αὐτοῦ) and *Ws* 1:7 (πνεῦμα κυρίου πεπλήρωκεν τὴν οἰκουμένην) where the omnipresence of God is expressed, if not by the noun πλήρωμα, at least by the corresponding verbs (ἐμ-) πίμπλημι, πληρόω.

St Paul then found the idea of the universe as a 'Fullness' where God is present in all things, not only in the form of a pantheist immanentism in Stoic vocabulary, but already adapted to the transcendence of Biblical monotheism in some of the Books of Scripture. Then, when he wanted to refer to the Universe which is the frame for humanity, and which, without being the Body of Christ, was nevertheless encompassed in his recreative work, would he not have realised that πλήρωμα was a completely appropriate term? At any rate I propose to understand it in this way in the epistles of the captivity. I see in itthe Fullness of being, not only the Fullness of the divinity, an interpretation which we have refuted already, but also that of the Cosmos; and not only the Fullness of the Cosmos, as perhaps we are meant to think by the exegesis of Theodore of Mopsuestia, but also that of the divinity. It is the whole of this that is gathered up in Christ[2]. He is

---

[1] Cf. W.L. KNOX, *op. cit.*, p. 164; J. DUPONT, *op. cit.*, pp. 468–70.
[2] J. Gewiess, in the article quoted from the *Festschrift Meinertz*, sees a plenitude of divine life in the πλήρωμα of *Col* 1:19; 2:9f; *Ep* 1:23; 3:19; 4:13; but a cosmic

God and, through his redemptive work, he takes up into himself as
a New Creation, not only the regenerated mankind which is his Body,
but the whole new world which forms the frame of that Body.

To return to *Col* 1 : 19, πᾶν τὸ πλήρωμα includes τὰ πάντα, or again
εἴτε τὰ ἐπὶ τῆς γῆς εἴτε τὰ ἐν τοῖς οὐρανοῖς, the earthly world and
the heavenly world, including the divine world which Christ carries
within himself by nature since he is the Son, the 'Εἰκών. It is easier
now to understand how this presence in him of the πλήρωμα can be
called a 'dwelling' and be the result of the good 'pleasure' of God.
What cannot be true for his divine being is surely true for this taking
the universe in charge, which constitutes a new and gratuitous stage
in the divine plan of salvation. This stage certainly begins with the
Incarnation, but finds its full realisation in the Redemption. If we
lay the stress on the first aspect, the καί in v. 20 will have a consecutive
force: Christ, having through his Incarnation gathered into himself
the whole universe, divine, human and even cosmic, fragmented by
sin, was able to reconcile and bring peace back to everything through
his expiatory death and his resurrection. If we lay the stress on the
second, as I believe is preferable, the καί will have an explanatory
force: it was by reconciling and pacifying the fragmented parts of
this Universe through Christ's death, that God caused it to 'dwell' in
him as in the new Being, the New Creation, where Everything, God
and the World, is put in order again. We have already discussed the
way in which the redemptive act of the Cross and the Resurrection
are of interest even for the Angelic or material Cosmos, but only to
admit that Paul does not explain himself with complete clarity on this
point. In this context it is really the heavenly Powers who are his
principal preoccupation and whom he is anxious to integrate into the
new world ἐν Χριστῷ, and with them the material world which they

---

plenitude in the πληροῦν (– οῦσθαι) of *Ep* 1 : 23 and 4 : 10, and he tries to harmonise
these two senses which seem to him entirely disparate: 'Der Begriff der Erfüllung
hat einen ganz verschiedenen Sinn, je nachdem er auf die Kirche oder auf das
All angewendet wird' (p. 139). For my part, I recognise a slight shift in the use
of πλήρωμα between *Col* and *Ep*, but I would place it and explain it otherwise.
I think too that the opposition between the order of creation and the order of
recreation must not be taken too far, but on the contrary that they should be
seen as continuous, a fact which authorises the way the term shifts under the
fingers of St Paul. God fills the world with his creative power; when he takes it
in hand again, after the catastrophe of sin, in the person of Christ, he fills it
with new life, but in different modes according to whether it is a matter of saved
mankind or the cosmos which is his frame. On the particularly 'soteriological'
way in which Paul envisages the creation and the cosmos, J.M. Gonzalez Ruiz
(*art. cit.*) has some good things to say but they need some qualifications.

rule through their Law and their observances. It matters little whether they have been stripped of their former prerogatives and ranged tamely under the domination of Christ or whether they have been reduced to impotence as conquered enemies. It must be – and this is sufficient for Paul – that the glorified Christ is their Chief, and through them the Chief of the whole universe, just as he is by a special privilege the Chief, the Head of the Body he has saved: in this way the whole 'Fullness' truly does dwell in him –the Fullness of God which he is by nature and the Fullness of the World which he brought back under obedience to him.

If this exegesis of *Col* 1:19 is correct, it ought to be verified also in regard to the other texts where the word πλήρωμα occurs, at least in regard to *Col* 2:9, which is so closely related to 1:19 by literary links. Here again it is a question of the dwelling in Christ of the whole Fullness. This time, it is true, the 'Fullness' is qualified by the genitive τῆς θεότητος which seems at first sight to give support to the exegesis we have rejected earlier: surely it is merely the 'Fullness of the divinity' which dwells in Christ in its entirety, as opposed to those Aeons of the Gnostic which share this Fullness between them? But again we have to take into account the adverb σωματικῶς which in its turn qualifies the whole idea. The supporters of the exegesis we are discussing find confirmation for their view here; it was by taking a σῶμα, that is by becoming incarnate, that Christ made the whole Fullness of the divinity dwell in a man. Of itself this interpretation is perfectly tenable; it is, I think, fundamentally true. But I believe too that it has to be completed and amplified to the cosmic dimensions which are envisaged in this epistle, and in particular in the immediate context. Paul is preoccupied with opposing Christ to the 'elements of the world' (v. 8), that is to the heavenly Powers and the whole former material Cosmos over which they ruled; and he is going to demonstrate straightaway that these Powers have been dismissed from their cosmic role, because Christ has become their 'Chief' (v. 10) and has stripped them of their empire (v. 15). From now on it is he who holds the entire new world of the eschatological era under his sway. And this idea, which seems clearly to be demanded by the context, is expressed in v. 9, which takes up the exact thought of 1:19, but makes it more precise. That which dwells in Christ is indeed the same Pleroma such as we have already understood it: the Fullness of Being, of God and of the world; but this time the two components of this Fullness are expressed analytically; God (τῆς θεότητος) and the world (σωματικῶς). It is in fact permissible to give σῶμα which is at the root of this adverb a wider extension than the single individual body of Christ. I said above that in Paul's eyes this risen body was enlarged by all the human bodies that link themselves to it through the sacraments of salvation, and we have seen too that in the Stoic philosophy known to St Paul σῶμα was in current use to describe the whole Cosmos in its diverse unity. This cosmic sense seems to me to fit here[1]. In Christ the divinity dwells according to a corporeal mode, first certainly by reason of the individual body which he took when he became incarnate, but following that through the whole of mankind whom he unites to himself, and lastly through the whole of the frame of humanity, the whole renewed Universe which he carries in embryo in his state as the New Creation. At the bottom of all this there is indeed the Incarnation, which brought the divinity to dwell in a human body, but there is also and especially the Redemption, the Resurrection through which there overflows from this risen body a new life in the Spirit which spreads to all the saved, and indirectly to the whole Universe.

The words which follow at the beginning of v. 10, καὶ ἐστὲ ἐν αὐτῷ πεπληρωμένοι describe the privileged situation of Christians in this new order. Before the Sovereignties and the Powers which are set beneath Christ as their Head (v. 10b), Christians are *in* Christ and are 'filled', not of course with the divinity, but with the incarnate divine life of Christ the Pleroma which is poured out over the new Universe and of which they are the privileged beneficiaries. It seems to me to be necessary to interpret this participle πεπληρωμένοι in the light of the noun πλήρωμα which is close by; but at the same time we have to take account of an earlier theme of Paul's which is re-introduced. Paul has often already spoken of the Christian 'filled' with consolation (*2 Co* 7:4), with joy and peace (*Rm* 15:13), with knowledge (*Rm* 15:14), with the fruit of justice which Jesus Christ produces (*Ph* 1:11); here too (1:9) he has prayed that the Colossians may be 'filled' with the full knowledge of the divine will, and in *Ep* 5:18, he is to exhort his readers to be filled, not with wine, but with the Spirit. This use of the theme of 'fullness' suggests simply and in a wholly spontaneous manner the outpouring of divine graces in the human heart; it owes nothing to the more precise concept of cosmic fullness

---

[1] Cf. Theodore of Mopsuestia (ed. Swete, I, p. 286): quoniam omnis creatura in eo inhabitat, hoc est, ipsi coniuncta est, et quasi quoddam corpus in se retinet aptatum, propter illam copulationem quae ad eum est.

and is prior to it. It was inevitable however, since the latter had arrived on the scene, that the two forms of the theme should come to be combined, since they used the same words and were both linked to the same fundamental idea of the life flowing from God to accumulate in his creatures, on this side as spiritual benefits, on that as cosmic recreation. We do in fact find the two themes fused, and first of all in this v. 10a: Christians are 'filled' because they exist from now on, in the first place, in Christ who is the Pleroma of the new world; but this also means, and more profoundly, that they are filled with the new risen life which he gives them by their being incorporated into him through baptism (vv. 11–13). These are not two different ideas, but two aspects of the one idea, the second being the only one that is important in Paul's eyes and being linked to earlier expressions of his, while the second has appeared late in his work to answer the speculations of the Colossians.

Can we pursue the same sense of πλήρωμα in the epistle to the Ephessians? Yes and no. Yes, because the term reappears there three times and manifestly in the line inaugurated in *Col*; no, in so far as it gets a slightly different application from a context of thought which is not exactly the same. In his epistle to the Ephesians, which is composed at least logically after the epistle to the Colossians, Paul is no longer so much anxious to refute the error of the latter as to re-think, on the cosmic plane to which that had lifted him, the great problem so close to his heart, that of the reunion of humanity in the salvation of Christ. The cosmic supremacy of Christ and his triumph over the heavenly Powers are facts acquired by the exposition of *Col* which it is sufficient to recall (*Ep* 1:10, 20–2), even to illustrate with a piece of midrashic exegesis (4:8–10)[1]. What is important from then on is to re-think and, in this fresh perspective, to resolve the anguishing problem of *Rm* 9–11, that of the juxtaposition of Jews and Gentiles in one and the same salvation. Whence the increased importance of the theme of the Body of Christ, which is the Church (1:23; 5:23–32) and the insistence on its unity (2:16; 4:4; 4:7–16). Whence a more marked transference of the image of Christ the Head of the Powers to Christ the Head of the Church (1:22; 4:15f; 5:23). Whence lastly, and this is what interests us at the moment, a kind

---

[1] Cf. BÜCHSEL, *TWNT*, III, pp. 641–3; J. GEWIESS, *art. cit.* (Festschrift Meinertz) p. 129ff; P. BENOIT, 'Les Épitres de la captivité' (*Bible de Jérusalem*), 2nd ed., 1953, p. 96f.

of identification of the πλήρωμα with the Body/Church. The Pleroma as equalling the Cosmic Fullness, including God and the World, no longer interests the mind of Paul for its own sake. The Church invades the whole field of his thought. And he restricts the idea of the Fullness to her or, if you prefer, he extends the Church to the dimensions of the Pleroma, giving her thus a cosmic dimension[1]. This is not a substantial modification such as would demand the intervention of another author. It is simply a return on Paul's part to what has always been at the centre of his interest. He occupied himself with the heavenly Powers and the Cosmos only because there were those at Colossae who were too much occupied with them; and it was only to insist that all that is also encompassed by the re-creative work of Christ. The alarm over, he returns to what alone really interests him, the salvation of man, the Body of Christ, the Church; and now to describe it as occupying the whole field of the new world in Christ.

This identification of the Church/Body with the Pleroma appears clearly with the first occurrence of the word, in *Ep* 1:23; τὸ πλήρωμα is in apposition to τὸ σῶμα which is itself said of the Church. It manifests itself again in 4:13 where the πλήρωμα τοῦ Χριστοῦ, figuring in a context which deals with the construction of the Body (vv. 12 and 15f), is clearly co-extensive with that Body. It has however, in this context of 'growth', a suggestion of accomplishment, of achievement, which underlies the πληρόω theme and which cannot be eliminated *a priori*[2]. The dwelling of the 'Fullness' in Christ is a fact acquired in principle from the Incarnation on but crowned by the Resurrection, and *Col* could be content with affirming this fact. But it is also the object of a process of becoming, a result to be obtained by applying the salvation of Christ to all those to be saved in the concrete, and through them to the whole Cosmos, and this throughout the entire intermediate period between the Resurrection and the Parousia. On this score, the Fullness takes on the aspect of an achievement which is realised little by little up to the appointed day when it will attain the 'mature stature' of the 'perfect Man'[3], εἰς ἄνδρα τέλειον, εἰς μέτρον ἡλικίας τοῦ πληρώματος τοῦ Χριστοῦ. Combining

---

[1] Cf. SCHLIER-WARNACH, *Die Kirche im Epheserbrief,* pp. 30ff, 88ff.

[2] Cf. WARNACH, *op. cit.,* p. 13, who upholds the double force, both active and passive of πλήρωμα; compare SCHLIER, *ibid.,* pp. 90, 110.

[3] This 'perfect man' is often understood of the individual Christian, but the context suggests rather the collective sense of Christ uniting Christians to himself in one 'New Man' to which the divine plan assigns a growth into maturity; cf. WIKENHAUSER, *op. cit.,* p. 182. E. MERSCH, *op. cit.,* I, p. 184, n. 3, quotes numerous Fathers in support.

these themes as they are in this text, we can say that the individual Christ has already arrived as 'Head' at the perfection of the new order, in the heavens (4:15, cf. 1:20–2), but that his Body, made up of all those who are saved, is still being constructed on earth (vv. 12: 16; cf. 2:20–2) and that, growing in this way, it completes and achieves the 'Fullness of Christ' in its perfect state determined by God (cf. *Col* 2:19 τὴν αὔξησιν τοῦ θεοῦ)[1].

This idea of Christ being realised in his Fullness is found again in 1:23; τὸ πλήρωμα τοῦ τὰ πάντα ἐν πᾶσιν πληρουμένου. Many exegetes want to take this particle as a middle with an active sense: Christ fills all things[2]. But the passive sense, supported by philology[3], and adopted by the majority of the ancient versions[4] and the Fathers[5], seems clearly preferable[6]. It takes up the well-known double meaning of the Stoic theme, where God 'fills' and 'is filled by' the world[7], and applies it to the case of Christ: Christ 'fills' the new world by taking possession of it with the cosmic extension of his recreative influence, but he 'is filled' too by this world in the degree to which he is progressively completed and achieved in his total Fullness by the growth of the Church and of the world which the Church draws after itself into Christ.

In these last words of v. 23, some old interpreters wanted to see the Fullness of God, not of Christ[8]. This exegesis is not supported by the immediate context; but is in line with an idea which is not incorrect and which is expressed in *Ep* 3:19. Here we find ourselves

---

[1] This idea of a 'fullness' assigned by the divine plan to the growth of the Body of Christ can be compared to other measures which are to be 'filled', equally foreseen for the end of time in God's design: sins (*1 Th* 2:16; cf. *Mt* 23:32), time (*Ga* 4:4; cf. *Ep* 1:10), pagans to be converted (*Rm* 11:25), the preaching of the Gospel (*Rm* 15:19; *Col* 1:25), Messianic trials (*Col* 1:24), martyrs (*Rv* 6:11); cf. J. JEREMIAS, on *2 Tm* 2:10 in *N.T. Deutsch*, Göttingen, IX, p. 44. — To admit the Stoic origin of the term πλήρωμα in the vocabulary of *Col* and *Ep*, as we have just done with Dom Dupont, does not prevent our envisaging fresh shades of meaning which it could have got from earlier themes of Paul in which it had already been used. Dom Dupont himself recognises this (*op. cit.*, p. 475), but without drawing the full consequences.

[2] See, e.g., the well-documented discussion by J. SCHMID, *op. cit.*, pp. 187–92.

[3] The middle use of πληροῦν is very rare in secular Greek, and there is no other example in the N.T. Paul, in particular, is well able to use the active when he wants to express an active sense: cf. *Ep* 4:10; *Col* 1:25; 4:17, etc.

[4] The Peshitta is the only exception; cf. ROBINSON, *Comm. ad loc.*

[5] Origen, Chrysostom, Theodore of Mopsuestia, and all the Latins (Jerome, Pelagius, Ambrosiaster . . .), for whom the reading *adimpletur* left no doubt.

[6] τὰ πάντα ἐν πᾶσιν is then to be taken adverbially.

[7] Cf. DUPONT, *op. cit.*, pp. 457ff, 473ff.

[8] Theodore of Mopsuestia, Theodoret and Severian of Gabala here attribute the σῶμα to Christ and the πλήρωμα to the Father; cf. Swete's edition of Theodore of Mopsuestia, I, p. 141, note.

at the end of a prayer which has been sketched several times (1:16; 3:1) and is at last expressed (3:14–19): it is addressed to the Father with all the cosmic significance of that word[1], the Father from whom all fatherhood on earth and in heaven derives (v. 15), and it asks him to invade the spirits and the hearts of his faithful with the riches of his glory, through the gift of the Spirit and the dwelling in them of his Christ, to bring them to the knowledge which surpasses all knowledge, that of the love of Christ. The summit of this flight where Paul has accumulated everything that is strongest, most intense and most 'cosmic' in his vocabulary is 'the whole Fullness', no longer of Christ, but 'of God'. It is here that all else must lead. God is always the term of the work of Christ, the work which he has directed from end to end, by sending him, by having him put to death, by raising him and by glorifying him. It was *His* pleasure to cause the Fullness to dwell in Christ. It is He who is its first source and its ultimate end. It is he who fills Christ with the Fullness of his divine life and his recreated world. It is therefore in Him, in his total Fullness, that salvation is achieved: this is the final term (εἰς) to which the saved come, loaded with a fullness (ἵνα πληρωθῆτε) which integrates them into the whole Fullness of God (εἰς πᾶν τὸ πλήρωμα τοῦ θεοῦ). In this text which itself visualises a fullness as vast as possible, the expressions must be taken in their maximum amplitude. It is the whole fullness, not only of the cosmos but of the divine life as well, not only of Christ but of God as well, which is at the end of all things; and it is in constituting this Fullness, as well as being filled with it, that Christians find their consummation.

We have here the supreme flowering of one of Paul's essential ideas and of the expressions which he puts at its service. The sacramental union of the bodies of Christians with the risen body of Christ; the making in this way of a Body of Christ, which is the Church, and which grows continually; the governing and the enlivening of this Body of Christ conceived as its Head, first as the chief who rules it, but also as the principle that nourishes it; the extension of this influence of Christ to the whole universe which he holds within himself with his divinity in a Pleroma where all things are reconciled in a unity; finally, the Fullness of God himself who, through Christ, is at the origin and at the end of this whole work of recreation – such is the doctrine which we have seen being elaborated under our eyes, and it has an admirable coherence. It has been constructed with the

---

[1] Cf. DUPONT, *op. cit.*, pp. 340–5.

help of various themes, coming from various literary milieux, born of various needs and even of passing polemics. But far from embarrassing or contradicting one another, these multiple elements have found themselves organised, amalgamated and fused by a mind of exceptional power, of genius perhaps one should say, to produce a synthesis of an incomparable profundity. We have taken it for granted that all this while we have been listening to St Paul. And surely a constructive explanation like this, if it is admitted, is the best proof that *Col* and even *Ep*, even if they are not entirely from his hand[1], are at least the product of his heart and mind? In this view of Christ and the cosmic dimensions of his salvation, however developed it may be, there is still to be found the first insight that felled him on the Damascus road: Jesus is risen, he lives in his own, the eschatological era has begun, and now it is only Christ who counts, who is 'all in all'.

---

[1] The principal objection to the authenticity of *Ep* is literary: the phrases of *Col* are taken up, combined or divided, adapted and sometimes twisted, with a somewhat slavish application which it is difficult to attribute to Paul himself. Perhaps we should recognise in it the hand of a disciple, working under the direction of the Apostle and using the recently completed epistle to the Colossians to help him in editing this.

Primitive Christianity

Acts 2: 42-47

42 ἦσαν δὲ προσκαρτεροῦντες τῇ διδαχῇ τῶν ἀποστόλων καὶ τῇ κοινωνίᾳ, τῇ κλάσει τοῦ ἄρτου καὶ ταῖς προσευχαῖς.

43 Ἐγίνετο δὲ πάσῃ ψυχῇ φόβος· πολλὰ δὲ τέρατα καὶ σημεῖα διὰ τῶν ἀποστόλων ἐγίνετο.

44 Πάντες δὲ οἱ πιστεύσαντες ἐπὶ τὸ αὐτὸ εἶχον ἅπαντα κοινά,

45 καὶ τὰ κτήματα καὶ τὰς ὑπάρξεις ἐπίπρασκον καὶ διεμέριζον αὐτὰ πᾶσιν, καθότι ἄν τις χρείαν εἶχεν.

46 Καθ' ἡμέραν τε προσκαρτεροῦντες ὁμοθυμαδὸν ἐν τῷ ἱερῷ, κλῶντές τε κατ' οἶκον ἄρτον, μετελάμβανον τροφῆς ἐν ἀγαλλιάσει καὶ ἀφελότητι καρδίας,

47a αἰνοῦντες τὸν θεὸν καὶ ἔχοντες χάριν πρὸς ὅλον τὸν λαόν.

47b Ὁ δὲ κύριος προσετίθει τοὺς σῳζομένους καθ' ἡμέραν ἐπὶ τὸ αὐτό.

4: 32-35

32 τοῦ δὲ πλήθους τῶν πιστευσάντων ἦν καρδία καὶ ψυχὴ μία, καὶ οὐδὲ εἷς τι τῶν ὑπαρχόντων αὐτῷ ἔλεγεν ἴδιον εἶναι, ἀλλ' ἦν αὐτοῖς πάντα κοινά.

33 Καὶ δυνάμει μεγάλῃ ἀπεδίδουν τὸ μαρτύριον οἱ ἀπόστολοι τοῦ κυρίου Ἰησοῦ τῆς ἀναστάσεως, χάρις τε μεγάλη ἦν ἐπὶ πάντας αὐτούς.

34 Οὐδὲ γὰρ ἐνδεής τις ἦν ἐν αὐτοῖς· ὅσοι γὰρ κτήτορες χωρίων ἢ οἰκιῶν ὑπῆρχον, πωλοῦντες ἔφερον τὰς τιμὰς τῶν πιπρασκομένων

35 καὶ ἐτίθουν παρὰ τοὺς πόδας τῶν ἀποστόλων· διεδίδοτο δὲ ἑκάστῳ καθότι ἄν τις χρείαν εἶχεν.

5: 12-15

[11 καὶ ἐγένετο φόβος μέγας ἐφ' ὅλην τὴν ἐκκλησίαν καὶ ἐπὶ πάντας τοὺς ἀκούοντας ταῦτα.]

12a Διὰ δὲ τῶν χειρῶν τῶν ἀποστόλων ἐγίνετο σημεῖα καὶ τέρατα πολλὰ ἐν τῷ λαῷ·

12b Καὶ ἦσαν ὁμοθυμαδὸν πάντες ἐν τῇ στοᾷ Σολομῶντος.

13 τῶν δὲ λοιπῶν οὐδεὶς ἐτόλμα κολλᾶσθαι αὐτοῖς, ἀλλ' ἐμεγάλυνεν αὐτοὺς ὁ λαός.

14 Μᾶλλον δὲ προσετίθεντο πιστεύοντες τῷ κυρίῳ, πλήθη ἀνδρῶν τε καὶ γυναικῶν·

15 ὥστε καὶ εἰς τὰς πλατείας ἐκφέρειν τοὺς ἀσθενεῖς καὶ τιθέναι ἐπὶ κλιναρίων καὶ κραβάττων, ἵνα ἐρχομένου Πέτρου κἂν ἡ σκιὰ ἐπισκιάσῃ τινὶ αὐτῶν.

16 συνήρχετο δὲ καὶ τὸ πλῆθος τῶν πέριξ πόλεων Ἰερουσαλήμ, φέροντες ἀσθενεῖς καὶ ὀχλουμένους ὑπὸ πνευμάτων ἀκαθάρτων, οἵτινες ἐθεραπεύοντο ἅπαντες.

4. Some notes on the 'Summaries' in Acts 2, 4 and 5[*]

The narratives in the first chapters of Acts which concern the interior life and apostolic influence of the primitive community are separated and linked by 'summaries' the interest of which has long been noticed: they are a kind of broad outline which depict in a general way characteristics or attitudes of the community of which the adjacent narratives furnish particular illustrations. Three of them stand out by reason of their length: 2:42-7; 4:32-5; 5:12-16; and they are clearly distinguished from the notes on the continuous growth of the community, scattered throughout the book, which are equally general but much briefer[1]. These notes are in fact mere halts which mark out the course of the narrative, like the punctuation marks which emphasise and facilitate the progress of our speech: as J. de Zwaan has happily expressed it[2], they are 'stops' rather than 'summaries'. On the other hand, the three summaries with which we are concerned, although they do include examples of this constant refrain (2:47b; 5:14), set out to do more, to be brief but true pictures which recapitulate the life of the primitive community[3].

Their literary composition however, after a brief analysis, reveals some unusual features[4]. There seem to be additions which interrupt a

---

[*] Contributed to the symposium *Aux Sources de la Tradition chrétienne, Mélanges offerts à M. Maurice Goguel*, Neuchâtel-Paris, 1950, pp. 1–10.
[1] 2:47b; 5:14; 6:7; 9:31; 12:24; 16:5; 19:20. And see also, in the course of narratives, 1:15b; 2:41b; 4:4; 6:1a; 9:42; 11:21–24b; 13:48f; 14:1, 21; 17:4, 12; 18:8; 19:10.
[2] *HThR*, XVII, 1924, 103.
[3] The summaries in the Gospels with which some are ready to compare them, such as Mk 3:7–12, Lk 6:17–19 and 4:41, are a little different and occupy an intermediary position between 'stops' and 'summaries'; they are longer than the former, but their content is more general and vague than that of the latter. Elsewhere the gospel of Luke provides some excellent examples of 'stops'; 1:80; 2:40, 52; 4:14, 37 (cf. Mk 1:28), etc.
[4] As well as the commentaries and works which study the sources of Acts in general, more detailed studies of these summaries are to be found in JUNGST, *Die Quellen der Apg.*, 1895, 51–6; K. LAKE, *The Beginnings of Christianity*, vol. V, p. 141ff; H.J. CADBURY, *ibid.*, p. 397ff; L. CERFAUX, *Ephem. Théol. Lovan.*,

primitive and simpler substratum and break the thread. Each of these summaries includes, in addition to elements which belong to it alone, other features which are to be found again, and better situated, in the other two; the result is that there are, between these three brief pictures, striking parallelisms which look like actual doublets. It is the general opinion, for example, that the natural thread of the second summary is broken by the intrusion of v. 33 and that, in the first summary, vv. 44-5 are a condensed anticipation of the second.

However, the explanation of this literary fact varies considerably according to the critic and seems to need further review[1]. We shall demonstrate this in particular with reference to two more recent attempts, those of Canon Cerfaux and Professor Joachim Jeremias[2]. For the latter, the primitive state of the summaries was made up of 2:41-2, 4:32 and 34-5, and 5:11-14; all the rest would be due to editorial expansion, 2:43 being inspired by 5:11-12a; 2:44-5 by 4:32, 34-5; 2:46a by 5:12b; 2:46b by 2:42; 2:47 by 5:13b-14; 4:33a by 5:42; 4:33b by 2:47a; lastly 5:15-16 by 8:6f and 19:11f. M. Cerfaux, on his part, makes the primitive layer consist of 2:46-7a, 4:32 and 34-5, and 5:11-16; he attributes 2:41-2 to Luke's editorial activity and derives 2:43 from 5:11-12a; 2:44f from 4:32 and 34-5; 2:47b from 5:14; 4:33b from 5:13b: as for 4:33a, in its primitive state this appeared between 5:12a and 12b.

These analyses agree on several points, which are in fact indisputable, such as the borrowing of 2:43 from 5:11-12a and that of 2:44-5 from 4:32, 34-5, but they diverge considerably on many others. Would it not be possible to envisage a different analysis, which would have the advantage of distinguishing in the three summaries a similar distribution into a primitive layer and editorial additions? I propose in fact to treat 2:42, 46-7; 4:32, 34-5; and 5:12a, 15-16 as primitive and 2:43-5; 4:33; and 5:12b-14 as secondary (see the table on p. 94).

As regards the second summary everyone is very nearly in agreement: 4:34-5 should follow on from 4:32 since these three verses provide a continuous and homogeneous picture of the sharing of possessions in the primitive community, while verse 33 interrupts

---

XIII, 1936, pp. 673-80 and XVI, 1939, p. 5ff; JOACHIM JEREMIAS, *ZNW*, XXXVI, 1937, p. 206f.

[1] The old school of source criticism of Acts, represented by SPITTA, JUNGST, etc., attempted to explain the composite character of these passages by the fusion of the same two sources A and B, plus editorial activity R, which it distinguished in the remainder of Acts. But the results obtained in this way do not carry conviction.   [2] See note 4.

this picture with a different idea, that of the apostolic preaching and its success with the crowd. But the situation is surely the same for the third summary, where vv. 15–16 would follow on very well after v. 12a[1] to describe the wonders worked by the apostles, whereas the intervening verses introduce ideas which are, if not contradictory, at least disparate: the diligence of the faithful (?) in meeting at the Portico of Solomon, the complex reactions of the crowd, and lastly the well-known refrain which runs all through Acts about the continual growth of the young community. The ὥστε καί of verse 15 and the consequence which it introduces (the crowding in of the sick) are surely better explained if they follow v. 12a (the miraculous powers of the apostles) than if they follow v. 14 (the growth of the community)[2]. It seems difficult therefore to allocate 12b–14 to the primitive substratum of the third summary as do Cerfaux and Jeremias. Lastly, to come back to the first summary, it again seems evident, as both realised, that 2:43–5 are secondary elements taken from elsewhere, but I myself would add that there too they have been inserted between verses of an older layer whose thread they have broken: verses 46–7 in fact follow very well after v. 42, since they describe in detail the common life of prayer and apostolic influence which v. 42 has enunciated in a balanced and lapidary formula, while the ideas of fear among the people (v. 43a), of miracles and wonders (43b) and the sharing of possessions (44–5) are foreign to the subject matter of this first summary[3]. This presupposes, against Cerfaux, that v. 42 indeed comes from the primitive layer and not from secondary editorial activity[4]. It is true that the two elements of the διδαχὴ τῶν ἀποστόλων and the κοινωνία may seem to go beyond the horizon of the first summary and to anticipate that of the other two; this is what

---

[1] Thus WELLHAUSEN, *Kritische Analyse der Apg.*, 1914, 10; GOGUEL, *Introd. au N.T.*, III, 1922, p. 186f; and many others.

[2] Cf. among others JUNGST, *loc. cit.*, 51f, and LAKE, *Beginnings*, IV, 53f, who rightly compare it with the construction of 19:11 which is analogous. On the other hand H.H. WENDT (*Komm. Meyer*) succeeds in finding a satisfactory logical sequence in the third summary as it now stands, as in the other two. HARNACK (*Die Apostelgeschichte*, 1908, 167) links v. 15 to v. 13 and regards only v. 14 as interpolated; similarly, V. ROSE, *Revue Biblique*, 1898, 341.

[3] It is hardly natural to explain the fear of v. 43 by the impression that the events of Pentecost made on the crowd; thus WENDT, LOISY and others.

[4] Besides, Cerfaux himself, in other passages in his article (pp. 673 and 680), seems disposed to link 2:43 to the 'Document' received and utilised by Luke. As for v. 41, I prefer to see it as the conclusion of the narrative of 2:1–40 rather than as the beginning of the summary in 42–7, while acknowledging the fact that Luke has formulated this conclusion as a transition (οἱ μὲν οὖν) which carries forward the progress of his narrative and introduces his favourite theme of the growth of the community.

influences Cerfaux to see it as a little editorial prelude in which Luke synthesises in advance all the different aspects of the life of the primitive commumity. But this observation may be taken into account, in so far as it is well founded, simply by admitting that the primitive opening of the second summary, the traces of which are still to be seen in 42b, has in fact been expanded by the editorial addition of the two first terms enunciated in 42a. But this concession may perhaps not be necessary. The διδαχή τῶν ἀποστόλων may very well not be so foreign to the subject-matter of the first summary as it appears at first sight: isn't this apostolic teaching closely associated with the life of liturgical prayer?[1] didn't it have a privileged place in the course of those meals in which the 'breaking of bread', perhaps the Eucharist, was celebrated?[2] and isn't it discreetly conveyed in v. 47a in that 'praising God' which found favour with all the people (compare 4:33, which derives as we shall see from 2:47a; and also v. 42 which while resuming 2:46–7 in addition makes the notion of preaching more explicit)?[3] As for κοινωνιά, it is perhaps unnecessary to see it as a technical term, of Pythagorean origin, for the sharing of *possessions*[4], since it can be understood simply of that union of heart and spirit which is described in the first summary[5] and is to be found expressed by the same term in other passages of the New Testament (*Ga* 2:9; *Phm* 6; 1 *Jn* 1:3, 6, 7)[6].

In order to explain the editorial additions with which the primitive form of each of these summaries has been expanded, it is sufficient to have recourse to the other summaries and also to the narratives which

---

[1] WELLHAUSEN, *loc. cit.*, regards this διδαχή as teaching inside the community, distinct from preaching to people outside it. The observation may be valid for the context under discussion, but it is certain that διδάσκειν is used in these chapters to mean preaching outside the community, cf. 4:2, 18; 5:21, 25, 28, 42.

[2] O. BAUERNFEIND (*Theol. Handkomment.*, V, 1939, 54) relates all four terms of v. 42 to the celebration of the Eucharist: it was at these liturgical gatherings that they 'taught', that they brought 'alms' (for this meaning of κοινωνιά, cf. *Rm* 15:26), that they 'broke bread' and that they 'prayed'.

[3] The possible translation 'giving thanks (to God) in the presence of the whole people', proposed as an alternative by LAKE (*Beginnings*, IV, 30)—for this meaning of χάριν ἔχειν, cf. *Lk* 17:7; *I Tm* 1:12; *2 Tm* 1:3; and the classics and papyrus, BAUER, *Wört* 3, col. 1454—seems less probable. The idea of 'favour with the people' (thus PREUSCHEN, BAUERNFEIND . . .) fits the context better and is confirmed by the resumptions of 4:33 and 5:13.

[4] CAMPBELL (*JBL*, LI, 1932, 374f) sees here, as in *Heb* 13:16, the spirit of generosity, which expresses itself by contributions of money.

[5] BAUER, *Wört* 3, 729: 'the community (brotherly), togetherness. Similarly the commentaries of WENDT, ZAHN, PREUSCHEN and A. CARR, *Expositor*, May 1913, 458–64.

[6] The Latin (*communicatione fractionis panis*), Coptic and Syriac translations have the communion of the Eucharistic rite in mind.

they enclose. 2:43 is an obvious borrowing from 5:11–12a as has already been noticed; this unexpected mention of fear among the people (43a), which is followed without any perceptible logical connection (notice the clumsy succession of two δε) by the announcement of the miraculous powers of the apostles (43b)[1] is explicable only in 5:11–12, where these two disparate ideas represent respectively the conclusion of the episode of Ananias and Sapphira, where the fear is properly motivated, and the beginning of the third summary. In the same way, 2:44–5 is a résumé of 4:32, 34–5; on this point too everyone is agreed[2]. In this case, it is simpler surely to explain the addition made in the second summary, 4:33[3], as inspired by the first (2:47a). To make 4:33a derived from 5:42, as Jeremias wants to do, seems unnecessary, especially as this latter verse is itself plainly editorial and for resumes 2:46–7a. For the same reason I refuse to follow Cerfaux in explaining 4:33b by 5:13b which I believe to be equally editorial. As for thinking that in the primitive state 4:33a appeared between 5:12a and 12b, this seems even more difficult, since on the one hand the two halves of this verse do not belong to the same layer and on the other the editorial re-working of these summaries is never done by cutting back and displacing texts but much more by making additions which complete and create doublets. It will be admitted that 4:33a is to be explained as a resumption of 2:47a if one recognises that the χαρίς μεγάλη of 33b means, not the divine grace which assists the apostles, but the high regard they meet with from the people, as in 2:47a[4], and on the other hand that the apostolic witness of 33a has already been hinted at in the 'praising God' of 2:47a; if this last comparison appears too weak, it is sufficient to hold that the editor introduced this mention here of the witness given to the resurrection of Christ so frequently spoken of in Acts (1:22; 2:32; 3:15; 5:30–2). The editorial expansions of the

[1] Certain witnesses (א A C Vg) tried to remedy this stage of things by placing the mention of fear after the mention of miracles. But it is difficult to see this as the primitive arrangement of the text as does ROPES, *Beginnings*, III, 24.

[2] However it incorrect to present the whole of the first summary, 2:43–47, as a résumé of the second, 4:32–5; thus GOGUEL, *Intr. au N.T.*, III, 186; and cf. LAKE, *Beginnings*, v, 142ff.

[3] For HARNACK, *Die Apostelgeschichte*, 167, it is not a question here of addition but of displacement: v. 33 should be attached to v. 31, and v. 32, the opening of the fragment 32–4–5, has been inserted later inadvertently; similarly MOFFAT, *Introd. N. T.*, 1918, 311.

[4] This idea will be taken up again in the additions to the third summary, and one might suggest the following channel of verbal dependence: χάρις (2,47a) – χάρις μεγάλη (4,33a) – μεγαλύνειν (5,13).

third summary can easily be explained in the same way[1]. 5:12b is taken up from 2:46a, with the additional influence of 3:11; 5:13 repeats the idea of 2:47a, already taken up again in 4:33b, with the addition of a rather strange expression concerning the way in which the crowd kept their distance out of reverence (5:13a) which seems to resume the idea of the people's fear (5:5, 11) in the form of the general meaning it received in 2:43a. As for 5:14, this verse does no more than take its inspiration from 2:47b and from other similar passages such as 14:1; 17:4, 12; and 18:8, in order to introduce the theme of the continuing growth of the community. The following verses of the third summary, 15‑16, belong as we have already said to its primitive state and there is no reason to be seen for regarding them as Jeremias does, as being imitated from 8:6f and 19:11f. 8:6f does not present any notable similarity unless it is perhaps that we meet, quite naturally, 'unclean spirits' in connection with miraculous healings[2] and, if 19:11f constitutes a fairly striking parallel, this is no doubt because Luke himself wanted to make this parallelism between the miracle-working of Paul and that of the first apostles.

The greatest recommendation of the literary analysis proposed here is that it ends with the realisation that the three summaries have each received similar treatment from the hand of the editor. In each case he has made an addition which expands the meaning of the summary in the light of the themes developed in the other two; to the theme of the life of piety and edification, approved by the favour of the people, he has added brief anticipations of the themes of miracle-working and sharing of possessions; in the case of the sharing of possessions he has briefly recalled the first summary, the influence of the apostles and the people's favour; lastly, in order to reinforce the theme of miracle-working, he has made a further mention of the edifying life of the community and of the mixture of favour and fear felt by the people.

Furthermore, in each case, the editor has made the addition *in the middle of the already existing summary*, or, more exactly, shortly after its beginning. This interruption was conscious and calculated; it had no doubt the disadvantage of breaking up to some extent the logical sequence of the text, but it had also the advantage, great enough in his eyes to compensate for the disadvantage, of keeping intact the

[1] L. Dieu, *RBibl*, 1921, 93ff, sets out to explain matters in the opposite direction and makes 2:46-7 derive from 5:12b-14.
[2] This association, which results from the very nature of things, was already abundantly provided in the Gospel, cf. *Lk*, 6:18; 7:21; 8:2 etc.

beginning and end of the primitive summary, i.e. the points at which it was linked to the narrative context.

This leads us to the important conclusion that the editor found these summaries already organised with the narratives which they resume and generalise. This fact is probable enough in itself, but it is decisively confirmed by the proof that he read the beginning of the third summary (5:12) immediately following the Ananias and Sapphira episode (5:11), since he left these two verses very closely linked, awkward though this is, in the borrowing he carried out for 2:43.

Is this editor who intervened so clumsily Luke himself? It is difficult to believe so. Whatever may have been the part played by Luke in the composition of 2:42–5, whether he himself organised this grouping of three summaries and three narratives, or whether he received it in the form of a preceding Judaeo-Christian document, as Cerfaux thinks, it seems certain that he is principally responsible for chapters 2:42 to 5 in the state in which we have them[1]. Was it then Luke himself who, in putting the final touches to his work, remodelled the summaries in the way we have just analysed? The clumsiness of the remodelling prevents us believing this.

There is more: the language of these additions presents several peculiarities which work against our attributing them to Luke. Certainly there are some terms which do indeed belong to his vocabulary, such as for example 2:44f οἱ πιστεύσαντες, ἐπὶ τὸ αὐτό, καθότι; 5:12b ὁμοθύμαδον; 5:14 προσετίθεντο; but it is plain that the editor owes these to the passages which he has drawn on to make his additions. There are three terms alone to be noted that the editor cannot have got from the immediate context but which are nevertheless characteristic of Luke: they are διαμερίζειν (2:45; cf. Lk 11:17f; 12:52f; 22:17; 23:34; Ac 2:3), κολλᾶσθαι (5:13; cf. Lk 15:15; Ac 8:29; 9:26; 10:28; 17:34), and μεγαλύνειν (5:13; cf. Lk 1:46, 58; Ac 10:46; 19:17). But these words are in no way rare and could have been used by any writer, especially if he were familiar with the work of Luke. The contrary indications are, besides, much more striking. These are to begin with turns of speech which Luke does not ordinarily use or at any rate that he does not use in this way:

2:43 ἐγίνετο πάσῃ ψυχῇ φόβος: Luke's normal phrase is φόβος ἐπὶ with the accusative, cf. 5:5, 11; 19:17 and also Lk 1:12, 65; further,

---

[1] The 'Lucan' character of this group, as also its dependence on earlier sources which were probably written, emerges clearly from a study of its vocabulary and style; cf. particularly, L. CERFAUX, *Eph. Theol. Lovan.*, xvi, 1939, 6ff.

he uses πᾶσα ψυχή only in 3:23 in a quotation from the Septuagint (but cf. *Rm* 2:9; 13:1; *Rv* 16:3); διὰ τῶν ἀποστόλων seems contrary to the usage of 5:12; 14:3; 19:11 διὰ τῶν χειρῶν (τ.ἀπ.), although one might quote 2:22 and 4:16 in support of the briefer phrase;

2:45 ὑπάρξεις is a rare word that Luke never employs since he writes τὰ ὑπάρχοντα, cf. 4:32 and eight examples in the Gospel;

4:33 τὸ μαρτύριον is never met with this meaning in the work of Luke; but cf. *1 Co* 1:6; 2:1;

5:12 ὁμοθύμαδον, so frequent in the Acts, is there always found accompanying a verb which expresses action or progress which is carried out 'together' 'with one accord'; with the static verb 'to be', Luke prefers ὁμοῦ, ἐπὶ τὸ αὐτό, cf. 2:1; *Lk* 17:35;

5:14 πλήθη; Luke always uses this word in the singular; cf. with this meaning of 'a mass', 'a great number', 14:1; 17:4; 28:3; *Lk* 6:17.

In addition attention is to be drawn to the awkwardnessses, not to say mistakes, in the style which are to be observed in these verses and cause exegetes so much worry. The repetition of ἐγίνετο in 2:43 is weak and graceless. It is not easy to know to what we should refer the ἐπὶ τὸ αὐτό of 2:44, a fact which has led numerous texts to add ἦσαν. In 2:45, αὐτά is less clear than τὰς τιμάς in 4:34. The order of the words in 4:33a is so obscure and ambiguous that none of the textual variants has really succeeded in remedying it. Exegetes have not succeeded in deciding whether the πάντες of 5:12b are the apostles of 12a or the assembly of the faithful implicitly suggested by the opposition to the λοιποί. Lastly the manifest exaggeration of 5:13a, which contradicts 13b–14, denotes more zeal than skill in improving on the given text of Luke.

Such indeed seems to have been the intention of the editor who composed these interpolations; he wanted to reinforce Luke's summaries in order to adapt them better to the double role of preparing and generalising that they play with regard to the narratives. It is in this way that the addition of 2:43 anticipates the miraculous healing of the lame man and that of 5:13–14, underlines the popular enthusiasm which is going to force the members of the Sanhedrin to intervene while at the same time it prevents their taking too drastic measures against the apostles. And at the same time the additions improve on the generalising character of the primitive summaries. For example, 2:44f presents as realised and practised by the entire community a sharing of possessions which is described by the second summary with greater subtlety as an ideal in the hearts of all (4:32), realised in practice only by the rich (44) and under the control of the Apostles (35)[1]. Compare in the same way πάντες οἱ ἀκούοντες of 5:5–11 and πᾶσα ψυχή of 2:43; χάρις in 2:47 and χάρις μεγάλη in 4:33; the fear and the intimidation of 5:5, 11 and οὐδεὶς ἐτόλμα κολλᾶσθαι αὐτοῖς of 5:13a.

Whatever the intentions of the author of the additions in the summaries may have been, it seems to be established, by the clumsy nature of his interventions and by the colouring of his style, that that author was not Luke. Luke had composed pictures that were homogeneous and quite distinct and which showed none of the repititions, doublets and incoherences which spoil the present text. These irregularities are the doing of a later editor who had disfigured Luke's work while trying to perfect it.

It will be noticed that this literary analysis is opposed to Harnack's famous hypothesis, in so far as it suppresses several of the doublets which led him to distinguish two parallel sources A and B: 2:43 (B) and 5:12a (A); 2:44–5 (B) and 4:32–5 (A); 2:46–7 (B) and 5:12b–4 (A). It maintains the existence in the same document of two appearances before the Sanhedrin, but we know that that is not a true doublet: the two scenes are quite distinct and the duality corresponds no doubt to a well-known rule of Rabbinic jurisprudence, as K. Bornhauser and Joachim Jeremias have shown[2].

As for the intervention of an editor who touched up the work of Luke, this should cause no surprise if we remind ourselves that the book of Acts offers many other inconsistencies in the style or in the arrangement of the subject matter[3]. Certain critics have suggested that we should regard Acts as an imperfect and unfinished work to which Luke was unable to put the final touches and which was edited by one of his friends or disciples[4]. This plausible hypothesis may perhaps find some confimation from the literary analysis which I have put forward on these pages.

---

[1] Cf. J. WEISS, *Das Urchristentum*, 1914, 49ff. – We realise too that the second summary itself already represents a certain idealisation of the historical reality when it describes the sharing of goods as the ordinary and most obligatory rule of the first brethren, whereas the narrative of Barnabas's gesture presents it as an unwonted generosity, worthy to be remembered, and the episode of Ananias reminds us of its optional nature through Peter's own mouth (5:4a).

[2] Cf. *ZNW*, XXXVI, 1937, 208–13.

[3] Cf. in particular HARNACK, *Die Apostelgeschichte*, ch. VI: 'Die Inkorrektheiten und Unstimmigkeiten'.

[4] Cf. J. DE ZWAAN, 'Was the book of Acts a posthumous edition?', *HThR*, XVII, 1924, 95–153.

5. The origins of the Apostles' Creed in the New Testament*

For a long time it was believed that the 'Apostles' Creed' had really been composed by the Twelve Apostles, that the latter, at the moment when they separated to go out and conquer the world, had fixed the formula of the common faith they preached and that this formula, to which each had contributed an article, was no other than our apostolic creed. This belief, which appears at the end of the 4th century and probably goes back to still more remote times, flourished until the 15th century, at which time the critical spirit of the Renaissance became aware of its legendary charater.

The reaction that followed was necessary and healthy, but it went too far, so that modern scholars of the 19th and early 20th centuries were able to go to the opposite extreme and deny that the apostolic age had had a datum of faith solidly established and professed by everyone. Deceived by an analytic method which was useful in itself but was practised in a one-sided fashion, they happily emphasised the divergences between St John and St Paul, and even between St Paul and Jesus himself, and concluded that the first century of Christianity had seen only a flowering of disparate and even contradictory doctrines. It would have been only from the beginning of the 2nd century that the Church, now an organised institution, would have undertaken to unify these multifarious data and to canonise the result in a formula of faith; and this unification and canonisation, it is well understood, could not have been carried out without choosing, forcing and in part sacrificing the diverse tendencies of the first epoch.

But this extreme opinion has been corrected in its turn and work carried out in the last few years has given us a more exact picture. It has become apparent that, behind the indisputable divergences of theological development discerned by analysis, a profound unity concerning the essentials of the Christian message reigns throughout the

* Published in *Lumière et Vie*, 2, 1952, pp. 39–60.

writings of the New Testament. Furthermore, it has been recognised that this nucleus of the message is to be found enunciated more or less by everyone in similar stereotyped terms which, without having the fixity of the formulas to be elaborated in the end, nevertheless foreshadow and prepare us for them. In the light of this it again becomes true to say that the 'Apostles' Creed', in content as well as in form, derives in a direct line from the datum furnished by the writings of the Apostolic age; even if it was not composed by the Apostles in its present state, it still represents a faithful expression of the message they transmitted to the Church and in terms which even reflect the form in which they transmitted it.

This is what I propose to show in this essay, by studying (1) the content and the form of the apostolic preaching, especially the 'Kerygma' and (2) the content and the form of the first 'Confessions of Faith' which in certain privileged circumstances issued from the life of the nascent Church, since it was from the combination of these two elements that the Creed was born and it is through them that it really is linked to the Apostles.

1. THE APOSTOLIC 'KERYGMA'

What the Kerygma is

The Greek word *Kerygma* is used in the New Testament to denote the first triumphant preaching that the witnesses of Christ addressed to the world to bring to its notice the 'Good News' (the meaning of the word *euangelion*, gospel) of the salvation which God the Father had just achieved in his Son and through his Spirit. It differed from *Catechesis*, *Didache* and *Didaskalia*, which followed up and taught the converted doctrine they were to hold in a more systematic fashion, and from *Paraenesis*, which inculcated the moral obligations of their new way of life, by having a shock-effect – it was an announcement, a proclamation addressed to men still ignorant of Christ to call them to believe.

In this first contact only the essentials mattered. Like the 'heralds' (in Greek *Kerux*) of a great King, these messengers proclaimed before the world the astounding news that God, in the person of Jesus, had just intervened all-powerfully in the history of mankind: no one could remain indifferent in the face of this divine initiative, it was necessary to surrender to the evidence of the facts they witnessed to, to believe, to be converted. Peter preaches in Jerusalem in the very first moments of the Church. Paul carries the gospel to the Jews and Gentiles of the Graeco-Roman world. Matthew, Mark, Luke and John write out the one Gospel in more developed forms, setting out this primitive, essential Kerygma in ways that vary according to their aims and their audiences. The author of the epistle to the Hebrews, the Seer of the Revelation, know no basis for their wonderful theological or prophetic elaborations other than the common faith in the dead and risen Christ. Everywhere we find the same doctrine, the same message, the same language, not yet enclosed indefinitive formulas but always sounding the same unique note.

The Kerygma in the Acts of the Apostles

For the study of this primitive Kerygma, discourses contained in the first part of the *Acts of the Apostles* form an especially important source. Admittedly this work, although it tells the story of the first steps of the Church, is not the earliest of the New Testament writings; its author, St Luke, the disciple of St Paul, belongs to the second generation of Christians. But it is equally certain that in the composition of this work he used sources that were earlier, and that these sources, whether spoken or written, go back to the first years of the Church in Jerusalem, shortly after the departure of Jesus.

Proof of this is to be found in the way the Aramaic language in which they were first formulated makes itself clearly heard behind the Greek of Luke's translation; and also in the still very simple way, prior to all theological speculation, that the person of Christ is presented. His divine pre-existence is not denied but it is not yet clearly enunciated. We are at the very first stage, when the dazzling conviction of the triumph of Jesus, raised to the right hand of the Father in heaven after the humiliations of the Passion, occupies the whole field of Christian awareness and does away with the need to reflect on the heavenly existence which might have preceded these humiliations. On this point, a version composed some thirty or forty years after the death of Jesus would have expressed itself much more explicitly. If we cannot be certain that these discourses give us the *ipsissima verba* of the Apostle Peter, we can be certain that in them we hear a direct and authentic echo of the way in which the first community from its very beginnings understood and preached the message of salvation.

We can therefore make use confidently of these precious documents to isolate the essential elements of the primitive Kerygma.

There are five of these discourses of Peter. The first (2:14–39) was addressed, on the day of Pentecost, to the crowd which had been attracted by the news of this extraordinary event. The second (3:12–26) was delivered a little later to a crowd which had gathered in a portico of the Temple following on a miraculous healing. When the leaders of the Sanhedrin wanted to control the agitation this miracle had led to and which seemed disquieting to them, Peter had the chance to defend the new faith in front of them in a third (4:9–12) and fourth (5:29–32) discourse. Lastly, later still, having been summoned to Caesarea by the centurion Cornelius who asked to be instructed, the prince of the Apostles gave him an exposition which constitutes the fifth discourse (10:34–43). To these five proclamations of Peter, we can add the discourse given by the Apostle Paul in the synagogue at Antioch in Pisidia (13:16–41), since this discourse differs considerably from the other discourses of Paul reported in the Acts, in being based plainly on the same outline as those of Peter. These discourses of course all differ notably in length and importance, and they show appreciable variations due to their varying occasions. Nevertheless they all resemble one another in the elements which make up the underlying structure and which are precisely the elements that constitute the primitive Kerygma. It is these elements which we are concerned to disengage.

At the very centre there stand the death and resurrection of Jesus. This is the essential fact that must be brought to the notice of all men, since it contains the whole substance of salvation: Jesus of Nazareth has just been put to death, rejected by the Jews, handed over to Pontius Pilate, executed by the Pagans; but God has raised him on the third day and has exalted him in glory to his right hand with the title of 'Lord' (*Kyrios*) (2:23f, 32–6; 3:13–15; 4:10; 5:30f; 10:39f; 13:27–30).

This cardinal fact, which is presented as a historical event, duly proved, occupies the centre of the Kerygma of which it is the real essence. But if does not stand alone and is surrounded, as by concentric circles, with a halo of other historical facts, antecedent and consequent, which prove it and give it its full value.

A first circle is composed of the facts which immediately preceded and followed this drama. Before the Cross, there was the earthly life of Jesus, the marvellous features of which guarantee his divine mission; he was announced by John the Baptist, and anointed by him with a baptism at which God declared him to be the Messiah (10:37f; 13:23–5), then he went about in public, in Galilee and Judaea, doing good and working miracles (2:22; 10:38f). After his resurrection and exaltation to heaven, there were the signs that proved his triumph: the appearances in which he showed himself alive to his disciples (2:32; 3:15; 5:32; 10:39–42; 13:31) and the outpouring of the Holy Spirit which, in confirmation of his promise, came to confer the first-fruits of the new life on them (2:33; 5:32).

A second circle then surrounds this nucleus of facts and places them in a wider historical perspective, looking backwards to the past as well as forward to the future. In the past, there were the prophecies in the Scriptures which had been announcing these events for a long time and which receive a startling confirmation from them: his Davidic descent (2:30; 13:34), his Messianic sonship (13:33), his mission as 'Prophet', successor to Moses (3:22f), his sufferings (3:18), his role of the stone rejected by the builders (the Jews) which becomes the keystone (4:11), his resurrection (2:25–31; 13:34–7), his exaltation to the right hand of God in heaven (2:34f) – was this not all announced by the Prophets?

To this long preparation in the past corresponds an indefinite repercussion in the future. With the resurrection of Christ and the outpouring of the Spirit, the messianic times have begun (2:17–21), the era of salvation has opened: to it are invited not only the Jews but also the Gentiles (3:25), all those who call on the name of the Lord Jesus (2:39), in whom alone is salvation (4:12). It is a period of waiting during which Christ Jesus remains in heaven; but one day he will return, and then all things will be restored (3:20f). For the moment it is necessary to be sorry for one's sins, to believe in the Lord Jesus and be baptised in his name; in this way one will be granted the forgiveness of sins and the gift of the Holy Spirit (2:38; cf. 3:19–26; 5:31; 10:43; 13:38).

It is, as we can see, *the whole divine plan of salvation* that this schema of the primitive preaching passes in review. This review has a clear historical character, because salvation in the Judaeo-Christian revelation is a history, the history of God's intervention in the progress of human events to bring his creatures dispersed by sin back to him. In this history the kerygmatic schema which we have just analysed isolates three stages: at the beginning, the preparing of salvation in the prophecies of Scripture; then in the centre the work of Christ, his dying and rising; lastly, the fruits of his salvation communicated to men by the forgiveness of sins and life in the Holy Spirit, while they wait for the restoration of the universe at the Parousia. It is easy to relate these three stages of salvation to the Three Persons of the Trinity, the Father who creates, the Son who saves, and the Spirit who sanctifies. We shall have to remember this when we discuss the Trinitarian scheme adopted by the Creed.

The Kerygma in the Epistles

If the discourses in Acts are an especially important source for the study of the Kerygma, because they present it in a complete form and in a logical order, or rather a chronological order, they are not the only witness nor even the earliest. The epistles, especially those of Peter and Paul, also bear witness in their own way, not in the form of a consecutive exposition but of brief allusions.

These writing are adressed to the converted and are answering special questions of doctrine or morals, and in them the Apostles are carrying out catechesis, distributing 'didache', or even 'didaskalia'. They did not have to reproduce the Kerygma, which they had already preached and which they took for granted as known. They do, however, sometimes remind their readers of it quickly, and these brief mentions, which could almost be called quotations, are very precious to us since they allow us to see the substantial identity of the primitive Kerygma, in its foundation and even to a certain degree in its form. These isolated fragments, buried in theological or polemical elaborations, have been compared to the first crystals that form in a substance which is in process of crystallisation: in them we see the first signs of the formulation that will grow more and more stereotyped and will end one day in the Creed.

They are brief assertions, easily recognisable from their style, which is simple, declaratory and often rhythmic. It is not rare either for the context to betray their origin; for example when they are quoted as that which it is necessary to 'believe' and 'confess' (*Rm* 10:9), ys that which has been 'received' from tradition and which must be 'handed on' (*1 Co* 11:23; 15:1-3). Paul is glad to remind his readers that assertions like these have their origins in 'his Gospel' (e.g. *Rm* 2:16; *2 Tm* 2:8).

All the elements of the Kerygma that we have encountered above

can thus be found again threaded through the epistles. The proclamations of the death, resurrection and exaltation of Christ to heaven,
which we saw were the centre of the Kerygma in Acts, are also the
most frequent in the rest of the New Testament, and this is an interesting confirmation of their primordial value in the Christian message.
Take for example the passage in *1 Co* 15:1ff, whose introduction and
style are particularly typical of 'Kerygmatic' quotations; 'Brothers, I
want to remind you of the gospel I preached to you, the gospel that
you have received . . . I taught you what I had been taught myself,
namely that Christ died for our sins, in accordance with the scriptures; that he was buried; and that he was raised to life on the third
day, in accordance with the scriptures; that he appeared first to
Cephas and secondly to the Twelve, etc. . .' We realise that Paul is
here quoting – he tells us so himself – a fundamental proclamation of
the faith which is already clothed in a 'traditional' formulation and
handed on like that.

This text is particularly clear, but there are many others as well in
which we can sense the existence of formulas which are already half-
fixed, for example: that 'Christ died (was delivered up) for our sins' or
'for us' (*1 Th* 5:10; *Ga* 1:4; 2:20; *2 Co* 5:14; *Rm* 4:25; 5:6–8; *1 Tm*
2:6; *Tt* 2:14; *1 P* 2:21f; 3:18; cf. *Mt* 20:28; *Mk* 10:45), that he
'died and rose again' *1 Th* 4:14; *Rm* 4:25; 8:34; 14:9; *1 P* 3:18 etc.),
that it was 'God who raised him from the dead' (*1 Th* 1:10; *1 Co*
6:14; 15:15; *2 Co* 4:14; *Ga* 1:1; *Rm* 4:24; 6:4; 10:9; *Col* 2:12;
Ep 1:20; *1P* 1:21), that he is 'seated at the right hand of God'
Rm 8:24; *Ep* 1:20; *Heb* 1:3–13; 8:1; 10:12; 12:2; *1 P* 3:22; and
cf. *Mt* 22:44; 26:64; *Mk* 16:19; *Ac* 7:55f) and that he is established
there as 'Kyrios', that is, as 'Lord' (cf. *1 Co* 12:3; *Rm* 10:9); and the
use of this title throughout the New Testament) of the living and the
dead (*Rm* 14:9) and even the heavenly spirits (*Ph* 2:10f; *Ep* 1:20f;
Heb 1:4; *1P* 3:22). All these stages that Christ traversed when he
passed through death to regain life are to be restated in almost the
same form by the Apostles' Creed. One article alone, the Descent into
Hell, is less powerfully attested in the New Testament; even so the
kerygmatic passage in *1 P* 3:18–22, alludes to it without any doubt.
Besides, as we know, it is an article of lesser importance, and did not
appear in the primitive Roman form of the Apostles' Creed, just as it
is still missing from the Nicene.

In the Kerygma in Acts the central fact of the Death and Resurrection were surrounded and as it were prolonged by preparations in the

past and consequences in the future. These elements do not fail either to appear in the remainder of the New Testament, ordered here, as they were there, to placing the Cross and Easter in the full sweep of the divine plan. It was in this way that the earthly life of Jesus, his work and his teaching, although it is true that they play a very small part in the epistles whether Paul's (*1 Co* 7:10; *2 Co* 8:9; see also 5:16) or the others (*2 P* 1:16–18), became the object of a broad catechesis which was gathered up in the gospels. It was in this way too that the prophecies and the prefiguration of the work of Christ in the Scriptures were exploited as a theme by all the authors of the New Testament, whether they make it their business to emphasise the fulfilment of prophecy (the Gospels, especially St Matthew), whether they draw material from it for a theological explanation of salvation (St Paul), to the point where this exegesis becomes the principal object of a treatise (the epistle to the Hebrews), or whether they derive inspiration from the oracles of the past to announce the future of the Church (the Revelation of St John). And it is finally in this way that the divine origin of Jesus, which the discourses in Acts still pass over in silence, very quickly becomes one of their most constant affirmations: not only does his descent from David form part of the Kerygma (cf. *Rm* 1:3; *2 Tm* 2:8), but his title 'Son of God' appears in it too (*Rm* 1:3f; *Heb* 4:14), as well as in the confessions of faith (*Ac* 8:37; 9:20; *1 Jn* 4:15; 5:5, etc.), not to mention a large number of texts where it has spread from the Kerygma into the epistles and the gospels. The only thing to notice is that the conception by the Holy Spirit and the virgin birth never appear explicitly outside the infancy gospels of Matthew and Luke (and perhaps in Jn 1:13, according to a form of the text which seems very early). It may be that the Church did not feel the need to assert these truths of faith explicitly until a little later, on the occasion of certain heresies. Even so, this happened very soon: St Ignatius of Antioch always includes the virgin birth in his statement of faith.

As for the future, all the New Testament writings are unanimous in what they affirm of its ultimate perspectives. The expectation of the 'Day of the Lord', of the day when he will 'come', of his 'Parousia', appears so often, from the gospels through the epistles to Revelation, that it is unnecessary to quote texts. It is sufficient to remind ourselves of the liturgical appeal: *Marana tha*, 'Our Lord, come!' (*1 Co* 16:22; *Rv* 22:20). This return of the Lord will be the signal for the general Resurrection and the Judgement, two points of faith which the epistle to the Hebrews (6:2) ranges among the fundamental articles of the elementary teaching. These two points were new to the pagans, to whom they had to be preached and defended (*Ac* 17:18–31f; *1 Co* 15:12), but in fact they originated in traditional Jewish belief (with the exception of the Sadducees, cf. *Mt* 22:23ff; *Ac* 4:1f; 23:6–8).

The new element in the Christian message was to associate these strictly with the person of Christ, and this is precisely what happens in many texts of the New Testament in which we seem to hear an echo of the apostolic Kerygma. The 'resurrection of the dead' is announced by Peter as 'in Jesus' (*Ac* 4:2), which evidently means in relation to the resurrection of Jesus, which is its prelude; and Paul for his part never ceases to base the assurance of our own resurrection on that of Christ (*1 Th* 4:14; *1 Co* 6:14; 15:12–23; *2 Co* 4:14; 13:4; *Rm* 6:4f; 8:11; *Ph* 3:10f; *Col* 2:12f). Similarly, the traditional Jewish doctrine of the eschatological judgement is renewed by the assertion that it is Jesus who 'will judge the living and the dead', a formula which is already fixed in the New Testament (*2 Tm* 4:1; *Ac* 19:42; *1 P* 4:5; *Rm* 14:9f; cf. *1 Co* 3:13; 4:5; *2 Co* 5:10; *Rm* 2:16; *Ac* 17:31; *Mt* 25:31–46) and which will be taken up again by the Creed just as it is.

The Kerygma, whose essential content we have just reviewed, is therefore seen to be the basis of the faith in the first Christian communities. We have shown that its major pronouncements are to be found again in all the New Testament writings, with a strong basic similarity and often even with one of outward form. In it we can perceive a well-defined nucleus of fundamental beliefs which characterise the faith in its primitive state. It is a boon which comes from the Apostles, which we 'receive' from their witness and which must be 'passed on' in its integrity (*2 Th* 2:15; *1 Co* 11:1, etc.). It is a 'rule of doctrine' which we must obey with all our heart (*Rm* 6:17), a 'deposit' which must be kept (*1 Tm* 6:20; *2 Tm* 1:14), a 'sound teaching' (*1 Tm* 1:10; *Tt* 1:9; *2 Tm* 4:3), 'sound words' *1 Tm* 6:3; *2 Tm* 1:13) which must be opposed to 'strange doctrines' and 'subtleties' (*1 Tm* 1:3f) which restless spirits occupy themselves with. It is a 'profession of faith' of which we must never let go (*Heb* 4:14; cf. 3:1; 10:23), a 'faith' which has been 'entrusted' to the 'saints', i.e. the Christians, 'once and for all' and for which they must fight (*Jude* 3).

Behind the inevitable, and fertile, divergences that distinguish the theological elaborations of the different New Testament writers from one another, there is then a fundamental datum from which they all start, on which they all build, and which they all begin by preaching when they want to conquer the world for the faith of Christ. On their lips and in their writings this datum is clothed in a formulation which is already fairly homogeneous, governed by the simplicity of the message itself and by the frequency with which it was repeated. It is not yet a 'Creed' with a definitively fixed text, but it is its prelude and its authentic source.

II. THE CONFESSIONS OF FAITH

Another kind of literary formation however appeared on the scene to combine with that of the Kerygma and prepare for the establishment of the Creed; that of 'confessions of faith'. These are formulas, often very short, which the Christians uttered on certain special occasions when they had to proclaim their faith. Issuing from the apostolic preaching, from which they drew their entire substance, these formulas are nevertheless distinguished from it, first by the precise occasions which determined their employment, and secondly by their literary form, which is even more lapidary and more stereotyped that that of the Kerygma. They seem to take pleasure in being as concise as a motto, a pass-word or a slogan. And this stripped and trenchant stylisation played its part in the composition of the Creed.

We can get some idea from the New Testament of the principal circumstances in the life of the Church which called out such confessions of faith. The first and most important of course was *Baptism*. In this act of initiation into the Christian life, the neophyte had to profess the faith which justified his admission; being baptised 'in the name' of Christ or of the Trinity (*Ac* 2:38; 8:16; 10:48; 19:5; *1 Co* 1:13–15; *Mt* 28:19); he had to proclaim his faith in that name (*Ac* 22:16). In fact, one passage in the Acts of the Apostles shows us the deacon Philip saying to the Ethiopian eunuch who had asked for baptism: 'If you believe with all your heart, you may', and the latter replying, 'I believe that Jesus is the Son of God' (*Ac* 8:37).

Other texts again could be explained very well as formulas having a baptismal origin: for example, *1 P* 3:18–22, where the elements which have a kerygmatic character (vv. 18, 19, 22) enclose an explicit mention of baptism; or *Ep* 4:4–6 where too baptism is mentioned: 'One Body and one Spirit . . . one Hope; one Lord, one Faith, one Baptism; and one God who is Father of all, over all, through all and within all'. *Rm* 10:9 and *1 Tm* 6:12, which we are going to examine shortly, could also have a baptismal origin.

The *Eucharist,* which was celebrated intimately among the baptised, was not of a nature to call out such confessions of faith. It would rather have been the occasion for kerygmatic catecheses on the institution of the rite by the Lord, such as that which St Paul utters in *1 Co* 11:23–5 and that which served as a basis for the narrative of the Last Supper in the Gospels (*Mk* 14:22–5). In return for this, however, *Exorcisms,* which also introduced the invocation of the Name of the Lord, must have used formulas of faith which would have been imposed to be respected and obeyed by the demons (cf. *Jm* 2:19; *Mk* 1:24; 3:11; 5:7). *Miraculous Cures* can also be assimilated to exorcisms, since sickness was believed to be of demonic origin and was expelled by invoking the Name (*Ac* 3:6; 3:13–16; 4:10). As for the 'profession' which Timothy made 'in front of many witnesses' (*1 Tm* 6:12), some interpreters believe it was made at the moment of his ordination to the priesthood (cf. *1 Tm* 4:14; *2 Tm* 2:2). It is true that others place it at a time of persecution, before a pagan tribunal, because of the allusion in v. 13 to the 'profession' made by Christ before Pilate; and it could again be merely a question of the profession of faith uttered by Timothy at his baptism.

We can be certain too that *persecutions by the pagan authorities* also called out confessions of faith: Christians, pressed to utter blasphemous formulas, opposed them victoriously with the profession of their faith in Christ. The detailed episode in the Martyrdom of St Polycarp (VIII, 2), where the old bishop refuses to say 'Caesar is Lord', (*Kyrios Kaisar*) throws a striking light on the formula of faith 'Jesus is Lord' (*Kyrios Iesous*) which St Paul quotes on two occasions: *Rm* 10:9: 'If your lips confess that Jesus is Lord and if you believe in your heart that God raised him from the dead, then you will be saved', and *1 Co* 12:3: 'no one can be speaking under the influence of the Holy Spirit and say "Curse Jesus", and on the other hand, no one can say, "Jesus is Lord", unless he is under the influence of the Holy Spirit'. The first of these texts has been taken by many interpreters to be a profession of baptismal faith, and this is very probable, but it is very attractive to follow O. Cullmann and recognise in the second at least an allusion to these declarations that Christians had to utter before the public authorities and in which they had the confidence to see the inspiration of the Holy Spirit (*Mt* 13:11).

Polemic against the enemies of the faith, whether Jew, pagan or heretic, was another occasion for the creating or propagating of confessions of faith which condemned their errors. It was necessary to prove to the Jews that 'Jesus is the Messiah' (*Ac* 5:42; 18:5–28), and many exegetes have thought that John has his eye on their refusal to believe when he exclaims: 'The man who denies that Jesus is the Christ – he is the liar' (*1 Jn* 2:22). However, the particular way in which John uses the word 'Christ' suggests that he is here visualising rather the Docetist heresy, which denies the Incarnation. In fact, the struggle against this heresy inspires him a little further on with another formula which this time leaves no doubt: 'You can tell the spirits that come from God by this: every spirit which acknowledges that Jesus the Christ has come in the flesh is from God; but any spirit which will not say this of Jesus (or, according to certain witnesses, which dissolves Jesus) is not from God (4:2f). It is then the Incarnation and the Divinity of Jesus that John proclaims in the two confessions of faith that follow, which are practically equivalent: 'Whoever believes that Jesus is the Christ has been begotten by God' (5:1) and 'If anyone acknowledges that Jesus is the Son of God, God lives in him, and he in God' (4:15). – As for the pagans, what has to be maintained against them above all is monotheism; and this is clearly the intention that inspires St Paul, in a contest where he is combating idolatry, to utter this confession of faith: 'for us there is one God, the Father, from whom all things come and for whom we exist; and there is one Lord, Jesus Christ, through whom all things come and through whom we exist' (*1 Co* 8:6).

Finally, in the heart of the Christian community itself, the *solemn oath* which took the divine Name to witness could have been an occasion for the use of professions of faith: this is how *2 Tm* 4:1 is to be explained; and it throws some light on *1 Tm* 6:13 also.

It is evident that the various occasions we have just been envisaging are not mutually exclusive and the same confession of faith, for example 'Jesus is Lord', '*Kyrios Iesous*', could be used at Baptism (*Ac* 8:6; 19:5; *Rm* 19:9) as well as in exorcisms (*Ac* 19:13) or before a tribunal (*1 Co* 12:3), and even as a mere liturgical invocation (*Ac* 7:59; *Rv* 22:20). These formulas were important in their own right, independently of the use that could be made of them, and there are some, like that in *1 Tm* 2:5, whose context no longer allows any precise circumstances to be assigned to them.

To these various circumstances in the life of the Church which gave rise to professions of faith, another cause must be added, *Liturgical Worship*. It too necessarily led to the expression of the faith in stylised and stereotyped formulas, but with a rhythm different from that of the confessions of faith, broader, less lapidary and more lyrical. In the New Testament we have traces of liturgical formulas of this kind. Sometimes they are very short invocations like the *Marana tha* of *1 Co* 16:22 (cf. *Rv* 22:20) or like 'The Lord is very near' of *Ph* 4:5. Sometimes they are doxologies as in *1 Tm* 1:17: 'To the eternal King, the undying, invisible and only God, be honour and glory for ever and ever. Amen' (cf. also *Rm* 11:36; 16:27; *Ph* 4:20; *Jude* 25; *Rv* 5:13; 7:12). Sometimes they are benedictions like that in *2 Co* 13:13: 'The grace of the Lord Jesus Christ, the love of God and the fellowship of the Holy Spirit be with you all'. And it has been suggested that the formulary of greetings and thanksgivings with which all the epistles of St Paul begin may take its inspiration from the words he uttered at the liturgical assemblies. Lastly, they are sometimes actual hymns that the Christians sang at their prayer-meetings (*Col* 3:16) and of which it is thought there are traces in *Ph* 2:6–11 and *1 Tm* 3:16, and perhaps also in *1 P* 2:21–4. It will be noticed that the content of these hymns is no other than the Kerygma of the abasement and exaltation of Christ, presented in a rhythmic and poetic mode..

But we must return to 'Confessions of faith' properly so-called, that is to those formulas which proclaim the Name to which the believer declares his allegiance. This name is ordinarily that of Christ, but it happens sometimes that the name of the Father is linked to it, and even that of the Spirit; this structure can develop from a simple to a tri-partite one, and it deserves to hold our attention since it is of interest for the trinitarian scheme of the Creed.

In actual fact, the simple or Christological formulas are the more numerous. Whether they record the work of salvation achieved by Christ, or select his titles of 'Messiah', 'Lord' or 'Son of God' from it, the kerygmatic proclamations and the confessions of faith mention most often only the person of Christ: it is he who is truly at the centre of the message. The 'by-partite' formulas, those which associate the person of the Father with him, are relatively less frequent. Besides *1 Co* 8:6 and *1 Tm* 6:13, which we have quoted above, there are two other texts from the pastoral epistles which are particularly adduced: *1 Tm* 2:5 'There is only one God, and there is only one mediator between God and mankind, himself a man, Christ Jesus, who sacrificed himself as a ransom for all', and *2 Tm* 4:1 'Before God and before Christ Jesus who is to be judge of the living and the dead, I put this duty to you'. As for the tri-partite form, which juxtaposes the three Persons of the Trinity, it is to be found, we are told, only in the

order of baptism given in *Mt* 28:19 and in the liturgical blessing in
2 Co 13:13.

From this state of affairs the conclusion has sometimes been drawn
that the trinitarian form of the confession was later and was the result
of an evolution which had slightly vitiated the meaning of the primitive faith. Not of course that faith in the Father and the Holy Spirit
was not as primitive as that in Christ. But for the very first Christians
of all, the former was a function of the latter: they believed in the
Father and in the Spirit because of and in relation to the Son, in the
Father as the One who raised Christ from the Dead, and in the Spirit
as the Gift granted by Christ through Baptism. Christ being at the
centre of the faith, to relegate him to the second place in a trinitarian
confession would therefore be a distortion of tradition, it would be as
it were to displace the centre of gravity in the object of faith.

This complaint, presented in particular by O. Cullmann, does not
seem to be justified. It derives from a mistaken perspective which
places too much importance on the confessions of faith and too little
on the totality of the apostolic preaching contained in the Kerygma.
The fact that the confessions of faith put the emphasis on the person
or the work of Christ and most frequently do not go beyond that, can
be explained easily by the very special circumstances that gave rise to
them – the Christians were invoking the name of the Saviour to whom
they were attaching themselves through a sacred rite, or affirming
their belief in his true dignity as Christ, Lord or Son of God, against
the false brethren, the Jews and the pagans who attacked him. But if
we turn from the confessions of faith to the Kerygma in all its richness, we find the persons of the Father and the Spirit linked in an
indissoluble fashion to the work of Christ from the very earliest epoch.
Texts abound in the New Testament which associate either the Father
and the Son, or the three Persons of the Trinity; and often they are
expressed in formulas which, without being confessions of faith,
nevertheless, with their stereotyped form, give us a glimpse of a very
primitive tradition common to all.

It will be sufficient to quote as an example the formula 'Blessed
be the God and Father of our Lord Jesus Christ' (*2 Co* 1:3, 11:31;
Ep 1:3; cf. *Col* 1:3) whose origin as a docology is obvious (cf. also
Rm 15:6, where it is a question of being 'united in mind and voice'
in the utterance of this formula); or again the formula of greeting
adopted by St Paul in all his epistles from *2 Th* on: 'Grace and peace
to you from God the Father and the Lord Jesus Christ'. It is a

118

THE ORIGINS OF THE APOSTLES' CREED

remarkable thing that the other epistles, which do not adopt this specifically Pauline expression, nevertheless are careful to associate God and Christ in their prologues: cf. *Heb* 1:1–2; *Jm* 1:1; *2 P* 1:1–2; *Jude* 1; *1 Jn* 1:3; *2 Jn* 3. Alongside these liturgical formulas many others could be adduced which reveal the constant habit of naming the Father and Son together: for example, *1 Th* 3:11, 'May God our Father himself, and our Lord Jesus Christ, make it easy for us to come to you'; *2 Th* 2:16, 'May our Lord Jesus Christ himself, and God our Father . . . comfort you . . .'; *1 P* 4:11, 'So that in everything God may receive the glory, through Jesus Christ'; *Rv* 1:2, John has 'written down . . . the word of God guaranteed by Jesus Christ', etc. etc.

The harvest of texts with a manifestly trinitarian intention would be no less rich. Here are some characteristic examples: *1 Co* 6:11, 'You have been . . . justified through the name of the Lord Jesus Christ and through the Spirit of our God': *1 Co* 12:4–6, 'There is a variety of gifts but always the same Spirit; there are all sorts of service to be done, but always to the same Lord; working in all sorts of different ways in different people, it is the same God who is working in all of them': *Ep* 2:18, 'Through him (Christ), both of us have in the one Spirit our way to come to the Father': *1 P* 1:2, 'Peter . . . to all . . . who have been chosen, by the provident purpose of God the Father, to be made holy by the Spirit, obedient to Jesus Christ and sprinkled with his blood', etc. etc.

In reality, the whole message of the New Testament is founded on faith in the concurrence of the Three divine Persons in the accomplishment of salvation. And if it is true that the Father and the Spirit are ordinarily considered in relation to the work of the Son, it would be wrong to conclude from this that the latter takes place in the faith. It is not possible to subscribe to O. Cullmann's phrase[1], 'Because he believes in Christ Kyrios, the first-century Christian believes in God and in the Holy Spirit'. It is the contrary which is true: it is because he believes in the Father who raised him and in the Holy Spirit whose outpouring manifests his triumph in heaven that the Christian believes in Jesus *Kyrios*. And if he wishes to express the totality of his faith in the divine Name in a single formula, it is logical that he should place the Father before the Son, as being the one who sent him, delivered him over to death for our salvation, then raised and exalted him, and that he should place the Spirit after the Son, as being the one who is sent us from heaven by the risen Christ to continue his

[1] *Les premières Confessions de foi chrétiennes*, Paris, 1943, p. 42.

work of salvation in us. And in fact, this order is not only 'logical', it is 'chronological'; it is the very order of the history of salvation, such as it emerges from the Holy Books and as we realised its presence behind the Kerygma in Acts, such too as it is to be found again in the sublime panorama of the divine plan of salvation at the beginning of the epistle to the Ephesians (1:4–14). This order is no other than that of the interventions of God in our human history. It is the order of our knowledge of the Trinity itself. Our faith in the Three divine Persons did not spring from speculations about their own intimate relations: these came later, in the course of theological elaboration. It is the Scripture itself that reveals the divine Persons through the actions which they have performed for us, creating, saving and sanctifying us. And it is this concrete faith, soaked in history, that is expressed by the trinitarian formula. By taking this as the framework of the Creed, the Church has perfectly preserved the authentic Scriptural orientation of primitive Christianity.

CONCLUSION

The historians of the Apostles' Creed have shown that it sprang from the combination of two formulas with different origins: on the one hand, the trinitarian confession of faith, and on the other a kerygmatic statement of the incarnation and redemption of Christ. These two types of formula, which arose in different circumstances and existed separately to begin with, were naturally brought together and associated in the life of the Church, notably in the liturgy of baptism. The association could be a mere juxtaposition (cf. Irenaeus, *Adversus Haereses*, I, 10:1); but more often it was managed by combining them, the Christological statement being inserted after the mention of the Second Person in the framework of the trinitarian confession. In this way our Creed was constructed. This elaboration took place in the second and third centuries, and we do not have to study it in this article. Our task has been to observe, from the first century, from the very beginning of the Church, the birth of these two types of formula which were to be fused in the Creed and we have been able to show that both equally issued from the teaching of the Apostles: the Christological statement was the result of the fixing of the Apostolic Kerygma the essential elements of which we found in all the New Testament writings; the trinitarian confession of faith derives from the earliest confessions and, if it is from the literary point of view the end-product of a certain evolution, it is no less a completely authentic expression of the way the first Christians came to know the Three divine Persons through the revelation of the history of salvation.

We have therefore very good reasons for saying that our Creed is truly 'Apostolic'. It is true that it was not composed in its present form by the Apostles: but it descends in a direct line, both in content and in form, from formulas received from the Apostles which expressed the essentials of the Christian message at the beginning of the Church. This is an assurance of the first importance for the firmness of our faith. And another no less fruitful lesson may be drawn from this study. It was in order to convert the world, to gather men to Christ, to conquer devils and fight the enemies of the faith, that our first brethren solemnly proclaimed their belief. Let us, when we utter again with our lips substantially the same formulas which they uttered before us, let us in our turn make them, not a formal and individualistic declaration, but a proclamation intended to conquer the world, which is sure of its power because it is based on the witness of the Apostles, and through them on Christ.

6. The Primacy of St Peter in the New Testament*

The study devoted by Mgr Cassien Bésobrasoff to the problem of *St Peter and the Church in the New Testament* deserves to hold our attention for its width of exegesis and its care for objectivity. Since I have been invited to express my reactions to his enquiry and its results, I shall try to show how the examination of the texts of the New Testament seems to me to lead necessarily to conclusions which are sensibly different. I shall begin by putting forward some reflections on method. After that I shall in my turn pass in review the various passages of Scripture that bear witness to the person and the role of Peter.

*   *   *

It does not seem to me to be happy to make such a sharp distinction between the historical facts, such as they can be gleaned for example from the Acts of the Apostles and the Epistles of St Paul, and the theses of the 'theologians', in this instance St Matthew, St Luke and St John. On the one hand the history narrated in the Acts is written by a theologian who, without seriously deforming the facts, has nevertheless presented and organised them according to his own idea of the nature and the origins of the Church; we shall see this for example in connection with the Council of Jerusalem. On the other hand, the theologically-minded evangelists, even if each in his own way developed the themes which were dear to him, nevertheless founded these themes on words and actions of Jesus which they wanted first and foremost to report faithfully; and this is true, the necessary allowances being made, even of the fourth gospel. If then it is legitimate to try and understand the individual conceptions of the sacred writers,

---

* This article was originally published in *Istina*, 1955, pp. 305–34, and followed the study by Mgr Cassien to which it refers.

it would be insufficient to rest on that and it will be necessary to
strive to reach behind them to what the Lord said and did. This
principle being safeguarded however, the manner in which Mgr
Cassien has set out the New Testament material is logical and con-
venient, and I shall follow it myself in order to evaluate his interpretations.

A second warning is necessary to remind ourselves that Scripture
cannot be the only source of our information; alongside it, or better
still all around it, like an atmosphere in which it exists, is Tradition[1].
In the living community of the Church, God spoke otherwise than by
writings; he poured his light and his power into the hearts of a privileged generation, which then found itself charged with the responsibility for transmitting his message to subsequent generations. It is of
course permissible for an isolated work to make a special scrutiny
of one of these sources. Mgr Cassien, who as an orthodox theologian
cannot underestimate the importance of Tradition, has a perfect
right to abstract from it in a study which is by definition exegetical;
and, following his example, I shall do the same. It was however
opportune to remind ourselves that by doing so our enquiry becomes
incomplete and that we must not be astonished if it does not provide
an entire solution of the problem. The revelation brought by Christ
became the object of the Church's reflection and understanding, after
the Resurrection, in the light of the Holy Spirit; a process of understanding, a passing from the implicit to the explicit, that did not take
place in one day and was not even brought about with the same speed
on every point. Certain essential truths like the divinity of Christ and
his redemptive Death and Resurrection were the first to shed the fullness of their light and thus occupy a central place in the writings of
the New Testament. Others could wait longer to appear in their full
clarity because they responded to needs that were less immediate or
less quickly to be discussed; it is possible then that although they
receive their fundamental expression in the New Testament they are
definitively unfolded only later, in a living Tradition which surrounds
and prolongs the first witness of the Scriptures. It seems to me that
the organisation of the Church, and in particular the problem of its
unity under a unique Head, belong to this order of truths that began
by being lived in a spontaneous manner before seeing their content
made precise and in a sense regulated in consequence of difficulties

[1] See my review, in *RBibl*, 1955, pp. 258–64, of the short work by O. CULLMANN,
La Tradition, Paris, 1953, which is reprinted on pp. 176–85 of the present volume.

that arose later[1]. However, I shall take this idea up again and give it more concrete expression in connection with a last remark on the subject of principles.

This third question concerning method, which seems to me to be the most important here, is to do with a certain anachronistic way of posing the problem which may prevent one reaching a valid understanding and solution. I feel that it is at work in many of Mgr Cassien's expressions. He speaks of 'jurisdiction', 'hierarchical' or 'canonical primacy', 'monarchic power', 'absolute and personal power'. Even if we acknowledge from time to time that this is talking in terms of 'canon law', it is to be feared that the continual employment of such expressions reveals an incorrect attitude to the problem. If it were no more than imprecision of terminology, this would be pardonable; but it seems that there is more than this, and that, in order to prove a primacy of Peter in the primitive Church, it has to be carried out in an exercise which in fact derives from a later and more developed age. Later, indeed, the withdrawing of the Church's origins into the past no less than the withdrawing of the Second Coming into the remote future, the considerable growth in the number of Christians, and the confrontation with the political powers of this world obliged the Church to organise itself more and more, to reinforce the effective authority of its central power and to systematise the different exercises of that power, doctrinal, legislative and disciplinary. In the first years of the Church all this was there in bud, but still latent and embryonic, and only the most simple and democratic manifestations of the primacy are to be expected from it as it existed then. To look anachronistically for it in more developed forms is to expose oneself to a failure to find it.

This is to be seen from the very first pages of Mgr Cassien's study, on the primacy of the church of Jerusalem and on that of Peter. In a word, he seems to me to grant the church of Jerusalem a hierarchical and universal primacy which it did not have and to refuse Peter a personal primacy which he did have.

With regard to the church of Jerusalem an essential distinction must be made from the very beginning: between the very first years when it was still the only expression of the universal Church in terms

[1] See the interesting remarks of P. H. MENOUD, ΜΙΑ ΕΚΚΛΗΣΙΑ, in *Hommage et Reconnaissance* . . . *à Karl Barth*, Paris, 1946, pp. 87–91: if the affirmation of 'one Church' does not appear in the powerful text of *Ep* 4:3–6, is this perhaps because the unity of the Church had not then become a matter for discussion? (Cf. *RBibl*, 1947, p. 157).

of a community and the later years when, after the birth of other communities in other centres, it no longer appeared as anything more than a particular church. In the first case the Apostles are still living there, it is the whole Church and does not have jurisdiction over other churches because there are no others; in the second case it has its own local head, St James with a college of presbyters round him, and it is only then that the problem may arise of its jurisdiction over the new communities which are being formed in different parts of the Empire. However, even if we can admit such a jurisdiction over the churches that were in a way founded by it, in Judaea, Galilee, Samaraia (*Ac* 8:1ff; 9:31; *Ga* 1:22) and as far as Antioch (*Ac* 11:19ff; 15:1; *Ga* 2:12), I dispute that it can be admitted for the churches founded by Paul as well. A division was consciously made between the regions of the 'circumcision', that is to say Judeao-Christian, which had Jerusalem as centre, and those of the 'Gentiles' where the apostolate of Paul was to be exercised (*Ga* 2:9). A union of heart and mind was of course to reign between these diverse parts of the growing Church, but it was not to be assured by means of an effective 'jurisdiction' of the Jerusalem community over those of Asia Minor, Greece or Rome. The collection for the poor of Jerusalem which was asked of St Paul (*Ga* 2:10) was to be a living witness of this union – which is why Paul attached so much importance to it –, but there was about it nothing of an 'obligation' deriving from a 'jurisdiction' of Jerusalem to which Paul 'submitted'.

Nor is the universal jurisdiction of Jerusalem proved by the famous Decree of the 'Council of Jerusalem'. For here we must make use of a little criticism and acknowledge with many modern exegetes, even Catholic ones[1], that St Luke has combined the narratives of two distinct discussions: one which bore on the obligation of the Mosaic Law, especially circumcision, for converts from paganism; the other, no doubt later, which determined the indispensable observances in the matter of food which would permit a common table for and good everyday relations between converts from Judaism and converts from paganism. The first debate which was of decisive and universal import was settled, not by the particular church of Jerusalem by itself, but by the Apostolic College assembled at Jerusalem, with which James,

[1] Cf. S. GIET, 'L'assemblée apostolique et le décret de Jérusalem', in *RSR*, XXXIX, 1951 (Mélanges Lebreton, I), pp. 203–20, who has a good idea of the problem even if his particular explanation of the person of Simeon is hardly plausible. See also the notes by Dom J. DUPONT in the fascicule of the *Bible de Jérusalem* devoted to the Acts of the Apostles.

the 'Brother of the Lord',[1] was certainly associated, but without his being accorded the presidency. The second debate, which was of less importance and more of local interest since it concerned especially the regions where Judaeo-Christians were numerous (*Ac* 25:23), must have taken place later, perhaps after the 'Antioch incident', and this time James certainly was the principal authority, while Peter and Paul were no doubt absent. The proof of this, in regard to the latter, is that he was ignorant of the Decree concerning observances about food, whether in his presentation of the Council of Jerusalem (*Ga* 2:6), or on other occasions when he should have made use of it (*1 Co* 8–10; *Rm* 14), and has to hear it from the lips of James at the close of the third journey (*Ac* 21:25)[2]. It is therefore doubtful to say the least whether we should attribute to the church of Jerusalem a jurisdiction 'competent to pronounce decisions binding on the whole of Christianity': what is true for the Apostolic college gathered *de facto* at Jerusalem is not true for the church of Jerusalem as such when, under the direction of its local head James, it makes regulations valid only for the neighbouring communities which are of its province. And beside this case which we have just restricted to its proper compass, it would be vain to look for others which would witness to an authority of a 'juridical' or 'canonical' order of the church of Jerusalem over those of Ephesus, Corinth or Rome.

Nor is such an authority exercised over the apostolic activity of Paul. For it is not correct to see in his journeys to Jerusalem so many visits *ad limina*. Those which he made three and then fourteen years after his conversion (*Ga* 1:18; 2:1) were, it is true, carried out with the intention of winning approval for his gospel, but from the 'columns', not from the local community as such; the people who Paul

---

[1] Like Mgr Cassien, I am inclined to think that this James was not part of the group of the twelve Apostles.
[2] It is true that Luke (*Ac* 16:4) shows us Paul passing on 'the decisions reached by the apostles and elders in Jerusalem' to the faithful in Lycaonia. But this is a necessary consequence of the combination which he has made earlier on and which he pursues in his role of a historian conscious of his right to synthesise facts. In addition, the Decree itself, with its restricted destination to the brethren 'in Antioch, Syria and Cilicia' (*Ac* 15:23), has received under his pen an enlarged formulation which includes the non-obligation of the Mosaic Law (*Ac* 25:28). The historical distinction of the two debates, which is rendered necessary by many considerations which I cannot deal with in detail here, cannot be followed out on the literary level in the sort of enquiry which discovers break between the phrases of documents which have merely been juxtaposed. Linking two problems which rightly appeared to him to be connected, Luke fused them into a powerful literary unity. He had the right to do this as a historian, and as an inspired historian; but this does not deprive us of the right to distinguish in our turn what he has linked together.

visits are first Cephas and James, then 'James, Cephas and John'[1].
Later, when the apostles are no longer there and the Jerusalem
community figures instead as a local Judaeo-Christian church, Paul
is to visit it again at the end of the second and third journeys, but
this is in no way to acquit himself of a 'duty' and 'give an account of
his works' as though to his 'hierarchical authority'. Without insisting
on the visit of *Ac* 18:22, which is quite possible but of which all that is
said is that Paul 'greeted the Church', that in *Ac* 21:17–26 certainly
does not authorise us to believe that Paul submitted to James as to
his superior in the hierarchy. Nothing is more natural than that he
should tell the brethren at Jerusalem about the success of his ministry
among the Gentiles: but this is not an inferior's 'rendering an account', and the joy of the brethren who glorify God is not the official
approval of a hierarchical authority. When in addition Paul accepts
James' suggestion that he should associate himself with the vow of
the four Nazirites, this is not an act of obedience but a fraternal concession, and even an act of prudence destined to appease the animo-
sity of certain intransigent Judaeo-Christians[2]. If Paul had to render
an account of his mission, this would have been to the church of
Antioch who had sent him (*Ac* 13:1–3)[3], it would certainly not have
been to the church of Jerusalem.

And yet it is a fact that he keeps going there often. But this is better
explained by a prerogative of Jerusalem other than universal jurisdiction, I mean that of a pre-eminence of honour. This latter is
indisputable and it is this that has put Mgr Cassien on the wrong
scent. Jerusalem had the prestige of antiquity in the faith. After being
the centre of the old dispensation, it had become the cradle of the
new religion and for several years had represented the whole of the
young Church. There was the Temple, where the Judaeo-Christians
still loved to pray and which kept, even in the eyes of Christians

---

[1] The dignity of 'brother of the Lord', as well as and even more than his as yet ill-
defined title as head of the local community, raised James to the level of the
Apostles. The fact that in *Ga* 2:9 he is named first does not authorise us to
conclude Paul ranks him higher than Peter. The order of the names is easily
explained by the context. In the debate over the obligation of the Law, James
was certainly, in the eyes of the Galatians and their Judaizing teachers, the most
likely to be thought of as opposing the gospel of Paul. This is why the latter
puts his name at the top of the list; even James imposed nothing on me, but
instead gave me his hand!
[2] Or even of the Jews themselves, if we are to admit the conjecture of J. MUNCK,
Paulus und die Heilsgeschichte, Copenhagen, 1954, p. 234ff.
[3] It is however necessary to make strong reservations on this point: though
originally under the patronage of the church of Antioch, Paul must have freed
himself later from dependence on it.

liberated from the Law such as Paul, the prestige of the sacred place where God had prepared the way for fulfilment of his promises. This primacy of honour can and must be conceded; but it must not be transformed into a primacy of a 'juridical' or 'canonical' kind, which would make Jerusalem, up to the catastrophe of 70 A.D., 'the hierarchical centre of the Christian world'. Far from putting this latter 'beyond the bounds of doubt', 'our scriptural sources' exclude such a primacy, and the epistle of James is certainly not a kind to contradict what we have just concluded from the texts of Acts and of St Paul. St James, with his prestige as 'brother of the Lord' and local head at Jerusalem, had a perfect right to send an authoritative letter to 'the twelve tribes of the Dispersion' (*Jm* 1:1), especially if he meant by this the Judaeo-Christians scattered through the Greco-Roman world; this is not an act of 'universal jurisdiction' any more than the epistles of St Peter, in which Mgr Cassien rightly refuses to see 'the expression of the canonical consciousness of the church of Rome' and which nevertheless present themselves under the same conditions as the epistle of James.

To these arguments of fact may be added a theoretical one. By its very nature Christianity does not have a hierarchical centre attached by divine right to a particular city. The old dispensation, entrusted to the chosen people Israel by themselves, was expressed in physical terms in a worship the sole legitimate site of which was the Temple at Jerusalem; the new religion with its worship 'in spirit and in truth' could not be attached to any particular place; 'the hour is coming when you will worship the Father neither on this mountain nor in Jerusalem' (*Jn* 4:21). Although he believes that the facts demonstrate a universal jurisdiction of Jerusalem, Mgr Cassien acknowledges that 'all dogmatic justification is lacking', that on this point there is no 'commandment of the Lord'. Indeed, there could not be. In fact, Jesus made Jerusalem no more than the starting-point of the great movement of universal expansion (*Ac* 1:8) and announced its destruction. When this destruction came about, this was no catastrophe for Christianity as it would have been if the 'hierarchical centre' of Christianity had been established there; it was no doubt a source of sorrow, tempered by the Lord's prediction and the conviction that it was in precisely this way that the universality of the new form of worship was affirmed.

Jerusalem had been the necessary centre of Judaism: with Christianity it ceased to be, and this not in order to make room for any other city whatsoever, neither Antioch, nor Alexandria, nor even Rome. It seems to be believed sometimes that the right of the church of Rome to dictate to other churches is a necessary article of Catholic belief. It is no such thing. We do not attribute a primacy to this particular church as such; it enjoys this privilege in our eyes only in virtue of the personal primacy of the Head who resides there. We believe from tradition that Peter exercised there the personal power he had received from Christ and that at his death he handed it on to a successor: it is to this fact and to the long succession which has flowed from him through the centuries that the church of Rome owes its place in the life of the Church. If the successor of St Peter were to decide authoritatively to move his residence to some other place, the 'hierarchical centre' of Christianity would for that very reason also move[1].

Thus we are prepared to concede to Mgr Cassien that the primacy over the universal Church is not a permanent privilege bestowed by divine right on any particular church whichever it may be. We do not even acknowledge that it was possessed by the church of Jerusalem at the beginnings of the Church by an exceptional privilege, as Mgr Cassien believes. We believe only in the personal primacy of Peter and his successors; as, however, it is disputed that this is founded in the New Testament, we must now proceed to evaluate this judgement.

First of all, the historical facts, such as they can be isolated from the Acts of the Apostles and the Epistles of St Paul.

In the first period when Peter had his headquarters in Jerusalem (*Ac* 1–12), there is an abundance of texts that witness to hie pre-eminent position at the centre of the young Church: whether it is a question of the election of Matthias, the miracle at Pentecost, the healing of the lame man and the appearances before the Sanhedrin, or the punishment of Ananias and Sapphira, it is Peter who speaks in the name of all, Peter who takes the initiative and makes the decisions. There is no need to insist on this: Mgr Cassien himself acknowledges this 'role of director'. But elsewhere he seeks to limit it: Peter is not alone, at his side are the Eleven, St John in particular; later especially, when he goes to Samaria, then to Lydda and Joppa, and finally to the house of Cornelius, it is as a delegate of the church of Jerusalem who has to render an account of his activities to this

---

[1] Cf. *RBibl*, 1953, pp. 574–8, in my review of O. CULLMANN, *Saint Pierre, disciple, apôtre, martyr*, Paris, 1952. See also below pp. 167–74.

church and get its approval. His power then is not 'monarchic', his authority does not have 'an absolute and purely personal character'. This way of reasoning seems to me to be vitiated by two faults: a certain misuse of texts and the anachronistic demands to which I drew attention earlier. That the primacy of Peter was not invested with a dictorial character, we are perfectly prepared to concede. Absolutism in the central direction, which would be open to criticism at any epoch in the life of the church anyway, was certainly not in favour in these early years when the community still felt itself very vividly to be a family, whose Master had hardly disappeared and was due to return shortly, and in which the head delegated by him appeared as a brother, the first among the brethren, whose part was less to promulgate authoritative decisions by himself than to take the leadership of the apostolic movement, in harmony with all the others. That John or the Eleven are not eclipsed by him but assist him and help him out, does not detract a whit from his authority; it would have been a pity if it had been otherwise. When the apostolic college send Peter and John to Samaria (*Ac* 8:14), it does not delegate them as though they were inferiors, but rather sends them as its two most remarkable members, certainly with their agreement and no doubt on their initiative. If Peter then goes to Lydda, Joppa and Caesarea, it is not as a subordinate charged with the mission, but as the head of the mission who himself takes the first steps in the expansion of the apostolate. If he then returns to his brethren in Jerusalem to report the novel decision he has had to make, prompted by the Holy Spirit, to associate with and baptise one of the uncircumcised, this is the least of matters; and a great deal of good will is necessary to see in this step the rendering of account by a simple missionary 'obliged to justify himself' in front of his leaders, as also to see in the agreement of the brethren 'the approval of the competent authority'. I would not dream of denying the astonishment and even the stirrings of irritation (*Ac* 11:3) which so novel an attitude on Peter's part must necessarily have provoked among the circumcised brethren of Jerusalem: but when Peter calms and enlightens them, this is not by soliciting a 'verdict' of approval which they could have refused him[1], but by informing them with as much gentleness as firmness of the divinely irresistible nature of the stance he has just taken, and they have nothing further to do than to assent to this decision, so heavy with

---

[1] It is remarkable that there is no mention of James here, as would have been normal if it had been a question of a 'verdict' by the supreme authority.

consequences, of which God has just notified them through the mediation of their head.

It is still less difficult to interpret the words with which Peter takes leave of James and the brethren of Jerusalem (*Ac* 12:17). Nothing there suggests a transmission of power by which Peter would be giving up the direction of the Church in order to entrust it to James and to submit himself to James from then on as delegated for the Judaeo-Christian mission. Anyway, Mgr Cassien does not accept this highly questionable interpretation of Cullmann's[1] and favours a perfectly natural interpretation of this very simple phrase: Peter warns the head of the local church, James, of his departure since this very departure is going to mean fresh responsiblities for the latter. But if he does not dare to make Peter dependent on the 'personal jurisdiction of St James', he nevertheless takes Peter as being under 'the jurisdiction of the centre of Jerusalem represented by St James as its local head'. The proof of this is to be found in the incident at Antioch where Peter is seen to be 'obliged to repudiate his behaviour in front of the emissaries of James (*Ga* 2:12)'. Here again we see a practical attitude which has a bearing only on a secondary matter of everyday behaviour and in which St Peter's deficiencies are sufficiently explained by his own character, elevated into a question of 'jurisdiction' and used to attack the primacy. For, as I have said, not only must we not expect in these first years of the Church an absolutist exercise of the primacy which would forbid Peter any concession to the other brethren, but we must also bear in mind the elements of his own actual character: ardent, generous and impulsive, he was also rash and changeable, too ready with spontaneous reactions which exposed him to blunders and obliged him to make corrections. Jesus was well aware of this side of his qualities and, though he chose him nevertheless and promised him assistance, this did not totally suppress the faults of Peter's temperament. In the present case Peter showed hinself weak and pusillanimous and this deserved Paul's correction; but it would be a gross exaggeration of the affair to understand this too human fear of the opinions of the Jewish Christians as an abdication of principle in face of the superior authority of the church of Jerusalem.

The 'council of Jerusalem' can also be used to uphold the notion of Peter's inferiority in relation to the mother-church in the person of James its head. Mgr Cassien does this however only with moderation;

[1] Cf. *RBibl*, 1953, pp. 566ff; and below pp. 156–9.

and I have said earlier how we are to take the presidency that the narrative of Acts seems to attribute to James, as well as the fact that his name heads the list in *Ga* 2:9. I shall therefore not repeat myself, but only draw attention to the fact that our scriptural texts are full of gaps since they are episodic, and that if they do not illustrate the authority of Peter over James after the former's departure from Jerusalem in a decisive fashion, they certainly do not authorise the contrary affirmation: 'it is absolutely certain that St James, in his role of head of the church of Jerusalem, was independent of St Peter'. So categorical a declaration lacks all basis and goes clean against the totality of the New Testament texts, and those of Acts in particular.

Let us turn to the relations between Paul and Peter, in so far as they can have relevance for the primacy of the latter. Here again, to begin with, it is conceded that on various occasions Paul regards Peter as 'the highest authority' to whom appeal can be made (*1 Co* 9:5), as 'the last degree before Christ' (*1 Co* 1:12), as the first witness of the risen Jesus (*1 Co* 15:5). It was in order to see Cephas that Paul went to Jerusalem (*Ga* 1:18). But he did see others too, James, John (*Ga* 1919; 2:9), and above all in his letters he makes a point of maintaining that he 'yields nothing to the other apostles, not even St Peter'. This is indisputable, and there can be no doubt that, at the level of apostolic witness, Paul holds himself Peter's equal. But this equality, which is real because Paul too has seen Christ (*1 Co* 9:1), does not throw doubt on Peter's primacy, which operates on a different level: not the level of the apostolic witness (however, even from this point of view, Peter remains the one who was the first to see), but that of the direction of the Church, including the right to lead and the obligation to correct the other apostles. In order to settle the question of the relationship of Peter and Paul on this point, we need some actual occasion on which the exercise of this primacy can be established. But what I have said earlier about the democratic atmosphere of the Church at the beginning and what we know in addition to the powerful personality and peculiar vocation of Paul scarcely allow us to expect such an occasion.

There is however the 'Antioch incident', and it is here precisely that it is thought that a case had been found in which Paul shows clearly that he does not attribute any superiority to Peter: 'he could reprimand him only if he were equal to Peter in principle'. I doubt however whether the precise character of the incident authorises such a conclusion. Or, more exactly, here too as on other occasions, Paul demonstrates that he believes himself to be Peter's equal as an apostle of Christ; but I do not think that this permits us to draw any conclusions for or against Peter's primacy, since I do not believe that it is involved here. As I have said earlier, the incident has no more than an episodic and disciplinary importance. Certainly, Paul links it to the fundamental question of the obligation of the Mosaic Law for converts from paganism. But he does also say that at bottom Peter and he are in agreement (*Ga* 2:6-9, 15f)); what he reproaches Peter for is an inconsistency in his behaviour, due to a moment of cowardice and lack of foresight. In showing Peter the dangerous tendency of his conduct and calling him to order, Paul is only exercising with a kind of holy liberty the right of fraternal correction which can be employed even towards a leader, more than one example of which could be quoted from the history of the Papacy. He does not call in question the fundamental role of Peter, he rather presupposes it and this is why he takes care to show the brethren at Antioch as well as his Galatian readers, that Peter is fundamentally in agreement with him, even if in a moment of weakness he adopted an ambiguous attitude which could lead to a misunderstanding of his deeper convictions. Mgr Cassien sees this clearly himself: 'If (Paul) mentions this incident it is because for him St Peter is the first'. 'The primacy of St Peter is presupposed in this passage. St Paul means that he yields in nothing to the first', on which he comments correctly, 'It is always the equality of his apostleship that Paul is defending'. But if this is so then I fail to understand his concluding phrase: 'St Paul's witness is formal, he does not deny the hierarchical primacy. The primacy of St Peter does not put him above the apostles.' What are we to understand by 'Hierarchical primacy' if it is emptied of its content? I would prefer to say: 'The primacy of St Peter does not put him above opportune corrections and the latter do not call it in question'.

Little light is thrown on the later apostolate of Peter and his arrival in Rome by our scriptural sources. It is here especially that they must be filled out from the evidence of Tradition. Since, like Mgr Cassien, I am restricting myself to the texts of the New Testament, I shall be as reserved as they are and more so than Mgr Cassien. I doubt for example whether the absence of the mention of St Peter in the epistle to the Romans, in the closing of the Acts, in the epistles of the captivity and in the pastoral epistles authorises us to conclude that he arrived in Rome only after the death of Paul. This argument from silence does not seem decisive to me. Whatever may be the case, Peter came to Rome, Mgr Cassien admits, but in his opinion this was only in the role of a simple 'apostle', that is to say as an 'itinerant minister'. 'In the historical situation – between 64 and 67 – there can be no question of his primacy. The centre at Jerusalem was still in existence, and its hierarchical primacy was acknowledged by the whole of Christianity. As for St Peter, we have seen that he possessed it neither before nor after his departure from Jerusalem.' Let us pass over this obstinate expression of the arguments that have preceded it: it is worth only what they are worth.

Have we, to say the least, any positive scriptural testimony for the activity of St Peter at Rome? Mgr Cassien here calls only on the two epistles that claim him as their author and indirectly the gospel of Mark. He does not mention another text which deserved to draw his attention, *Rv* 11:3-13, in which some recent works have recognised an echo of the apostolic action and the martyrdom of Peter and Paul at Rome[1]. If this exegesis is correct, the passage certainly does not give us any actual information about the primacy properly so called of Peter, but it does throw a very interesting light on the importance attributed to his witnessing and his death in the capital of the Empire, as well as the connection, at least on the theological level, of the martyrdoms of the two great Apostles.

As for the two epistles which bear Peter's name, Mgr Cassien holds the first to be authentic, and the second to be at least derived from an authentic document, but using a partial re-working which had already been drawn from it by the epistle of Jude. For my part I would prefer to believe that the Second Epistle of Peter frames a re-working drawn from Jude between two sections which could go back to a Petrine writing; I think that *2 P* 3:3 is dependent on *Jude* 17-18 and not vice versa. On the other hand I wonder whether the similarities between *1 Peter* and *Ephesians* are really due to the fact that Peter has borrowed from Paul, as Mgr Cassien envisages, or whether they are not instead to be explained either by the use of traditional common formulas or by the activity of the same disciple-editor. Whatever may be the case with these delicate literary distinctions which there can be no question of our pursuing further here, they dispose me even less than Mgr Cassien to examine these two writings

---

[1] Cf. M.E. BOISMARD in *RBibl*, 1949, pp. 533f and 540; J. MUNCK, *Petrus und Paulus in der Offenbarung Johannis*, Copenhagen, 1950 (Cf. *RBibl*, 1951, p.627f).

to see what they have to suggest concerning a consciousness of canonical primacy. I concede gladly that they are to be explained well enough by an apostolic consciousness which gives authority for the instruction of the faithful, even in distant regions. There is nothing to compel us to see a 'universal jurisdiction' here, I agree; I am only astonished that Mgr Cassien has not reached the same conclusion in regard to the epistle of James. These letters which claim Peter as their author are indeed not yet Encyclicals; and it would perhaps become necessary to look in a quite different direction if the hypothesis, not mentioned by Mgr Cassien, were verified, which sees in the First Epistle a baptismal catechesis presented subsequently in the form of a letter. Neither, lastly, would I claim that the approval given to the epistles of Paul in *2 P* 3:15–16, represents an exercise of superiority, 'the judgement of the Church in the matter of St Paul's teaching'. Again let us beware of anachronisms: there were as yet no Imprimaturs.

If the epistles of Peter fail to provide us with decisive evidence of his hierarchical primacy at the time of his stay in Rome, can we not expect more light from another scriptural source? Here it is that one thinks of the gospel of St Mark, which is commonly believed to have been written in Rome, as an echo of Peter's catechesis. We shall therefore examine it, and then the other three gospels. When we have seen what the New Testament can tell us about the actual exercise of Peter's primacy at the beginning of the Church, we shall thus get back to the period of the ministry of Jesus himself during which this primacy was founded.

Truth to tell, Mgr Cassien does not claim to go back this far, since what he is looking for in the gospels is less the words and deeds of Jesus than the thinking of the authors. This attitude to research, made fashionable by Form-criticism, has its interest, but it remains limited and I have drawn attention earlier to its inadequacies. Here it takes the form of examining the second gospel to discover 'the opinion held by its author concerning the ministry of St Peter'. And as in addition it is admitted that all he has done is to collect the 'memories' of the apostle, this comes in the end to mean the personal recollections which were dear to St Peter and which he was fond of recounting. This way of tackling the text is a little narrow. It runs the risk of emptying out the importance of so many details which already in the second gospel bear witness to the predominant place of Peter in the apostolic college: but, we are told, this point of view is not surprising,

since it is Peter we are listening to and quite naturally he insists on the
events in which he was involved! There is nothing in all this that
suggests the primacy of the apostle: it is simply that 'Peter cherished
these details of his relations with the Master. He kept a vivid memory
of them that Mark was able to reproduce'.

This way of understanding the second gospel does not appear to me
to be very correct. First of all, Mark is more than an 'interpreter' in
the narrow sense of a disciple who reports faithfully the account
given by his master and nothing but that. He is a theologian, a fact
that recent critivism is realising more and more[1]; he writes his
gospel to illustrate a thesis: Jesus was in truth the Messiah and the
Son of God, but hidden and suffering ,and this is why his contemporaries did not understand. On the other hand it is oversimplifying
things to make Mark dependent only on the oral catechesis of Peter.
Serious critics, especially among Catholics[2], think that he is also, and
most of all, dependent on an earlier writing, which could well be the
enigmatic but probable 'Aramaic Matthew'. No doubt he uses the
living preaching of Peter, but it may be that all he owes to it is a certain way of presenting things, the addition of some picturesque details:
the substance of his work must go back beyond St Peter to the primitive catechetical tradition of Jerusalem. This way of looking at things
is not without importance. The predominance given to the person of
Peter ceases to be a merely optical effect, due to the fact that he
preferred to relate what he had himself seen close to; it becomes the
echo of a more general and more profound conviction, the conviction
natured by the primitive Church concerning the original role of Peter
in the apostolic group. And this evidence is the more valuable because
it appears in Mark as imposed by the power of Tradition, not in
virtue of a thesis of his own that he was trying to establish.

For indeed we have to concede that St Mark does not make the
primacy of St Peter one of the major subjects of his gospel. Not only
are there lacking certain significant elements or episodes that Matthew
and Luke have in addition; but he even omits from the scene of the
confession at Caesarea the Petrine Logion which Matthew records
there (*Mt* 16:17–19) and to which *Lk* 22:31-2, and *Jn* 21:15–17,

[1] Vincent TAYLOR for example recognises in Mark a Christology as lofty as any
other in the New Testament, including John (*The Gospel according to St Mark*,
London, 1952, p. 121).
[2] For example, CERFAUX and VAGANAY. Cf. also among Protestant critics,
P. PARKER, *The Gospel before Mark*, Chicago, 1953 (*RBibl*, 1954,. pp 454f).

provide equivalents at least. It is legitimate to be astonished by this omission and it requires an explanation. If it does not actually go against the primacy, it at least denies it a support which would have been considerable. I want to put forward three considerations in regard to it. In the first place, we cannot be sure that there has been any 'omission', because we cannot be sure that this Logion was originally to be found in this place in Aramaic Matthew. I find Cullmann's arguments on this point persuasive and am inclined to believe that the Logion on the primacy in the narrative of the Confession represents an insertion due to the editorial activity of the Greek Matthew. This does not call its authenticity into question, as Cullmann again admits; it is sufficient for the Greek editor of the first gospel to have found it in another source and to have combined it with the scene at Caesarea, following a procedure which is habitual with him. In this case Mark has 'omitted' nothing; on the contrary he represents a purer and more primitive state of the episode of the Confession, which is reproduced also by St Luke. This solution seems a happy one, but several exegetes are opposed to it, especially those who, believing in the existence of Aramaic Matthew as a source of Mark, hold that it contained the Logion on the primacy in this place. For them Mark has really 'omitted' something. If we adopt their hypothesis, I would put forward two further suggestions which are complementary. The manifest plan of the second evangelist was to present the person of Jesus the Son of God and to explain his mysterious destiny as the Messiah who suffered and was rejected and yet triumphed. This plan guided his choice of materials and led him to suppress a number of things, especially 'words' of the Lord, since he was not concerned to report his teaching in detail. Here he could well have omitted the Logion about Peter, which was not directly useful for his purpose; he preserved the essentials about which he was deeply concerned: Jesus is the Messiah, his own acknowledged him, but even they did not understand his way of suffering! If however we still feel astonishment that he could have eliminated so important a Logion, a last consideration will not be out of place: that is, that this Logion on the primacy did not have the decisive importance at the origins of the Church that we give it nowadays because of the discussions which have centred on it. On the one hand, as I have said, the primacy of Peter was lived before ever it became a subject of reasoning and discussion: the need to prove it by argument was not so strongly felt. *Mt* 16:17–19 did not become the *locus classicus* for the

Roman primacy until later[1]. On the other hand, there were other passages in the gospels to justify it, such as *Lk* 22:31-2, and *Jn* 21:15-17.

In contrast to the strictly 'personal character of Mark's references' touching St Peter, Mgr Cassien acknowledges the considerable importance given to the primacy in the gospel of St Matthew. 'The primacy of Peter is asserted throughout the gospel.' 'Matthew's references have a doctrinal character witnessing to the hierarchical primacy of St Peter. This is the thesis that St Matthew is exerting himself to prove.' This time we can only admit that he is right, and there is no need to duplicate his work by repeating all the texts which prove this point. It is indeed a thesis of the first gospel, among others as well, and it manifests itself especially in what can be called the 'ecclesiastical booklet'. I am thinking of those narratives in chapters 13 to 17 which lead up to the discourse about the relationships of the brethren in the future Church (ch. 18). In these appear the elements proper to Matthew which are plainly intended to emphasise Peter's pre-eminence in the apostolic group: the walking on the water which shows Peter to be more enthusiastic than the rest in following Jesus and strengthened by the Master in his still hesitant faith (14:28-33), the episode of the didrachma in which Peter is so closely associated with the person of Jesus (17:24-7), and lastly the Logion about the primacy which Matthew is alone in inserting in the Caesarea Confession (16:17-19).

This last text is evidently the principal document and deserves to retain our attention. Mgr Cassien himself acknowledges its considerable importance: the words of Jesus are indeed addressed to Peter in his own person, distinguishing him from the rest, and they grant him the privilege of being the rock on which the Church is to be founded. 'The primacy which is in question is a primacy which puts him, or rather is going to put him, above the other apostles. St Peter's place is absolutely unique.' We are the more surprised then to see him subsequently insisting on the obscurity of this Logion that he has just called 'clear', hesitating in an anachronistic way between a 'canonical', a 'moral' interpretation or a 'purely historical' one, and concluding that 'interpretation halts before an enigma it is powerless to penetrate ... The original meaning of the Logion on the Church remains and always will remain unknown to us.' 'Its interpretation in the light of

---

[1] See the work of J. LUDWIG, *Die Primatworte Mt* 16:18-19 *in der altkirchlichen Exegese*, Münster, 1952 (*RBibl*, 1954, p. 310).

parallels drawn from the Old Testament and from Judaism, which is very fashionable today, does not issue in any indisputable result.'

Such pessimism does not seem justified to me. After a period in which these words of Christ were either rejected or disfigured by polemical use, more recent works have done better justice to them. To quote only one of the more recent, and one which is not suspect for Roman prejudice, Cullmann has some excellent things to say[1]. Today, in the light of the Old Testament and of Judaism, not forgetting the Qumran texts, we can understand better how Jesus set out to found in his own lifetime, in the Messianic era inaugurated in his own person, a community of the saved which would continue and realise in a definitive manner the Assembly of the 'holy people', the 'Remnant' announced by the prophets. He was to found it as Son of Man, the representative and leader of the 'people of the saints' (*Dn* 7:13f, 18, 27), as the suffering Servant giving his life to save sinners (*Is* 53) and to make a 'new covenant' in his blood (*Jr* 31:31ff). This community, already sketched in his lifetime in the group of the apostles, was to be established and spread after his death and resurrection. To rule it and maintain its unity after his departure, it was necessary to give it a human head who would represent him on earth. It was Peter who was chosen for this office, and our Logion is one of the sayings by which Jesus made his choice solemnly known to the other apostles.

Our author is perhaps prepared to follow us thus far, but only to escape later. The power of the keys entrusted to St Peter is no more than the power to forgive sins which is to be granted to the other apostles as well (*Mt* 18:18; *Jn* 29:23). As for the personal privilege of being the rock on which the Church is to be founded, it is mysterious and perhaps represents something hardly more than a symbol, that must not be pressed too hard or it will be destroyed. In any case it cannot refer to a real hierarchical primacy, since that is not borne out by the practice of the primitive Church; there was no primacy recognised in the Church at that time other than that of the Church of Jerusalem, and it is perhaps because he has that in mind that Matthew projects on to St Peter the memory of the church which he directed for a time.

What I have said earlier is sufficient to refuse this last denial and the hypothesis which accompanies it. As for the expression 'bind and

[1] See the work already quoted and his article Πέτρος in the *Theol. Wört.z.N.T.*, vol. vi, especially pp. 106–8.

loose', even if it can be applied in a restricted way to the forgiveness of
sins and hence become valid for the rest of the apostles, it does have
also, in the rabbinic language which is its source, a wider significance,
that of forbidding or permitting, that is to say of passing judgements
of a doctrinal or juridical nature. In Peter's case it is rendered more
precise by another image, that of the 'keys' of the Kingdom of Heaven.
It is a question plainly of the office of major-domo (*Is* 22:22): among
the servants of the Master and at their head, Peter finds himself entrusted with the care of the House of God on earth. No doubt it would
be too far-fetched to bring the parable of the major-domo in here (*Mt*
24:45–51; *Lk* 12:41–7) and to suggest that we should see in the
steward put in charge of the other servants Peter directing the other
apostles; even if, according to Luke, the parable was sparked off by
a question from Peter, the latter nevertheless used the word 'us' and
was distinguishing only between the group of apostles and the crowd.
At least, to return to the immediate context, it is legitimate to understand the gates the keys of which Peter receives as being opposed to
the hostile gates of the Kingdom of the dead; it belongs to Peter to
welcome men to salvation and to protect them in their new refuge
against the assaults of evil. We sense here a power to govern which
goes beyond the simple power to forgive sins and also beyond the
mere function of apostolic witness.

For it is to this that Cullmann wishes to reduce the mission of the
Rock that is the foundation of the Church. Peter would be performing
this function by bearing witness to the resurrection of Christ like all
the other apostles, with the merely quantitative difference that having
been the first to see the risen Christ, his evidence takes on a special
dignity from this fact. It goes without saying that when reduced in
this way to apostolic witnessing alone, the role of Peter comes to an
end with his death and cannot imply any succession: Others can live
by the faith that he has planted but no one can take his place and say
that he has seen Christ! This interpretation seems much too narrow
to me; it corresponds neither to the image of the Rock-Foundation
nor to the Logion taken as a whole. Let us take notice that Peter is
not likened to the structural foundations of the building, that is, to
the first course, the θεμέλιος of which the other apostles are equally a
part (*Ep* 2:20). He is, by himself, the unique ground, the rock πέτρα
on which the θεμέλιος[1] of the apostolic witness is to be laid. We
realise that this is a special function, once again unique, and one

---

[1] The difference between the two terms is well illustrated in *Lk* 6:48.

which will last as long as the building lasts. The act of laying the first
courses will of course be done only once; but their role of support
will continue always, and, beneath them, the role of the Rock at the
base which supports even them[1]. The Church remains for ever solidly
founded on the witness of the apostles and behind them on the solidity
of him who was chosen as their leader. In the same way then that the
function of the apostles is to be continued through their successors
the bishops[2], so the function of the Rock is to continue in the person
of a successor who will play the part of Peter in their regard. We must
not however expect the whole answer from the image of the Rock; it
does not stand alone, but forms part of a passage which provides a
commentary on it, and on which in its turn the parallel passages in the
other gospels form a comment. In the saying reported by Matthew,
Jesus is clearly manifesting his desire to found a Church and give it a
leader, who will not only uphold it like a basis of rock, but will also
govern it like a major-domo. The very character of a human society
that he gives to his Church and which he wants to be eternal, demands
that he should expect this leader to perform the function of director
within the unity, a function without which no society can hold together. And since this leader is mortal, the demand implies necessarily
that his successors should take his place. One may regret that the
Logion makes no explicit mention of successors; one may also be
glad, since if it had done so, there are those who would have seen this
merely as another reason for rejecting its authenticity. It is sufficient
that Jesus' intention should be clear and that there should be no
deliberate refusal to accept its logical consequences, attested by the
life of the Church.

For the rest, this saying does not stand alone. The third and fourth
gospels record others which make a very useful commentary on it and
which are going to enlighten us still further on the fact and the manner
of Peter's primacy with regard to his brethren the apostles.

The gospel of St Luke also in its own way emphasises the pre-
eminence of St Peter in the apostolic group. Alongside elements which
he shares with the other evangelists, he has some of his own which are

[1] Cf. A. Vögtle, in the *Münchener Theologische Zeitschrift*, v, 1954, p. 20ff
(dealing with Cullmann's book).
[2] It is understood that the role of the bishops is not identical with that of the
apostles, but they are really the successors of the apostles. I have explained
myself on this point in my review of Cullmann (*RBibl*, 1953, p. 573f; and below
p. 166f) and I feel that Mgr Cassien, as an orthodox theologian, will not contradict me. In the same way we do not claim that the Pope is identical with
St Peter, but that he is really Peter's successor.

characteristic and to which Mgr Cassien has rightly drawn attention. In particular the miraculous draught of fish (5:1–11) which in Luke is the inaugural scene of the apostolate and in which the call addressed to Peter 'states the theme of St Peter as fisher of men and leader of the apostles'. And also the phrase in 24:34, which seems to attribute to Simon Peter the first appearance of Christ, according to a tradition found also in St Paul (*1 Co* 15:5) but nowhere else in the gospels.

The most important one however is the saying in 22:31–2, on which we must dwell. According to Mgr Cassien, St Luke here wanted to give an answer to the question that St Matthew had left 'open', to provide an interpretation of that primacy of Peter which had 'remained without explanation' in the first gospel. But this interpretation of St Luke's is not a 'canonical', but only a 'moral' one. From the 'canonical' point of view, the Twelve are to have the same power (v. 30). If Peter is superior to them, it is only through love. Tempted like them and more than them, he will fall and deny his Master; but this fall is to be followed by recovery. Then 'strengthened by the experience of his own faults and of the Lord's intercession, he will be able to anticipate their falls. St Peter's superiority is a moral one.' Then follows this unexpected conclusion: 'The idea of the ministers of the Church finding their final justification and their supreme meaning in a love which sacrifices itself for others is a biblical one. It was dear to St Matthew (cf. 24:45) as well as to St Luke (cf. 12:42). It is this apostolic love which is the secret of St Peter's superiority.' Thus the primacy of St Peter, according to St Luke, is a unique ministry, ordered towards the crisis of the Passion and solely 'moral', without any 'superiority of jurisdiction'.

Unfortunately this exegesis is arbitrary and without solid foundation. To begin with, it is highly doubtful whether Luke here wishes to reply to St Matthew: not only has the latter not left any question 'open', but Luke did not know the Greek edition of the first gospel. It is possible that this latter is earlier than 70 A.D., although this is not evident; but there is nothing to show why Luke must be later than that date. The argument drawn from *Lk* 21:20–4, does not hold water: C.H. Dodd[1] has proved that this passage is inspired wholly by the Old Testament and recalls the Fall of Jerusalem in 586 B.C. rather than describing that of 70 A.D. On the other hand, a literary comparison of the first and third gospels obliges us to admit, with the great

---

[1] 'The Fall of Jerusalem and the "Abomination of Desolation" ', in the *Journal of Roman Studies*, XXXVII, 1947, pp. 47–54.

majority of critics, that there is no direct dependence of one upon the other. The present case is only one more instance of it: the *logia* of *Mt* 16:17–19 and *Lk* 22:31–2 resemble one another only in the subject with which they deal; on the literary level they are entirely distinct. They are for that reason only the more interesting, as being two independent witnesses illustrating two different aspects of the primacy of St Peter.

In order to understand St Luke here, we must then rest content with his own text. But I have asked myself in vain what necessity there is to introduce the idea of Peter's love and sacrifice of himself for the other apostles. On the contrary it contains a phrase that Mgr Cassien does not seem to be aware of; *that your faith may not fail*. These words are, however, essential since they give the whole saying its meaning. That for which the Lord prays and which is to allow Peter to strengthen his brethren, is his faith. No doubt, shaken by the ordeal, he is going to utter his denial; but this cowardice is due precisely to the weakness of his love and of his spirit of sacrifice, rather than of his fundamental faith. Thanks to the intercession of the Lord, that will remain, provoking his remorse, forcing him to 'return' and then giving him the power to strengthen the weaker faith of his brethren. Peter is to be superior to them through the vigour of his faith. Is this a moral superiority? or a canonical one? Let us leave this dilemma on one side, it is a false problem here. What is important is that this Logion of Luke acknowledges that Peter has a primacy not merely of honour but one which is functional as well, and that it makes it consist in the exercise of faith; for it is in this way linked to the Logion of Matthew which attaches Peter's privilege to his great confession of faith[1]. In addition it makes it clear that this primacy of Peter is going to be exercised in regard to the other apostles, something which Matthew did not state so clearly, and it relates it to a crisis of fall and and recovery, which Matthew did not do: through these two aspects the passage of Luke prepares us to hear the witness of St John.

The gospel of St John holds Mgr Cassien's attention in a special way. It is here that he believes that he has found the definitive solution of the problem of Peter's primacy in the New Testament. And the exegesis that he devotes to it represents the most original contribution of his work. But is it also in my view the weakest.

[1] Or at least to some grace of revelation received from the Father, if the Caesarea Confession is not the primitive context of the logion.

Here again we have to begin by examining some points of literary criticism. It is not perhaps as unanimously admitted as Mgr Cassien thinks that John knows and is correcting the Synoptics: it seems to me very probable, though with certain refinements of course, and I shall not dwell on this point. I will only make some reservations in what concerns the relationship of Luke and John. The situation here is fairly complex. There are indeed some strange contacts between the last two gospels, but it seems to be oversimplifying things to say monolithically that John draws on Luke. In more than one case we get the impression that the influence must have worked in the opposite direction. The fourth gospel is not a work of a single growth, composed in its entirety after the other three. It is the result of a long preparation, the first stages of which could very well have been contemporaneous with the Synoptics, if not earlier than them. Thus I would prefer to believe that the final version of the Johannine gospel could have followed that of Luke and drawn on it, but that on the other hand Luke could have known certain Johannine traditions that were already in existence and himself also have drawn on *them*. To take only the texts which are related to our problem, I cannot admit that the miraculous draught of *Jn* 21 depends on that of *Lk* 5:1–11, nor that the running to the tomb in *Jn* 20:3–10, takes up and corrects *Lk* 24:12. In my view it is the contrary which is true: in his ch. 5, Luke has combined a narrative of a miraculous draught from a Johannine source with the scene of vocation from *Mk* 1:16–20[1]; and his allusion to Peter's running to the tomb (24:12) can only be explained as a summary of the longer and manifestly original narrative in *Jn* 20:3–10[2].

There is another note that must be made concerning Chapter 21 of St John. Mgr Cassien refuses to see it as an appendix: its structure is completely Johannine and it answers the questions left hanging in the air by the preceding chapters so well that it must have been planned by the author from the inception of the work. The last argument prejudges the issue of an overall solution which is precisely what is in

[1] One indication among others: *Lk* 5:8 is the only place where Luke uses the expression Σίμων Πέτρος, which is characteristic of John.
[2] Several terms in this verse are more Johannine than Lucan; yet on the other hand they are mingled with properly Lucan terms in an original composition which cannot be a mere copyist's gloss, as is no doubt the case with *Lk* 24:40. Luke must have drawn this brief note from the Johannine narrative, the eyewitness feel of the latter makes it impossible for us to believe that the dependence works the other way round, that *Jn* depends on the short note of *Lk*. In the same way, it is not John who has taken the washing of the feet from the simple phrase in *Lk* 22:27; it is Luke who here again is alluding to a Johannine scene he knows.

question. In any case it cannot use the fact that *Jn* 18 reports three denials by Peter as a support, since that was already common material belonging to the Synoptic tradition and John in his turn could have taken it over without already foreseeing that he would balance it with triple rehabilitation. No doubt the structure of the chapter is Johannine and so are many of the expressions. But they exist side by side in a curious way with others which are not[1]. It is enough to ask oneself, if not whether in the last instance the text issues from the Johannine circle, at least whether it formed part of the gospel in its original form, since it is separated from the rest by a conclusion (20:30-1) and in spite of everything this does pose a problem.

These remarks are of interest because they throw a certain doubt on the intention which Mgr Cassien attributes to John of putting foward from the beginning the problem of the primacy which had been bequeathed him by Matthew and Luke and of attempting throughout the gospel to provide a solution. We shall now have to see whether an examination of the texts themselves makes this intention seem likely and vindicates the manner in which it has been interpreted.

It is not possible that the first mention of St Peter (*Jn* 1:40-2) recalls certain elements of *Mt* 16:17-19. However, to see in this a deliberate statement of the problem of the primacy, we should have to adopt, in the wake of Cullmann, an explanation of πρῶτον which seems very forced. This reading is not certain either and one may feel inclined to prefer the reading πρωί which is not lacking in serious support and would fit in with a plan of John's which is much more obvious in these first chapters, to establish a chronological schema of a first week[2].

As for St John's solution of the problem of the primacy which he has thus started at the beginning of his gospel, Mgr Cassien sees it as having a two-fold orientation: to reduce the person of Peter to the level of the other apostles and to set over against him the person of the Other Disciple, more advanced than Peter in intimacy with the Lord and greater than Peter from the point of view of spiritual superiority. Part of this diagnosis is true but it is accompanied with exaggeration. For it cannot be denied that the fourth gospel puts beside Peter, and even raises above him in certain respects, the person of

[1] Cf. M.E. BOISMARD, 'Le chaptire XXI de saint Jean. Essai de critique littéraire', in *RBibl*, 1947, pp. 473–501.
[2] I owe this suggestion to my colleague P. Boismard who has since developed it further in his own work.

Another Disciple who does not receive a similar emphasis in the other gospels. Whatever may be the reason for this mysterious anonymity of the Other Disciple, the one whom Jesus loved, and whether or not he is identical with John the evangelist himself, it is clearly established that he seems closer to the Heart of the Master than Peter (*Jn* 13:23-6), that, alone of the disciples, he stands at the foot of the Cross (*Jn* 19:26-7) and that he recognises the risen Lord before Peter does (*Jn* 21:7). But it does not follow that this superiority in the order of intimacy and of spiritual perception overshadows the primacy of Peter, which is situated on quite a different level. It is not even certain that this superiority is emphasised with the intention of reducing Peter; it is sufficient if the Other Disciple is someone dear to the Johannine circle, even perhaps its head, for the gospel which issues from this circle to like to recall that even though Peter was the first in the apostolic group in certain respects, in others the Other Disciple was no less important. We shall return to this shortly in connection with ch. 21. For the moment let us observe that John's tendency to reduce the importance of Peter is not to be exaggerated.

In the confession which follows the discourse at Capernaum (*Jn* 6:67-71) Peter speaks in the name of the Twelve, true; but the same is true of the Confession at Caesarea in *Mk* and *Lk*. Only Matthew has added at that point a Logion concerning Peter especially, and, even if he knew it, John was under no obligation to repeat it here, especially if he was keeping in reserve an equivalent saying to record later. It remains that here, in John as in the Synoptics, it is Peter who speaks in the name of all to acknowledge Jesus; this is a lot, and John does not deny it.

When Jesus washed the feet of his disciples, did he begin with Peter or not? Exegetes are divided and the text does not allow us to decide with certainty. The least we can say is that the point remains in doubt and that anyway it is of little importance. The primacy does not depend on details like this and even if John had said clearly that Peter was not the first to be washed, a deal of good will would be necessary to see this as being intended to reduce his importance. Nor does this intention emerge from the fact that Peter is recalled to humility by Jesus; this is less serious than the reproach of being a Satan, which John has omitted from the scene of the confession, differing in this from the Synoptics, or which perhaps he has transferred to Judas (6:70). The fact that the prophecy of Peter's denial is

not accompanied by a promise of re-establishment, as it is in *Lk*
22:31–4, is significant only if we imagine John writing with the third
gospel under his eye and deliberately omitting this point. In fact, as I
have said, the literary situation is quite different. In his little discourse
after the Last Supper, St Luke is combining Synoptic material with
his own sources, part of which shows a Johannine influence (22:27).
Here St John does not depend on him and John's prophecy of the
denial contains nothing more shattering for Peter than that of Mark
and Matthew; it is perhaps even less shattering since it contains the
announcement that Peter will follow later, especially if we see here a
preparation for ch. 21.

Peter is introduced into the house of the high priest by the Other
Disciple, of whom nothing further is said while Peter's denial is
reported. 'The silence of the evangelist on this point suggests that
he himself did not deny the Lord.' Possibly; but it could also be that
since he was familiar to the high priest's household, he was not sub-
jected to the same danger, and hence cannot take any credit for it.

We next see Peter and the Other Disciple running to the tomb. Of
the latter we are told that 'he saw and he believed'. Mgr Cassien concludes, 'It was not St Peter, it was the Beloved Disciple who believed'.
I do not think that the text authorises this exclusion of Peter. It obviously dwells with pleasure on the enthusiasm and speed of the Other
Disciple, which brings him to the tomb first and it emphasises his
faith, no doubt because it is he who is bearing witness here. But it
adds an important detail which seems unfortunately to have escaped
Mgr Cassien's notice. Although he arrived first, the Other Disciple
yet took care not to go in, since he wanted to reserve this honour for
Peter, a delicate touch which acknowledges Peter's priority. The
Other Disciple may well recognise in himself a particular gift of
spiritual perspicacity; but for all that Peter must still go in front of
him; simply because he is the elder? much more because he is the
head.

This prolonged parallel between Peter and the Other Disciple is to
find its supreme expression in the decisive episode in Ch. 21. The
prerogatives of both are going to be explained, not to reduce the
importance of one for the benefit of the other, but to situate each
in its proper sphere. We find no difficulty in admitting that the Lord
is recognised first by the Other Disciple, on whose word Peter throws
himself into the sea. This in no wise prejudices the two passages that
are to follow, the one on the role personally entrusted to Peter by

Jesus (vv. 15–17), the other on the opposition then made between the martyrdom of Peter and the survival of the Other Disciple (vv. 18–23). It is here however that Mgr Cassien puts forward a minimising interpretation which is absolutely untenable purely from the exegetical point of view.

First, the pastoral charge to Peter, linked to his triple affirmation of love. It seems quite certain that this triple affirmation provoked by Christ corresponds to the triple denial and is to redress it. Before confirming Peter in his duty as Pastor, Jesus demands of him a proof of his love which, in his own and in the eyes of all, redeems his momentary weakness. But Mgr Cassien does not understand it like this; he perceives a 'regression in the three questions' thanks to which the 'supremacy of St Peter is expressly denied'. Jesus asks Peter first if he loves him more than the other disciples; alas, no, since the Other Disciple, by not denying him, has given convincing proof that he loved him still more (but did this Other Disciple, too, have to confess Jesus in the courtyard of the high priest? John does not say so.) Does Peter then love Jesus at least as much as the others? Alas, again no, it seems, since Jesus has to fall back on something even less exacting: he no longer asks whether Peter loves him with the authentic love of a disciple (ἀγαπᾶν), but simply with 'a purely human and personal attachment' (φιλεῖν). And it seems that Jesus is content with this minimum since he entrusts Peter with the cares of Pastor just the same . . . Before we go any further, let us say that this is frankly an abuse of exegesis. It plays in particular on an opposition between ἀγαπᾶν and φιλεῖν which is not legitimate in the vocabulary of St John, for whom φιλεῖν often serves to express the same spiritual love as αγαπᾶν (cf. 5:20; 16:27; 20:2; and φίλος 15:13–15). Why should it express a love of a different nature here? Because the two Greek words are juxtaposed? But this is a literary proceeding familiar to St John whose aim is only to vary the words in order to avoid monotony[1]. This procedure which is also responsible for the alteration of ἀγαπᾶν and φιλεῖν in regard to 'the disciple whom Jesus loved' (see Jn 20:2 and 13:23; also 19:26; 21:7, 20)[2] is found again in our passage in the alternation βόσκειν/ποιμαίνειν and ἀρνία/προβάτια. Mgr Cassien himself acknowledges that the latter are without consequence for the meaning; what right has he then to grant so much importance

---

[1] Cf. E. RUCKSTUHL, Die literarische Einheit des Johannesevangeliums. Freiburg, 1951, p. 146f.
[2] Compare again for example 14:27 and 16:27.

to the one which expresses in his opinion two different manners of loving[1]? I would explain in the same way why the second question does not develop πλέον τούτων: the omission of this serves to vary the style from the first to the second questions, just as the change of verb does from the second to the third. In brief, the subtlety that has been suggested is without foundation, and the supposed decline in the profession of love goes against the spirit of the passage. If Jesus confirms Peter in the charge of Pastor, this is because, in spite of his past weakness, Peter really does have the greatest love. The supremacy of Peter is not 'expressly denied'; on the contrary it is re-established and confirmed.

But in what does it consist? In order to refute it the more easily, our author has recourse to a very singular explanation of the pastoral function. First, it is carefully distinguished from the function of apostle: 'pastors' and 'apostles' are very different titles in *Ep* 4:11; and those who 'feed' the 'flock' in *Ac* 20:17 and 28, and *1 P* 5:1f, are 'elders', not apostles. Whence this unexpected result – as 'pastor' Peter is detached from the apostolic group, for he is not a 'pastor of pastors', 'he is not the first: he is one'. In short, there is no longer any question of primacy! And this is not all. The essential act of this pastoral ministry is to be the death of the martyr, as we are given to understand from the fact that vv. 18ff follow immediately on 15–17. 'This conception of the pastoral ministry which finds its accomplishment in death has an absolutely unique character. St Peter is a pastor in order to die.' Then, 'if death is the end and the supreme object of (Peter's) ministry, there can be no question of succession. For St John – even more than for his predecessors – the primacy of St Peter, which is a unique fact, is not and cannot be an ecclesiastical institution.'

In this there seems to me to be two pieces of false reasoning which give a wrong idea of Peter's pastoral function: the restriction which separates it from the apostolic group and the reduction which limits it to death as a martyr. The title of 'pastor' is susceptible, it is true, of a particular application which refers to the local head of a community as opposed to the itinerant witness, the apostle. But its primary significance is far more general; it indicates the direction of a

---

[1] To be logical, Mgr Cassien ought to have explained, as does the text of Origen he refers to, why Peter replies with a φιλῶ to the questions Jesus asks him about his ἀγάπη. Is there a subtle shade of meaning there too – I don't love you as a disciple, but I do love you all the same with a human love?

religious group which can be of very wide, even universal, extension. And it connotes therefore all the different activities that the shepherd has to employ to lead, nourish and save his sheep. Mgr Cassien shows himself well aware of this when he envisages 'a universal, ramifying ministry realised in a great variety of forms and extending over the whole flock of Christ'. It is in this superior and very wide sense that the title of Pastor is applied to Christ himself above all, in the New Testament: he called himself the Good Shepherd (*Jn* 10:11; cf. *Mt* 25:32; 26:31) and this supreme role of direction is attributed to him again in *Heb* 13:20; *1 P* 2:25; *Rv* 7:17; 12:5. He enjoys this title in so far as he is the Messiah King (*Ezk* 34:23; *Mi* 5:3; cf. *Mt* 2:60), representative of God the Shepherd of Israel (*Is* 40:11; *Jr* 21:10; *Ezk* 34:11–16; *Ps* 74:1; 78:2 etc.). In a word, the charge of Pastor is a charge to lead the people of God, a charge which belongs pro-perly to God and his Christ, but which is here delegated to St Peter! Mgr Cassien has seen this quite clearly himself: 'The Pastor is Christ, not the apostles. The pastoral office of St Peter brings him close to Christ'. Why does he not continue along this excellent line? Why oppose this ministry of Peter to that of the apostles, when all that needs to be done is to distinguish it from theirs as superior? It is not so far as he is an apostle that Peter is pastor, all right; but if he is an apostle like the other apostles, he is also, and he alone, pastor. That is to say, he is charged with directing them, and through them the whole flock of Christ. Jesus, the one and only Shepherd, at the moment when he is to quit the earth, charges Peter, as his unique representative, to feed his flock in his name. And as Jesus demands a love greater than that of the other apostles to make this privilege legitimate, everything suggests that these latter are to be the first of the sheep that Peter will have to feed. He is constituted leader of the apostolic flock, and ultimately of the whole Church.

But no, we are told, there has been a misdeal! The function of the pastor is only to die. I know nothing which authorises this restriction. Certainly not the sequel (vv. 18 ff), which can perfectly well link a new theme to that of vv. 15–17, but certainly cannot dissipate the proper content of the theme of Pastor. No doubt the supreme act of a good shepherd is to give his life for his sheep (*Jn* 10:11, 15); but the heroic sacrifice which can terminate his career is only the crowning phase of a whole activity of devotion, nourishing, leading and protecting the sheep. Before telling Peter of his martyrdom, Jesus says to him three times, 'Feed my sheep'. Here we are referred to the aorist στήρισον in

Lk 22:32, which is supposed to denote a unique act of love strengthening the brethren. But, apart from the fact that this unique act is much
more probably their re-establishment in the faith on the morrow of
the Passion (unless again this is a comprehensive aorist), the parallel
claimed with Luke cannot be valid here, where the command to feed
the sheep is given in the present imperative: βόσκε, ποίμαινε. This
fact, curiously neglected by Mgr Cassien, has its importance: before
foretelling Peter's death, Jesus prescribes him a whole, lasting pro-
gramme of activity at the head of his flock.

This fact is sufficient to reverse the conclusion drawn by Mgr
Cassien from Peter's death. From the moment, he tells us, that the
office of pastor consists in dying, it necessarily excludes all idea of
succession. It is the contrary that is true. The office of pastor consists
above all in directing the flock of Christ, to instruct it in the faith,
protect it against dangers and to keep it in the unity of the one fold
(*Jn* 10:9–16). In the same way that Christ as he quitted the earth entrusted this care to Peter, so Peter in his turn has to die and pass the
charge on to another. The heroic act of his martyrdom does not prevent the flock from carrying on and from needing always a pastor – a
pastor who, in his turn, will represent Christ and who, like him, will
direct the whole flock, including the bishops who are the successors
of the apostles.

Is this whole perspective, clear as it is, destroyed by the contrast
which follows between Peter who is going to die and the Other Disciple who is to remain? Certainly not. We find here again the particular interest the fourth gospel has in the mysterious disciple. In this
ending of the gospel care is taken to reiterate his authority as a witness, and perhaps it was also felt desirable to reply as well to rumours
that the longevity of the Beloved Disciple caused among the brethren[1].
Even if we were to admit strictly, as Mgr Cassien thinks, that the
office of St Peter was to feed the flock and die and that the office of the
Other Disciple was to live and bear witness, it seems to me obviously
exaggerated to say that 'the Beloved Disciple is greater than St Peter'
simply because in 'the era of the Spirit, he (John) belongs to the
superior level of the Spirit'. Besides, have we not been told a little
earlier, 'This pastoral ministry (Peter's, according to John) belongs

---

[1] In the case in which ch. 21 is taken as an appendix added after the death of
St John, it could be a question on the contrary of a reply by his disciples to the
astonishment of those for whom, according to a saying of the Lord, the Beloved
Disciple was not supposed to die. They are making clear that this is not what
Jesus said.

to the Christian era, it presupposes the presence of the Holy Spirit, it is guided by the Spirit'? No, let us not manufacture opposition between them. The Other Disciple arrived first at the tomb and perhaps understood sooner, but he let Peter go in front of him; in the evening of his life, he may have seemed the more important for the span of his testimony, but he does not claim precedence over him who is the Pastor.

The three principal texts concerning the primacy of Peter, *Mt* 16: 17–19; *Lk* 22:31–2; *Jn* 21:15–17 complement one another in a remarkable way. Mgr Cassien wants each of them to have known the preceding one, and to explain or correct it – a thesis which, joined to an often forced exegesis in detail, allows him little by little to empty the primacy of its content and in the end to dissolve it completely. I cannot share his opinions. Even if the evangelists were taking one another up in this way, I would still be unwilling to admit, from a theological point of view, that we can rest satisfied with the solution of the last as 'the answer of Scripture'; for Scripture is more than a human search striving to solve a problem, it is in all its parts a Word which commands faith. In fact, from a literary point of view, I think that the three texts in question are independent and are linked only by a common conviction, the tradition of the Church, founded on the words of Christ.

In these three cases at least, Jesus gave a solemn explanation of the role that he intended to entrust to the first of his apostles. Each time new details make his intention more precise. To the image of the Major-domo in the House of God is added that of the Pastor of the flock. The firmness of faith suggested by the image of the Rock-foundation appears as a privilege due to the prayer of Christ. Because through his own faith he had to strengthen his brethren the apostles, Peter was to be not only the first among them with regard to apostolic witness, a *primus inter pares*, but to be their head, charged with care for them as for the whole flock of Christ. In addition to his role as an apostle, a role shared with them, he was to have a unique superior role, that of the supreme direction and decision which is implied by the 'keys' in the hands of the steward and the office of 'pastor' responsible for his flock. He was to represent Christ.

We have noticed that the office of Pastor belongs in the first place to Christ. Now it is worth taking note that the same goes for the power of the Keys and the function of the Rock. These too are attributes of the Messiah. According to *Rv* 3:7, which takes up the

oracle of *Is* 22:22, Christ 'had the key of David, so that when he
opens, nobody can close, and when he closes, nobody can open'.
On the other hand, the designation of Stone and Rock is applied to
him in different ways; the stone of stumbling (*Rm* 9:33; *1 P* 2:8),
but also the foundation stone (*1 P* 2:6), rejected by the builders but
chosen by God as the keystone (*Mt* 21:42; *1 P* 2:7), and finally the
Rock which led the chosen people in the desert (*1 Co* 10:4). So that,
when he grants these titles to Peter, he is clearly nominating him to
continue on earth his mission to govern the Messianic people. This
is a unique but permanent mission, which cannot come to an end as
long as there is a flock to lead, a house to keep firm on its foundations
and to administer.

Of course Peter will have to die. What won him the privilege of
feeding Christ's flock was in fact his great love. And this he is to
prove by crowning his ministry with the glorious death of the martyr.
In foretelling this to him, Jesus did not add, at least according to our
texts, that he must therefore have a successor. But that went of its
own accord, and he did not have to say so. Since the Church was to
continue 'to the end of time' (*Mt* 28:20), it would always have need
of a head to direct it and keep it unified by assuring it, in a visible
manner, of the continuing presence of Christ, the Rock, the Key-
bearer and the Shepherd. Moreover Jesus spoke in the first place to
his apostles, whom he was sending out into the world; and it was
through them that he intended to reach those who, thanks to their
word, were to believe in him (*Jn* 17:18–20). He did not found a 'religion of the book' and he was not speaking for those who only wanted
to believe in a book. He was founding a living Community and en-
trusting to its first members the care of transmitting his wishes to
future generations. By its living Tradition enveloping and commenting
on Scripture, the Church has lived out this intention of its Master.

From its first steps, it grew under the guidance of Peter. Beyond all
the divergences and the gropings inherent in its prodigious development, it lived in so profoundly sincere a unity that it did not feel the
need, in its first writings, to make laws about all the aspects of its
'canonical' organisation. Later the divisions and discussions due to
the human weakness of its members led it to formulate more clearly
what it had begun by living. This unfolding was useful and even
necessary, but it was not wholly carried out in the New Testament.
Rather than creating stumbling-blocks and provoking interminable
discussions, this reserve in the Scripture and the holy and brotherly

freedom with which the first Christians lived in faith and love around the apostles and their head Peter, ought to invite the Christians to rediscover, in the charity of mutual support and reciprocal under-standing, the unity of a single flock under the guidance of a single shepherd, the legitimate successor of Peter and like him the repre-sentative of Christ.

7. St Peter according to Oscar Cullmann*

This is an important book,[1] by reason both of its subject and its authorship. It is divided into two parts, which deal respectively with the 'historical problem' and the 'exegetical and theological problem'.

The matter of the First Part is shared among three chapters: 'the disciple', 'the apostle', 'the martyr'. After studying the name, the origins and the profession of Peter, Dr Cullmann emphasises strongly the privileged position he holds in the group of Jesus' disciples. He is 'the first' among them. The three Synoptic gospels are unanimous in telling us this and in illustrating it with details. Even the fourth gospel acknowledges this pre-eminence, although it sets beside him another who is also 'first', but in other respects, the Beloved Disciple. But this pre-eminence does not yet imply the role of head: Peter is only the 'spokesman', the 'representative' of the Twelve. 'On the evidence of the whole gospel tradition, Peter occupies a particularly representative place among the disciples of Jesus' (p. 25). And this place was granted him by Jesus himself when he singled him out from the rest and gave him the name Cephas, that is, the 'Rock'. This choice may in part be explained by Peter's personal qualities, but these cannot be the whole reason; beside the disciple's temperament, there is a sovereign decision by the Master.

This privileged position is confirmed after the departure of Jesus. It emerges clearly from the first part of Acts, as well as from the attitude of Paul (*Ga* 1:18), that Peter is the director of the first community in Jerusalem, and *de facto* of the universal Church whose sole representative it is at that moment. This publicly recognised role of head Peter owes quite certainly to a mission received from Jesus; not only to that preference the Master showed him in his lifetime (the

* Originally published in *RBibl*, 1953, pp. 565–79.
[1] *Saint Pierre, Disciple-Apôtre-Martyr. Histoire et Théologie*, by Oscar Cullmann (Bibliothèque Théologique), Neuchâtel-Paris, 1952. (English trans., *Peter: Disciple, Apostle, Martyr*, trans. by F.V. Filson, S.C.M. Press.)

text of *Mt* 16:17ff is to be discussed later), but also and above all to
the mission with which Jesus entrusted him on the morrow of his
resurrection. He was the first to whom the risen Christ showed himself. This fact is guaranteed by a series of indications which overlap
one another: *1 Co* 15:5 and *Lk* 24:34 assert it; the lost ending of
Mk perhaps included it (it is postulated by *Mk* 16:7) and *Jn* 21 could
have been derived from this narrative; it is not certain, but *Lk* 5:1ff
(miraculous draught), *Mt* 14:28ff (walking on the water), *Mk* 9:2 and
its parallels (the Transfiguration), may be antedated echoes of this
Christophany; in return, it is permissible to find further allusions to
it in *1 P* 1:3 and *2 P* 2:16ff[1]. One may be surprised that this appearance is not reported in a clearer way, but one cannot doubt its
historical reality[2]. Now this must have had a decisive importance in
founding Peter's authority as head of the Church. First, because it
made him the first eye-witness of the Risen Christ, that is to say, the
first of the 'apostles', those men whose role was to be to bear witness
to the Resurrection of Christ. Secondly, because it was accompanied
by a special 'mission'; according to *Jn* 21:15ff, Jesus entrusted Peter
with the care of 'feeding his sheep', which can be understood only
of the direction of the Church and missionary preaching. But this
wholly personal mission was limited to the life of the apostle and was
to come to an end with his death (*Jn* 21:18ff 'attaches the prophecy
of Peter's martyrdom to the command to feed the sheep', p. 56);
furthermore, Peter was to exercise it only for a few years, at least
in so far as it concerned the direction of the Church. Cullmann insists
very strongly on this fact (pp. 35–45, 185, 202ff), which is evidently of
capital importance in his eyes. After a certain time during which he
directs the Jerusalem community, Peter quits this post to devote himself entirely to the mission and hands over to James who becomes the
head of the mother-church. Peter does indeed stay at the head of 'the
Jewish-Christian missionary work', but this is 'placed in dependence
on Jerusalem' (p. 37). I follows from this that he has to render an
account of his activity to the mother-church. We see him afraid of
the 'friends of James' (*Ga* 2:12) and 'pretending' because of them,

[1] It is usual to see in this text an allusion to the Transfiguration; but Cullman
prefers to discover an echo of the appearance of the risen Christ in it (p. 54, n. 2).
Elsewhere he dates *2 P* to the 'middle of the *2nd* century at the earliest' (p. 72).
[2] Cullmann suggests two possible explanations for this silence (p. 54): on the
one hand there may have been a preference for collective over individual appearances; on the other a polemical attitude which minimised the importance of
visions as a guarantee of the apostolate may have led them not to insist on this
kind of argument.

which brings down a rebuke from Paul. At the council of Jerusalem, it is James who directs the discussions and whose decision has weight. In short, Peter no longer plays the part of the head of the Church, but rather of a man who has abandoned this role for which he did not feel he was cut out, and instead is confining himself to the missionary apostolate in which he finds himself tossed about between two different currents, that of the Jewish-Christian mission, which he directs but in dependence on Jerusalem, and that of the mission to the Christians converted from paganism, in which Paul shows himself far more independent of the mother-church. This is not the part of a Primate, the Head of the universal Church!

But before we proceed any further, it will be opportune to make some observations. It is interesting to see Cullmann acknowledging, at least for a time, a real pre-eminence of Peter among the first Christians, and even in the group of the apostles, and granting a historical value to the choice made by Jesus which was the foundation of the pre-eminence. But it is already a little disquieting to find him insisting so strongly on the appearance of the risen Christ to the detriment of the declarations which Jesus could have made during his lifetime. It is true that he reserves the study of *Mt* 16:17–19, for later, and we shall see that he grants this saying real value. For the moment however, and due to the actual layout of his enquiry, it is the scene in *Jn* 21 which appears to be the decisive moment at which Peter's apostolic mission and his role as head of the Church receive their actual foundation[1]. Now it is true that this appearance of the Risen Christ, and the mission, are of great importance, but it is without doubt exaggerated to see it as the actual principle of Peter's primacy. It could be only its confirmation; we shall have to come back to this.

But there is another point where the historical explanation proposed by Cullmann seems to go beyond what is authorised by the texts. I mean Peter's resignation of the direction of the Church in favour of James and the subordinate position in which he found himself from then on. Cullmann is clear and precise on this point: once he has become the head of the Jewish-Christian mission, Peter is 'dependent on Jerusalem' (p. 37), he acts 'under the authority of

---

[1] Cullmann does in fact admit, because of *Lk* 22:31f, that 'it is not impossible that the position of director occupied by Peter at the centre of the Church at its beginnings may be founded on a distinction or a charge conferred on this disciple by Jesus during his lifetime' (p. 50). But this possibility or rather 'non-impossibility' is hardly envisaged in the conclusions on p. 56, where the mission received from the Risen Christ decidedly occupies the first place.

James' (p. 185), he is 'James' subordinate' (p. 202), and in return the latter 'is in fact the supreme head of the Church' (*ibid.*). This is going much, much too far. That James was the bishop of Jerusalem is not in doubt, in so far at least as one can talk of 'bishops' in this primitive period. Let us say 'head of the local church'. I am prepared to say that he was its first bishop, since Peter had been more than that, head of the primitive Church with all that is implicit in that. That this Church was at the beginning identical *de facto* with the mother-church of Jerusalem, does not mean that St Peter's authority was contained *de jure* within the limits of this local church. But on the contrary this is the case with James: from the time that the Christian movement extends itself outwardly through its mission, Peter is carried naturally towards fresh fields of action and it is at this point that James replaces him as director of the local church. Certainly this church, the cradle of every other, occupies an eminent position for that reason, but that does not imply that its particular head becomes the 'head of the universal church'[1]. Nothing in the texts authorises us to say so. Why Peter comes to give an account of the conversion of Cornelius to 'the apostles and the brothers' in Jerusalem (*Ac* 11 : 1ff) is easy enough to understand at this period when authority was still exercised in a very democratic way. There is nothing of an attitude of subjection in this; the brothers are content to rejoice in Peter's decision and to praise God (*Ac* 11 : 18) and it is noteworthy that James is not mentioned in this episode. When Peter sends word to James that he is leaving Jerusalem (*Ac* 12:17), this is not to be taken as his asking for permission, still less receiving a mission, but as his notifying his subordinate that he will have from then on to hold the reins of the local community. If James enjoys precedence at the 'council of Jerusalem', this is the normal consequence of his position as the head of the church where the assembly is being held[2]. Here we have to carry out a little criticism. Cullmann admits, with many modern scholars, that in ch. 15 of Acts Luke has mingled two debates and combined the

---

[1] Cullmann is to maintain later, with force, that the direction of a local church, whichever it may be, cannot itself confer on its holder a right to rule the universal Church. He has in mind here the church of Rome. This principle, which I concede, should also surely be valid for the church of Jerusalem, even with its character of mother-church. To rule the universal Church another title than that of the head of a local church is required, in fact a superior power, specially received from Christ, with which we shall see Peter was furnished.

[2] It is not even certain that James was an 'apostle'. Cullmann, who is doubtful of this along with many critics, nevertheless raises him with the admission that 'James, although not one of the Twelve, was very probably considered as an apostle' (p. 195, n. 1; cf. p. 207).

problem of circumcision with that of a common table: the Decree of 15:29 was in reality promulgated later (p. 42). Now it is noteworthy that the decisive intervention of James is closely linked with this decree (*Ac* 15:19f; 21:25)! We may therefore wonder if the first rank which the present narrative of Acts assigns to James in the apostolic debate on circumcision ought not to be restricted to another, later and more limited debate on the laws concerning food and if the perspective reconstituted by Luke is not the result of his telescoping his sources, one being of Jewish-Christian origin and naturally inclined to magnify the role of the Jewish-Christian leader. This leads me to mention another of Cullmann's arguments. To support the pre-eminence of James, 'bishop of bishops', 'head of the holy Church of the Hebrews and of the Churches everywhere founded by the Providence of God', he puts forward the evidence of the Pseudo-Clementine writings (p. 37, n. 2; p. 202)! But is there anyone who does not realise how suspect the testimony is of so notoriously Jewish-Christian a writing? To support his notion of Peter's subordinate position, he adduces also his timorous attitude to 'the friends of James' as well as to Paul (the Antioch incident). Here we must make an essential distinction: between the role with which Peter was invested and the manner in which he performed it. It is quite clear from what the gospel tells us that the apostle was an impulsive and somewhat unstable man, capable both of noble enthusiasms and of sudden retreats, and the choice of Christ, together with the charisma which accompanied it, could not change this foundation of nature. Peter had neither the energetic intransigence of James nor the theological power of Paul[1]. But the deficiencies of his nature cannot be a sufficient reason to deny a role entrusted to his person. Rather than seeing in Peter a subordinate 'whose hands are tied', we can see as easily in him a rather weak judge over whom the opposing parties dispute and who wants to make concessions to each side. Lastly, I cannot grasp how Cullmann's explanation reconciles the fact that Peter received from Christ a role of direction that he was to exercise throughout his life and up to his death (pp. 56, 187ff) and this other supposed

[1] Cullman however is anxious to raise Peter's theological prestige by attributing to him the merit of having been the first to see in Christ the 'suffering servant' and to have preached the expiatory value of his death. But he also acknowledges that this doctrine goes back to Christ himself. Is it then legitimate to give Peter the honour of this 'ancient solution of the Christological problem' (p. 58)? On this point as on that of universalism, he has taken up, after having at last understood it, the teaching of his Master. This is a lot; but is it sufficient to make him a theologian comparable to Paul?

fact that he abdicated this role after performing it only for 'a brief period' (p. 208). Even if he was conscious of his own deficiencies, was Peter the man to abandon a charge solemnly entrusted to him by his Master in this way? In short, I refuse to believe in the correctness of this picture of a Peter who is the head of the Church for only a few years, and who then becomes the mere head of a mission, with hardly more importance than another apostle, and is subordinate even to James; it does not issue from the texts, it does not conform to Peter's character, it does not correspond to the clear intentions of Christ. But to this we shall have to return shortly.

Dr Cullmann turns next to the study of the rest of Peter's life, after his departure from Jerusalem, only to have to admit that we are very ill-informed about it. What is the 'other place' (*Ac* 12:17) to which he goes on leaving the Holy City? We do not know, and nothing authorises our taking it to be Rome. He stayed at Antioch, according to the epistle to the Galatians, but for all that did not found the church there, as people wished to believe afterwards. That he went on to Corinth is made possible but not certain by some allusions in *1 Co*[1]; but there again he cannot have played the part of founder since that belonged to Paul. The most interesting stage certainly is that of Rome, for all the consequences with which it was pregnant; so Cullmann devotes a whole important chapter (pp. 61–137: 'the martyr') to this celebrated problem. He examines in succession the literary and liturgical sources and the archaeological data. The problem has different aspects which it is important to keep separate; on the one hand the fact of Peter's martyrdom, on the other Peter's connections with Rome, which latter involve several further questions – did he found the church of Rome, did he at least visit it, did he exercise an apostolate there, was he its first bishop, and finally was it there that he died? The fact of Peter's coming to Rome is hardly attested in itself. The epistle to the Romans on the contrary presupposes that he was not there when Paul wrote; but in hinting at the existence of a strong Jewish-Christian nucleus in the Roman community, it makes it probable that Peter visited it as head of the Jewish-Christian mission. The Acts of the Apostles tell us nothing, even though they were written after the deaths of Peter and Paul, but their

---

[1] Cf. *1 Co* 1:12 'I am for Cephas' and 9:5, the allusion to Cephas's missionary voyages. But it is surely a little rash to imagine (p. 46) that Paul could have reserved for Peter the task of administering baptism that he did not carry out himself. In any case the reference to *Ac* 8:14ff seems misplaced

silence is no doubt intentional. On the other hand, even if *1 P* is not authentic, it constitutes valuable positive evidence for the presence of Peter in Rome, since it is quite certainly Rome that we must see behind the 'Babylon 'of 5:13. But no more than any other does it mention the exercise of any apostolate in the capital, still less an 'episcopate'. As for what concerns Peter's martyrdom, without the explicit mention of place, it seems well attested by *Jn* 21:18, corroborated by *1 P* 5:1 and *2 P* 1:14. But the most important and decisive testimonies are those which link the two items, martyrdom and Rome. *Rv* 11:3ff would be very valuable if the hypothesis which sees Peter and Paul in the 'two witnesses' and Rome in the 'great City' were more certain; but Cullmann is reserved in this regard. In return however, he grants a lot of importance to ch. 5 of *1 Clement*: resuming a thesis which he has defended brilliantly elsewhere, he deduces from this text that Peter and Paul were martyred at Rome, victims of the jealousy of certain brethren, no doubt Jewish-Christians, who denounced and delivered them to the Roman authorities, a tragic end, humiliating for Christianity, which the Acts of the Apostles preferred to pass over in silence. This evidence, important for its authority and its antiquity, is again confirmed by St Ignatius' Epistle to the Romans (4:3) and the Ascension of Isaiah (4:2–3). Nothing much can be learnt from later literary sources; they must in fact be treated with caution in proportion to the degree to which they exaggerate the part played by Peter in the foundation of the Church of Rome (Dionysius of Corinth, Irenaeus). Exception however must be made for an indication of the Neoplatonist Porphyry, transmitted by Macarius of Magnesia (3:22), according to which Peter's ministry lasted only for some months, and for the texts of Caius and of Tertullian who are the first to witness, about the year 200, to a topographical tradition about the site of Peter's martyrdom, and perhaps even of his tomb.

This tradition leads Cullmann on to the examination of the liturgical and archaeological data. He pronounces against a transference of the relics of Peter and Paul to San Sebastiano in 258. Instead, in his view, this date marks the beginning of the cult of the apostles. They would have been venerated in this place because the pagan cemeteries of the Vatican and the Via Ostiniensis were not very accessible, and perhaps also because there was already a cult paid to them there, inaugurated by some schismatic sect such as that of Novation. It is noteworthy that the 29th of June, the date chosen for their feast, was the anniversary of the foundation of Rome by Romulus. The recent excavations in the Vatican probably rediscovered the 'trophaeum' mentioned by the priest Caius; they did not, according to Cullmann, discover the tomb of St Peter. In addition, he thinks it *a priori* almost impossible for such a tomb to be discovered: how could the first Christians have buried the apostle so close to the gardens of Nero? how could they have got possession of the body, since the victims of Nero's persecution were without doubt buried in a common grave or thrown into the Tiber? would they even have wanted to, in this primitive age in which a cult was not yet offered to the relics of the martyrs? They would only have kept the memory of the place of his death by a memorial such as the trophaeum of Caius. And it was only later, in the third century, when the cult of the martyrs had begun and the Eastern churches had put the tombs of their apostles in order, that the Church of Rome replied by pointing to those founders. It then looked for them spontaneously near the traditional places of their martyrdoms, at the Vatican and the Via Ostiensis.

I prefer to leave to those who are more competent the task of deciding whether Dr Cullmann has underestimated the importance of the excavations at St Peter's. The question is too fresh to be settled yet in any definitive way. The archaeological discoveries have not yet perhaps revealed all they have to tell us. Thus for example the absence of graffiti using Peter's name (p. 129) is not perhaps certain, if we are to believe some recent information. But this is not the essential point. The important thing is that Peter came to Rome and died there, since this is the sufficient and necessary basis for his having been able to transmit the personal power with which he was invested to someone else there. Cullmann, indeed, at the end of his critical enquiry, admits that the martyrdom of Peter at Rome is 'an almost certain fact for which the history of the early Church must definitively find a place' (p. 101). This is the basic thing. That Peter did not himself found the Church of Rome is possible, though it is better to say we are ill-informed on this point. Cullmann himself is hesitant: sometimes he admits that Peter could have come to Rome to visit the Jewish-Christians who belonged to his jurisdiction (p. 70), or more precisely to pacify the conflict between these and the converts from paganism (p. 94), sometimes he envisages him as coming merely as a prisoner to be executed there (p. 87, n.l.). He came to Rome, and that is sufficient, even if it is maintained that he was not its 'bishop' in the true sense of the word, since none of the apostles were ever bishops, but transmitted their power of direction to the bishops. We shall return to this point when we are examining the end of the work.

The Second Part, which deals with the 'exegetical and theological problem', is the more important. It begins with the exegesis of *Mt* 16:17–19 and then discusses the dogmatic problem posed by the application of this text to the later Church.

After a brief history of the principal interpretations to which this celebrated text has given rise and which, as Cullmann observes have been too often influenced by 'confessional prejudices', comes an exegetical study of the greatest interest. To put it in a nutshell, Cullmann thinks that these vv. 17–19 are no longer in their original context, but maintains that they reproduce an authentic saying of Jesus, whose meaning he endeavours to arrive at. It is the detailed comparison of *Mk* with *Mt* which leads him to see in these verses an addition due to *Mt*. In *Mk* the scene at Caesarea Philippi appears in all its freshness and its fundamental truth: the point of the narrative lies as much, and more, in the announcement of suffering and the reprimand inflicted on Peter as in the confession of this latter. Questioned by the Master, Peter, in the name of the Twelve, at last confesses, for the first time, that he is the Messiah. And this is considerable! But Jesus is not misled; in this decisive avowal there still lies hidden a profound misapprehension of the character of his Messiahship. This is why, instead of praising him without reserve, he orders their silence and hastens to qualify this acknowledgement of his Messianic role with the announcement of the sufferings it entails. Peter's misapprehension then betrays itself in his rebuke and Jesus has to reprimand him harshly by telling him, and all of them through him (he looks at them while speaking to Peter), that his concept of the Messiah is wholly human, or rather Satanic, analogous to that with which Satan had previously tried to dazzle him in the desert. Compared with *Mk*'s narrative understood in this way, *Mt*'s certainly sounds less pure. Not only does it not convey the same emotional force, not only does it substitute a less primitive 'Son of Man' for 'I' and leave the verb ἀπεκάλυψεν without its complement in an odd way, but above all its substitutes an unconditional eulogy of Peter for Jesus' sorrowful reserve, after which Peter's lack of understanding and the reprimand it draws on him are a considerable surprise. Matthew, according to a habitual procedure of his of which we have many other examples[1], has inserted into a groundwork of Mark a fragment taken from elsewhere. Although he has left some stitches which betray the insertion[2], he has carried it out not without certain skill which is equally customary: the correspondence between 'You are the Christ' and 'You are Peter', which, in the opinion of some, proves the authenticity of the entire passage, is an intentional effect of his literary talent, and it was perhaps because the isolated Logion began in this way that it occurred to *Mt* to insert it in this place. Where does this Logion come from then and what is its place historically in the life of Jesus? One suggestion might be the appearance of the risen Christ reported in *Jn* 21, but then it would be strange, says Cullmann, if Jesus had not explained the surname of Cephas during his lifetime. The episode in *Jn* 6:66ff, after the discourse at Capernaum, offers another suitable occasion . . . Finally Cullmann prefers to light on *Lk* 22:31f, as the most probable *Sitz im Leben*: it was after the Last Supper, on the eve of his Passion and of Peter's denial, that Jesus explained to the latter the role that was to be his and which was conveyed by his surname Cephas.

I have summarised this line of argument in detail because it seems to me very suggestive and largely worthy of agreement. Especially the first part: the more difficult it is to explain why *Mk*, then *Lk* have 'omitted' the saying about Peter the Rock from the scene at Caesarea, the easier it is to explain how *Mt* with his well-known talent for piecing bits together has inserted here a saying he got from elsewhere. About the primitive place of this saying I would be less positive myself and emphasise more than Cullmann does the hypothetical character of its link with the Last Supper. But it remains that the comparison of *Mt* 16:17–19' with *Lk* 22:31f and *Jn* 21:15ff is very enlightening and we shall see that it deserves to be exploited much more than Cullmann does.

Inserted though it may be, the saying of *Mt* 16:17–19, is no less authentic for that, and Dr Cullmann proves this by an excellent piece of exegesis which is the more precious because it is the opposite of so many denials that have come from the Protestant side. Not only does its archaic and semitic idiom manifest a very primitive Palestinian

---

[1] Another modification of *Mk*'s narrative, in *Mt* 14:33, has had the effect of weakening the importance of the confessions at Caesarea, since this latter now ceases to be the first and the quite new eulogy which it wins for Peter is less easily explicable.

[2] τότε and ἀπο τότε in vv. 20 and 21. See also the absence of the complement of ἀπεκάλυψεν which is to be explained literarily by a change of context.

origin, but its substance brings into play conceptions that can and must have been those of Jesus himself. The 'Church' is only a Greek translation of a pre-Christian notion that is profoundly Jewish and familiar to the Old Testament as well as to the sects of the last centuries (those of the Damascus document and now Qumran), the notion of the Holy People, of the little Remnant of the Community chosen for the end of time. If Jesus believed himself to be, as Cullmann admits, the Messiah, 'Son of Man' and 'Servant', he must have conceived this 'ecclesiology' as the necessary complement of his 'Christology'. 'As Messiah, Jesus cannot fail to have envisaged the formation of a community' (p. 171). When he speaks of a Rock and of building, these are images that have parallels in Jewish tradition too. And let no one object, with Albert Schweitzer, that Jesus expected an eschatological Kingdom at the end of time only, not already present on the earth. This opposition is a fallacy. In the thought of Jesus as in Jewish eschatology the present is not opposed to the future, but prepares for and anticipates it. Jesus thought of the Kingdom of God as being already begun in his own person (Mt 11:4-5; 12:28) and the little group of the Twelve, the institution and mission of whom during the lifetime of Jesus Cullmann regards as historical. Nor did Jesus believe that his death would bring the immediate advent of the eschatological Kingdom; rather, he regarded his death and resurrection as the decisive act which would found here and now his community of the 'new alliance', the anticipation on earth of the future Kingdom. The proof of this lies in the institution of the eucharistic meal and the saying about the new Temple that is to be built after the destruction of the old. He envisaged a delay of indefinite duration[1] between his resurrection and his return, during which the gospel was to be preached to the Gentiles (Mk 13:10), the companions of the bridegroom were to fast (Mk 2:20) and the Church was to be built (Mt 16:18). In resisting the attacks of the Gates of Hell – or even by assaulting them – this Church, like its Master, is to triumph over death through the power of his Resurrection.

Everything that Cullmann has just said about the Church as the Messianic community on earth is excellent, but the essential element of Jesus' saying lies in the relationship it establishes between this Church and the person of Peter by means of a triple image: the Rock-

[1] P. 181: 'Certainly Jesus did not have to envisage a period as long as several thousand years; it was a brief lapse of time that he had to admit between his resurrection and his return.' This affirmation however goes beyond what is given through exegesis, and does not change anything fundamentally anyway.

ST PETER ACCORDING TO OSCAR CULLMANN

foundation, the Keys of the Kingdom and the power to Bind and Loose. But on this precise point of Peter's prerogatives I am forced to say that Cullmann's exegesis seems to me less satisfactory since it minimises them in two ways: it eliminates as far as possible any difference between Peter and the other apostles, and in particular it excludes any eventual application to 'successors'. Is Peter the Rock on which the Church is to be founded? But so are the other apostles too; cf. *Ep* 2:20; *Rm* 15:20; *1 Co* 3:10; *Ga* 2:9 (columns); *Rv* 21:14. Does he receive the keys of the Kingdom? But these keys, like those of the Pharisees who travel over land and sea to make proselytes, (*Mt* 23:13, 15), signify scarcely more than the apostolic mission. He has the power to bind and to loose? This power which can mean 'forbid' and 'permit' here means 'condemn' and 'absolve', that is to say, the power to forgive sins which is to be conferred on the other apostles as well as Peter (*Mt* 18:18; *Jn* 20:23). Of course Cullmann does not want to deny 'the pre-eminence which is quite certainly accorded to Peter here', but for him it is reduced to that of a 'representative' of the other apostles; 'when he speaks, it is always in the name of the others as much as in his own; when one wants to speak to all the disciples, it is Peter one addresses' (p. 185). This exegesis is somewhat brief and refuses to see any real primacy of Peter over the other apostles, though this, as I shall be saying in a moment, is rendered necessary by the force of the texts as well as by Jesus' manifest intentions.

If Peter's powers scarcely surpass those of the other apostles, still less can they be bequeathed to 'successors'. Not only does the text of *Mt* 16:17–19, make no mention of such a transmission, but it must also be excluded *a priori* by a line of theological argument which Cullmann develops in the last, and most deeply-felt, pages of his book. This argument starts with a dilemma: a 'succession' to Peter can be envisaged either as to him as apostle or as bishop; but succession to either of these titles is not legitimate nor even possible. It is not possible to Peter as apostle, since the function of apostle is of itself untransmissible. The apostles are the witnesses of the earthly and the risen Christ; and the unique experience which they were granted cannot be repeated. It corresponds to a historical stage which will never again be repeated. It is possible for there to be men who will transmit their evidence; but there will never again be men like them who have *seen* Christ on earth. It is possible to build on the foundation they have laid; but this foundation, laid by them once and for all, will never have to be laid again. If Peter cannot have successors in the direction of the Church, as an apostle, still less can he have them as bishop. For he was bishop only of Jerusalem, and only for a short time; it is doubtful whether he was bishop of Antioch, still more so whether he was bishop of Rome; if then there are bishops who can claim to be his successors, they would have to be those of Jerusalem, at a pinch those of Antioch, but not those of Rome. In addition, it is illegitimate in itself for a particular church, whichever it may be, to claim to rule the universal Church. The bishops can be called the successors of the apostles in the limited sense that they have taken the place of the apostles in the government of the churches, but if 'their function follows on that of the apostles', it nevertheless 'differs radically from theirs' (p. 197). They no longer have to found the faith, they have to guard it, by watching over the construction of the building in the particular church with which they are entrusted. Not one of them can claim to govern the other churches of Christ, which ever apostle it was, even Peter, who founded it. Rome still uses as an argument the universal direction it exercised for so many centuries; but this *de facto* situation, which anyway did not go without opposition, appeared only in the post-apostolic period and cannot be used to support the notion of a primacy given by divine right and valid for all time. It was only from the beginning of the third century that the bishops of Rome conceived the idea, in order to back up their claims, of adducing the text of *Mt* 16:17–19, which is in fact no help to them.

These are the main outlines of Dr Cullmann's argument. Its principal weakness is to imprison the discussion in an unjustified dilemma and to exclude a third term which is nevertheless essential – Peter was more than a bishop, more than an apostle, he was the head of the apostles. But before I demonstrate this, I want to make some remarks about the branches of the alternative which has been laid down.

As to the apostolic function, in the strict sense of the word, it cannot be disputed that it is untransmissible. Nor has the Pope of Rome ever claimed to be an apostle on the same footing as St Peter. This is not the point on which I want to criticise Dr Cullmann. But in the course of his discussion he defines the role of the apostolic foundation of the Church in a manner which restricts it strangely; he reduces it, in fact, practically to the Scriptures! 'This unique element, which signifies the survival of the apostles in the age of the Church, is the apostolic writings' (p. 199). With this stroke of the pen he crosses off Tradition! Whatever one may think of the exact nature of the latter, and of the misuse which it has been possible to make of it, is it admissible to suppress the living, oral testimony of the apostles entirely and keep only the written? Even if we give the expression 'apostolic writings' a sense wide enough to take in all the works of the New Testament, even those which do not derive directly from an 'apostle', it still remains that the role of most of the Twelve is practically nullified for us, twentieth-century Christians. And even for those who left writings, do their works contain the whole of their testimony? It is impossible to prevent oneself sensing a Protestant viewpoint here. Cullmann, who foresees this objection, writes: 'It is not confessional prejudice which compels us to this affirmation: *it is exclusively the manner in which primitive Christianity understood the apostolate*' (p. 199). But these words which I have italicised contain a statement that is historically and theologically erroneous. The first Christians did *not* think of their apostles as nothing more than writers. The writings of certain among them are only one of the expressions, and one which can be incomplete, of the living Tradition which they bequeathed to the Church and which is perpetuated in it through the centuries.

Where the succession to Peter as bishop is concerned, I am prepared to concede Dr Cullmann much more than he perhaps expects from a Catholic. Indeed, no particular church, *as such and on those grounds alone*, can claim to rule the universal Church. In fact, the worldwide direction that the church of Rome *de facto* exercised through the centuries cannot, by itself, make this role into a divine right, but only confirm it. And I must also say that this historical role of the Roman church is not 'a decisive criterion' of the primacy in the eyes of Catholics (p. 208). Lastly, I do not take it as 'decisive . . . that Peter should have been the bishop of a particular church, that of Rome' (p. 204). I even dispute whether he was really the 'bishop' of any church at all, Jerusalem, Antioch or Rome. He was more than a bishop in as much as he was an apostle, *a fortiori* head of the apostles. The apostles were something other than and more than bishops. Their mission was never limited to the direction of a local community; they founded churches and entrusted the task of administering them to local heads, to supply for them during their absences and especially after their deaths – a mission which carried on their power of direction but not their unique role of witness, as Cullmann has well said. Paul was not 'bishop' either of Lystra, or Derbe, or Philippi, or Corinth, or Ephesus; even a Titus or a Timothy, a sort of apostolic superintendent in charge of several churches, was not yet a 'bishop' in the precise sense of the word; I cannot see therefore why there is this obstinate desire to make Peter the bishop of this or that church, muddling his role with that of a later generation. As an apostle he was able only to transmit his powers to the bishops of Jerusalem or Antioch or Rome.

But he was more than an ordinary apostle, and here we arrive at the essential point which is so sadly ignored in Dr Cullmann's argument. To the two terms of his mistaken dilemma, Peter as apostle and Peter as bishop, a third must be added which will break the deadlock – Peter as Prince of the apostles. I have said already that Cullmann acknowledges a certain pre-eminence of Peter in the college of the Twelve, but always to reduce it to the simple level of *primus inter pares*, of a 'representative' whom nothing distinguishes from the rest in an essential manner. 'Although he shares his dignity with the other disciples, he is especially representative within the group' (p. 196). Even the mission which he received from the risen Christ caused no substantial change in this situation. He is the beneficiary only of a 'chronological advance . . . over his equals', from the fact that 'he was the first to see the Risen Christ' (*ibid.*). By reason of this fact he is indeed 'particularly qualified to announce' salvation through the dead and risen Christ (*ibid.*), he is 'the principal witness of the resurrection of Christ' (p. 197), but these eulogistic qualifications must not make us victims of an illusion: 'first', 'most eminent', 'apostle above the rest' though he may be, Peter none the less remains, in Cullmann's eyes, on the same level as the rest as far as concerns the essentials of the apostolic function: he has no special mission in regard to the other apostles and through them in regard to the rest of the Church. To me, this way of looking at them does not do justice to the texts: for indeed the latter compel us to acknowledge in Peter *a role of direction even within the apostolic college.*

Let us take *Lk* 22:31f first; Cullmann has brought out the resemblances between this saying and that of Caesarea Philippi so well that he can see the framework of the Last Supper as the most probable moment at which *Mt* 16:17–19, could have been uttered. And yet he fails curiously to appreciate the force of this. We see Jesus announcing the trial of their faith that his apostles are to undergo, since it is with them (ὑμᾶς) that he is concerned in this intimate conversation at the Supper (cf. the promise of twelve thrones in the preceding verse!). Peter himself will be 'sifted' and will have to 'recover'; but, through

Christ's prayer, his faith will not suffer a complete 'failure' and he
will have to 'strengthen his brethren', who are without doubt the
apostles. Jesus could not have asserted more clearly than through this
saying the role of direction in the faith that he was reserving for
Peter *within* the apostolic group. The saying in *Jn* 21:15ff is strictly
related to the preceding, to the point of being 'the immediate replica'
of it, as Cullmann recognises (p. 165); and this is the governing factor
in his interpretation. At first sight, in fact, the order to 'feed the sheep'
could be understood of the direction of the faith in general, whose
pastors the apostles are, like the bishops (*1 Co* 9:7; *Ac* 20:28). But the
clear reference to Peter's triple denial and through that to the prophecy
in *Lk* 22:31–4 invites us to understand that the first sheep he will have
to feed will be his own brethren the apostles, whom he will have to
lead in their recovery just as he has led them in their desertion. This
mission of Peter in regard to the apostles themselves is also suggested
by Jesus' question: 'Do you love me *more than these others do*?': it
is because he loves Jesus more than the other apostles that he is given
charge of directing them, and with them the whole flock of Christ.
If we return now to the saying in *Mt* 16:17–19, where we have seen
that Cullmann offers a minimising exegesis on this point, we shall
recognise in it the same expression of a primacy which gives Peter
a rank to himself in the apostolic college. The one Rock (in the singular) is not identical with the foundation (*Ep* 2:20), or with the foundations (*Rv* 21:14) which the apostles are; if we may be permitted to
press the metaphor, we should think rather of the ground-rock on
which the foundations are laid and which assures their stability. The
Key of the Kingdom cannot be reduced to a simple symbol of the
apostolic mission through a factitious comparison with *Mt* 23:13, 15;
the obvious meaning of this image, well known in the Bible and the
Ancient East, suggests rather the charge of guarding and administering the house, confided to a single person. Cullmann, who quotes
Is 22:22, is not ignorant of this, but he does not make enough of it
when he speaks of a 'superintendent' (p. 183); we should rather think
in terms of a 'master of the palace' or 'vizier'[1]. Peter is established by
Jesus as the 'first minister' of his Church, in which he will have to
govern not only the mass of the faithful but also the officials themselves. As for the power to bind and loose, it does indeed imply

[1] Cf. R. DE VAUX, 'Titres et fonctionnaires égyptiens à la cour de David et de
Salomon', *RBibl*, 1939, p. 401f.

the forgiveness of sins[1], but it cannot be restricted to this: it designates a whole activity of decision and legislation, in doctrine as well as in practical conduct, which amounts to nothing less than the spiritual administration of the Church in general.

This power conferred on Peter concerns, among other things but before all, doctrine, that is to say, faith. This emerges from the connection between *Mt* 16:17–19, *Lk* 22:31ff and *Jn* 21:15ff, such as we just explained it, but also from the very terms used in *Mt* 16:17–19. Even if the original context of this saying was not the scene at Caesarea Philippi, and it cannot therefore be interpreted in relation to the profession of faith which Peter has just made (p. 186), it still begins with an allusion to a 'revelation' received from on high: it is because Peter has been favoured with this divine light that Jesus proclaims him blessed (compare *Mt* 13:16f and parallels) and entrusts him with a primacy in the Church which derives a primarily doctrinal character from this fact. This is not to say that the 'Rock' is simply Peter's faith. Cullmann is right to maintain, against the Reformers, that it designates rather the actual person of the apostle. But it is easy to reconcile the two: if the person of Peter is chosen as base, first minister and legislator of the Church, it is above all because of the faith which Jesus recognises in him (*Mt* 16:17), which he will protect and which he gives him the task of strengthening in the others (*Lk* 22:32).

The *personal* character of the privilege granted to Peter is of the first importance. Cullmann acknowledges it, but only to conclude that it is incommunicable and excludes all possibility of 'succession'. However, a quite different judgement must be passed on it, if one is willing to admit that this privilege resides in a power, a mission. Personal as it is, this power is *unique*, and the different sayings in which it is conferred on Peter allow us a clear perception of the deepest intentions of Christ, to give his Church *a single head*, who will maintain it in *unity*. This intention could have been foreseen already *a priori* in virtue of the very Biblical and Judaistic institution from which, as we have seen, the Church derives. The theocratic community of the people of God must be one. For that it needs a single head, representing on earth the One God. When Jesus chose from among his disciples a proxy, Peter, it was obviously with this inten-

---

[1] This is the meaning it gets in the saying in *Mt* 18:18, addressed to the disciples; but nothing obliges us to interpret 16:18 to fit this parallel, which also poses a delicate problem of literary criticism.

tion. He wanted his own people to remain united in faith and love once he himself had gone, and it is for this that he designates a head. But this intention implies, *pace* Dr Cullmann, that as long as the Church lasts this unity of direction must also last; and this can only come about through successors who, receiving their mandate from Peter, are to perform for their own generations the role Peter had to perform for his own. This is not mentioned explicitly in Jesus' words to Peter, but it is to be found implicitly in the intention behind those words.

Cullmann does not appear to feel this necessity for singleness in the direction of the Church. If some of what he says seems to concede the usefulness of such unity of government, though all the time refusing the manner in which the Roman tradition claims to ensure it[1], other expressions suggest that after all this unity is not necessary[2] and claim a precedent in the apostolic age which would authorise the division of the Church today (p. 38, n. 3). On these points I cannot agree with him either. On the one hand, the wretched experience of the profound changes in belief that separation from Rome has brought about in the Protestant churches[3] is sufficient to convince one of the necessity of the direction of the universal Church by a single head. And on the other hand, I do not allow that the Church of apostolic times offers any example of a division parallel to that of our own times. Of course, discussions and conflicts are to be seen, but they were the unavoidable crises of a creative epoch. There is a world of difference between the divergences within a unity that is being sought and the rendings of a

---

[1] p. 213f: 'To decide in each epoch *what personage ought to be at the head o, the universal Church*, we cannot start from an episcopal see fixed once and for all'. Similarly: '*One may be willing to deduce in addition from Mt* 16:17*ff that, even after Peter the Church will need a supreme direction, charged with administering the keys and the power to bind and loose.* But this cannot be done by reserving the role for the future occupants of a particular episcopal see'; or again '*to accede to the direction of the universal Church* cannot depend on a rule of succession which would make it the privilege of an episcopal see.' The words I have italicised suggest that the accession of a single person to the supreme direction of the universal Church appears all the same to be desirable and that this need ought to be satisfied if it were not for the insupportable pretensions of Rome.

[2] p. 204: 'Originally, a single "rock", between "columns", was to be found at the head of the Church. Is it necessary to deduce from this that, in all the generations to come, the universal Church must be directed by a single person? This is not a necessary consequence.' But the reason that Cullmann adduces is curious: 'in these early days the Church was limited to a local community, whereas nowadays the situation is entirely different'. Exactly! Surely the multiplicity of communities makes the need of a central authority all the more imperative?

[3] I have in mind the 'liberal' Protestantism which has so notoriously lapsed into rationalism, not those of our separated brethren who, like Dr Cullmann, are close to us in belief on many points.

unity which is breaking up. The unity of belief was then being built up; the workers tried loyally to understand one another; and they succeeded in doing so. This is why Paul goes to see the authorities in Jerusalem and the necessity of circumcision is discussed in 'council'. I do not see how Cullmann can write: 'They failed to reach understanding on this important subject: this is proved by the fact they parted company well and truly, that the dogmatic discussions on this theme continued, as the epistles of Paul show, and that there was no lack of collisions later on' (p. 38, n. 3). Of course there were still 'dogmatic discussions' and 'collisions', but with intransigent Jewish-Christians whose mandate from James has never been proved and who ended by leaving the Church. The responsible leaders gathered in Jerusalem on the contrary 'well and truly' understood one another and did not impose the obligation of circumcision and the Law on Gentile converts[1]. And 'the public task of the collection' which they asked Paul to undertake represented a sign of a unity that was fundamentally achieved, not a practical accommodation adopted as a last resource in default of an unrealisable dogmatic unity[2].

The unity of the primitive Church was realised round the person of Peter. The express desire of Jesus, recorded in the gospels, is sufficient to assure us of this, and the texts which narrate the beginnings of the Church confirm it, even if, as we have seen, the personality of Peter did not always respond to the loftiness of the role that had developed

---

[1] James himself, according to *Ac* 15:19, judges that they should not 'make things more difficult for pagans who turn to God', that is, in the context, impose on them the yoke of the Law and circumcision. It is noteworthy that in 21:21, the reproach he levels at Paul concerns the non-circumcision *of Jews*, not of pagans. James and his supporters were apparently anxious to maintain the Law among converted Jews, an attitude easily explicable in this age of transition and not of itself in any way heretical.

[2] Cullmann, who understands it in the latter sense (p. 38, n. 3), sees in this solution of charity an opportune lesson for the divided churches of today. Since it is perhaps unavoidable that 'the Roman Catholic Church should stand aside from all ecumenical conferences', would it not be better to 'abandon the aim, more elevated but Utopian, of a real union' and 'try to unite these two parts of Christianity (i.e., the Roman Catholic Church and the union of major churches independent of Rome) in a common task, at the same time renouncing expressly any reunion on the canonical and dogmatic planes'? This proposal springs from a profoundly Christian concern and is far from unrealisable: several times already, in recent years, the Catholic Church has joined forces with the churches separated from it to struggle against certain dangers threatening Christian civilisation. But a union of hearts like this cannot dispense us from reaching out towards, and against everything, the 'real union', in faith, which is not only 'more elevated', but indispensable, primordial, and intended above all by Christ. Desired by the Master and favoured with his grace, such a union cannot be 'Utopian'. All that is necessary is that the brethren who are separated should make an effort together and on this point, Peter's attitude, humble and conciliating, is an example to all.

upon him and if he exercised his authority with a conciliating kindliness which is not without a precious lesson for his successors.

This role – not of an apostle, nor of a bishop, but of the Prince of the apostles and Head of the Church – he handed on to someone else at the moment of his death, as he had to in order to respect the intentions of Christ and to ensure the perpetual unity of the Church. And, through Tradition, we believe that he bequeathed it to the place where he died, that is, to the head of the church of Rome[1]. It is not solely because he is the bishop of the local Roman church that we acknowledge the Pope's right to rule the universal Church; it is because he is the personal successor of Peter. To the power to direct a particular community, which he shares with all the other bishops in the world, is added in his case another power, unique of its kind, which he alone has received from Peter. The ground is thus cut away from under the complaint ceaselessly repeated by Cullmann, that a particular church cannot claim to rule the other churches, its equals. The bishop of Rome is not only a bishop, he is the head of the bishops, because Peter was not only an apostle, but the head of the apostles. The objection is brought against us that no text of the apostolic age records this transmission by Peter of his special powers to the bishop of Rome. This objection is valid for someone who believes only in texts and refuses all belief in the living Tradition of the Church. In the faith of Catholics, this Tradition exists; and it transcends the positive arguments of which it could avail itself. It is possible that this Tradition does not get itself affirmed in texts and historical monuments until a post-apostolic age; it is possible that the proof of the Roman primacy by recourse to Mt 6:17–19 appears in the texts only in the third century. It is the case with every truth of faith, even those propounded by Scripture, that it cannot impose itself on the mind by historical or rational evidence. That concerning universal authority over the Church, bequeathed by Peter to the bishops of Rome, does not escape this rule. A vicious circle, it is protested (cf. pp. 211, 213)! Perhaps, for someone who is willing to

[1] This head had not necessarily been appointed as bishop of Rome by St Peter, any more than the church of Rome had been founded by him. Peter could have found a bishop already established at Rome and bequeathed him the supreme power because he was going to die, and also because Rome was the capital of the Empire. We have here a knot of circumstances which is no less contingent for all its being providential. The bond which attaches the primacy to the former capital of the Roman Empire is not necessitated by divine right, but by ecclesiastical right. And this disposition could be changed if the official authority of the Church decided to transfer the pontifical primacy to some other episcopal see, or even to detach it from any particular one.

accept a truth of faith only when founded on historical evidence, but not for someone who is able to recognise the congenital insufficiency of history to prove a truth which transcends it. I concede that the universal authority of the Pope, founded on personal succession from St Peter, is in the end an object of faith for the Catholic. But this is neither escapism, nor a vicious circle, nor a leap into the unknown; it is an act of religious submission to the word, as it is manifested in the Writings and the Tradition of the Church. Besides, on this point as on every other, the faith of the Catholic is prudent, enlightened and well founded. In default of impossible historical evidence, it demands a human and divine probability which renders it reasonable and virtuous. And it finds this here: in the formal words of Jesus, which place Peter at the head of the apostolic college and of the Church, with a special mission in the order of faith and a manifest intention to ensure the perpetual unity of the Church in this way; in the effective and well-recognised role played by Peter in the beginnings of the Church, not merely for some years but during his whole lifetime; in the historically-proven fact that Peter came to Rome and died there; and lastly in the equally historical fact, even if the documentation is full of gaps, that from then on the head of the Church of Rome claimed to be and was recognised as the personal successor to St Peter. The Catholic faith in the Roman primacy rests on these bases, which it regards as firm, but it transcends them, as faith always transcends human motives. Those who are not open to this faith will without much trouble find exegetical or historical difficulties to legitimate their refusal; those on the other hand who accept it, do not do so without an assurance as complete as human knowledge is capable of furnishing.

In his Preface Dr Cullmann expresses his regret in a most moving way that he is unable to dedicate to his 'Roman Catholic' friends a work which he well realises cannot receive their approval. He has not ceased, however, in writing it, to recall his conversations with them and to foresee their objections. And he hopes that his sincere effort will encourage a dialogue and call forth useful reactions. For those who have had the advantage of a personal relationship with Dr Cullmann, this friendly sincerity cannot be put in doubt; and reading this work itself will confirm the impression. Without mentioning a competence which is not in question, one senses in it a perfect scientific loyalty in the service of an ardent pursuit of truth. Certainly this loyalty has not been able to guard Dr Cullmann, any more than any other man, from evaluating many facts and many texts in the light of his own profound convictions. So much so that a Catholic exegete and theologian will find himself obliged to dissent, not only on many a detail, but also on the essentials. 'Prejudices' on both sides? Let us say rather a differing religious attitude which necessarily makes itself felt in the interpretation of documents that are incomplete and limited. To the loyal frankness of this thesis, so authoritatively expounded, we can only reply with a parallel frankness. This is the attitude I have adopted in this review, the length and the detail of which will indicate clearly enough how highly I value Dr Cullmann's opinions. May God assist us, him and me and all our readers, to embrace his Truth with a heart always wholly sincere.

8. Tradition according to Oscar Cullmann*

One of the principal objections brought against Dr Cullmann's *St Peter* by Catholic critics reproached him with founding the whole of his argument on an exegesis, and a debatable one at that, of the Scriptural texts and ignoring the important part played by Tradition alongside the Scriptures (cf. *RBibl* 1953, pp. 573f and 578f; above pp. 167, 173). Anxious to pursue the discussion with the same sympathetic frankness which is able to make it fruitful, Cullmann published in the review *Dieu Vivant*, 23 (1953) an article entitled 'Écriture et Tradition' which brought fresh replies, in particular that of P. Daniélou (*ibid.* 24). This article he has reprinted as chh. 2 and 3 of the book under review[1], adding fresh material to reply to the objections which have been levelled at him, and introducing them with the reproduction of an article on 'Paradosis et Kyrios' which appeared in *RHPR*, xxx, 1950, pp. 12–30.

The first chapter establishes an interesting comparison between the *Paradosis* of the apostles, such as it emerges from the writings of Paul, and the *Paradosis* of the Rabbis. Beneath an indisputable similarity of origin, revealed by the vocabulary, there is an essential difference: instead of coming from 'men' (*Mt* 7:8), the tradition of the apostles comes from Christ, and not only from the historical Jesus as the origin of the series, but from the glorified Christ present there and then to the apostles through his Spirit, who confirms his teaching of them by direct revelation, without that excluding the action of human intermediaries; this is the way in which we are to understand the ἀπὸ τοῦ Κυρίου of *1 Co* 11:23. This is full of suggestion, but it is to be feared that Cullmann is generalising mistakenly, as P. Daniélou remarks (*Dieu Vivant*, 26, p. 74f), when he applies what was true in

---

* Originally published in *RBibl*, 1955, pp. 258–64.
[1] *La Tradition, Problème exégétique, historique et théologique*, by Oscar Cullmann (Cahiers Théologiques, 33), Paris, 1953.

the exceptional case of Paul to all the apostles. An apostle, in fact, whether we understand this in the strict sense reserved for the Twelve or in a wider sense of 'an eye-witness only of the resurrection of Christ' (Cullmann, p. 25), is by definition the witness of a direct experience of Christ living on this earth, even if this was after his resurrection. The 'revelations' he may receive will be at most a confirmation of his experience, a recalling of what Jesus said (*Jn* 14:26). The idea of apostles communicating the particular revelations they have received to one another (p. 26), appears to be more imaginary than based on the texts. And it is difficult to understand how this definition, 'The apostle is so to speak, by definition, one who transmits what he has received through revelation' (*ibid.*) harmonises with that of the apostle as 'eye-witness' (p. 25). Certainly the experience on which the witness of the apostle rests is of a spiritual order; but it remains linked to a historical contact, and distinct from what we normally call a 'revelation'. The definition which has just been quoted would be better applied to 'prophets'. It is understood that an apostle could at the same time be a prophet; but the present enquiry demands that his office be spoken of in its precise and specific sense. Paul, and only Paul among the apostles, needed a 'revelation' (*Ga* 1:16) to supply for the ocular testimony he lacked. I think one can see in Cullmann's writing a constant equivocation between two distinct aspects of revelation – that which Jesus communicated historically (either during his earthly life, or in the conversations which followed his resurrection) to the chosen 'witnesses' who are the 'apostles', and that which he grants later through his spirit to all the inspired people of the apostolic age, apostles, prophets and other charismatics, not forgetting, above all, the inspired writers. Objectively, these two aspects of revelation are expressed on the one side by the 'kerygma', on the other by the totality of the tradition of the apostolic age, such as it is preserved in the writings of the New Testament and in oral tradition.

These remarks will already give us some idea of the confusion which seems to reign throughout Cullmann's exposition between the Tradition of the apostles on the one hand and the writings of the New Testament on the other. In order to simplify the discussion I will state my own view right away: the Tradition of the apostles is at once narrower and wider than the content of these writings; narrower, in its strict sense of the kerygma, which is the foundation of, but does not include, all those theological developments evoked by the Spirit and recorded

in the New Testament by inspired men other than the 'apostles';
wider, in that it implies an oral tradition and a sense of the faith
which extend beyond the writings but have no less been transmitted
to the Church and confided to its authority. It seems that for Cullmann the Tradition of the apostles is identical with the tradition of
the apostolic age, and that both are identical with the content of
the New Testament writings. This is easily to be seen in ch. 2. After
a justifiable distinction between apostles and bishops, between 'apostolic' and 'post-apostolic' or 'ecclesiastical' tradition, a distinction
founded on the untransmissible character of the role of eye-witness
and on the closing of revelation at the end of the apostolic generation,
Cullmann asks (p. 33f) where this apostolic tradition which ought
to be 'the norm of revelation for all time' is to be found, and he
sees only one possible answer – in the writings of the New Testament.
Although he admits obviously that these writings 'were not all written
by the apostles themselves', he recognises in them 'the immediate
expression of their eye-witness testimony', which would be perfectly
correct if he did not apparently mean that they are *only* that and that
they contain the *whole* of their testimony, in short that between the
Tradition of the apostles and the Scripture there is co-extension and
identity. This latent presupposition manifests itself in expressions
such as 'the writings of the apostles' (p. 34). 'the written testimony of
the apostles' (p. 35). But this equation between the Tradition of the
apostles and Scripture is not posited without a *petitio principii*. If he
admits it, this is because he sees no means other than written ones to
ensure a living contact with the apostles, who are dead, for the Christians of succeeding ages; that is to say, he does not envisage, or *a priori*
refuses to envisage, the fresh slant given by a living, oral tradition,
which extends beyond the Scriptures and is entrusted to an Authority.
'The real presence of the apostles in the Church of all time is given
us in the New Testament' (p. 36). Of course he is not ignorant of the
mission of the Church, which is animated by the Spirit, continues the
history of salvation on earth, and is the repository of the sacraments
and responsible for revelation – in this he is some distance from many
Protestants and closer to the Catholic point of view (pp. 29, 31, 36,
47). But, in what concerns revelation, he subordinates the authority
of the Church to Scripture as a supreme and sufficient norm, and
limits its role to that of an authorised interpretation of the Sacred
Books. In Cullmann's work, the Church appears as an expert exegete:
it has the right and the duty to control individual interpretations and

would do well, in the Protestant churches, to take this role seriously (p. 39). But the 'post-apostolic tradition' which it thus creates remains 'at the level of a human idea, although the Holy Spirit can manifest himself through it as well' (p. 33); when the Church forgets this, claims infallibility and asserts that its decisions have 'the same normative value for all time as the apostolic norm itself' (p. 38), then the (Catholic) Church goes beyond its rights and 'by this claim of an authoritative norm the oneness of the apostolate is annulled' (*ibid.*). We find confusion to which we have already drawn attention between the Tradition of the apostles and Scripture again here: and we see linked to it this other error (from a Catholic point of view) in which Scripture understood in this way is superior to the living Magisterium of the Church. In this way two ideas which seem essential to us are ignored; (1) that Scripture is only one expression of the apostolic Tradition, this latter finding expression also in a living, oral tradition; (2) that both forms of expression, Scripture and oral Tradition, were elaborated from the beginning by the Church itself, as having been founded by Christ and charged with the deposit of the faith.

The discussion of these two fundamental points is also tackled head on in ch. 3. This time Cullmann faces squarely the oral tradition which he seems up to this moment to have ignored or avoided. But it is only to reject it by minimising it. First, it is dangerous *a priori*; to accept it is to minimise the Sacred Books; 'the writings of the apostles are then reduced to the point where they become instruments, useful of course but in no way indispensable' (p. 42). And then we know it, this oral tradition: it means the gossip of Papias of the apocryphal gospels (p. 43f). By arguing from it, the Catholic Church runs a grave risk of elevating a wholly human tradition such as that of the Rabbis, that Jesus rejected, into a norm[1]. If the apostles wrote their message, or had it written, down, it was precisely in order to limit their tradition, which was in fact oral to begin with, and to fix it in a written form which would constitute a definitive (p. 42) and sufficient (p. 45) norm for the Church. I will not insist further on what is inexact or narrow in this idea of the apostles writing the New Testament or having it written. There can be no doubt in fact that basically this idea is linked to the reality: it was on the authority of the apostles and armed with their guarantee that the writings of

---

[1] P. 40: 'The arguments by which the Jewish Rabbis justified their tradition considered as a norm were, in a large measure, exactly the same as those invoked by Catholic theology in favour of the tradition constituted by the dogmatic decisions of the Roman church.'

the New Testament were received as 'sacred' by the Church. I would not even dispute that they contain the essentials of the apostolic message, so much so that the admission alongside them of an oral tradition in no way lessons their 'indispensable' character. But I refuse to push this respect for the 'letter', sacred though it may be, to the point of making it exclusive. It may represent an excellent, inspired and, once again, essential expression of the message of the faith; it cannot claim to encompass all the potentialities of that faith, which Christ entrusted not to the lifeless pages of a book but to living persons. There is room, beside the fixed writings, for a whole commentary which surrounds them, extends them and helps us to understand them in the sense intended by their authors: a lived, moving, oral expression of the 'rule of faith' revealed to the apostolic generation, for whom the texts fixed in writing were indeed a norm, but not a limit. When we talk about an oral apostolic tradition, we are not thinking of the stories of Papias or the Apocrypha, but of beliefs and usages accepted from the beginning and on which the texts have not said the last word. We have more than one indication of these unwritten traditions in the New Testament itself; it has not been possible to put it all into books (*Jn* 21:25); after his resurrection Jesus had discussions with his disciples about the Kingdom of God (*Ac* 1:3), which no doubt cannot be reduced to what the evangelists have recorded; and those sayings of the Lord, not quoted in the Gospel, to which St Paul refers on occasion (*1 Th* 4:15; *Ac* 20:35; cf. Cullmann, p. 17), cannot be the only ones the memory of which was preserved[1]. Besides, most often it is a question of making explicit and applying teaching contained in substance in the summaries in the gospels, for example, on the primacy of Peter, the apostolic succession or the practice of the sacraments. But we need have no fear that these non-written traditions are infected with the decadence of rabbinic traditions, for the latter are attached to the revelation on Sinai by links that are fictitious and invented for the purpose (*Aboth*, 1:1), whereas the former really do go back through the apostolic generation to Christ, the 'New Law' (p. 22f) and the Sinai of the New Covenant.

It is well understood, in fact, that we grant this normative value equal to that of Scripture only to the *apostolic* oral tradition, not to

---

[1] Among the apocryphal Logia, which do not appear in the New Testament, Joachim Jeremias thinks there are twenty-one that can be retained as authentic (*Unbekannte Jesusworte*, 1948; cf. *RBibl*, 1949, p. 445).

the developments that may have issued from it later. But we maintain
that this apostolic Tradition can be transmitted to us through every
age, parallel to the Scriptures, by an authorised and infallible Magisterium, because this Magisterium itself was already in existence in
the first, apostolic, age and because it was this Magisterium which
received from Christ and carried in its midst both Scripture and the
Tradition which surrounds it. This point which is of capital importance needs further clarification. When we read what Cullmann writes
about the fixing of the canon in the middle of the second century
(p. 43ff), we cannot escape the embarrassing impression that the
Church was born at that moment. Before it, there had been the
apostolic generation; after it, the Church. Or rather, since that
expression makes his thought too rigid, we feel we are looking on at
a radical change in the Church. Before, it was living by a tradition
that was proliferating freely and even dangerously; after the Canon
of Scripture was fixed, the Church eliminates all tradition as a criterion of truth and submits itself 'by an act of humility' to the 'superior, written norm' (p. 44)[1]. I am afraid that Cullmann is exaggerating
– as he himself also seems to feel – the 'primordial importance' of
this fixing of the Canon in 'the history of salvation'. First, as to the
object of this decision, it consisted in distinguishing the writings
which had apostolic authority from those *writings* which could not
claim such an authority, not from the oral traditions which *ex hypo-
thesi* had the same authority. The 'stroke' with which the Church
'underlined the apostolic age' (p. 44) was rejecting the suspect writings
which were then in circulation, not the authentic traditions, even
though unwritten, which constituted a living commentary on the
faith recorded in the sacred books. For the remainder, Cullmann
admits the possibility of apostolic traditions, authentic even if oral,
but, from the moment that they fail to appear in the superior, written
norm on which the Magisterium of the Church has 'made its future
activity dependent' (p. 45), he refuses the Magisterium the right to
make use of them. This seems to me to ignore the value of a 'norm'
and the role of the Magisterium. A norm is a rule, a criterion; this
value being rightly allowed the writings of the New Testament,[2] if an

---

[1] p. 44f: 'Fixing the Canon meant saying: from now on we renounce the idea
that other traditions, not fixed in writing by the apostles, are norms . . . To say
that the writings gathered into a Canon were to be considered as the *norm*, meant
that they must be considered as *sufficient.*'
[2] In this sense they are 'sufficient' (p. 45), but this does not mean that they are
exclusive of every tradition which they do not contain in explicit manner.

oral tradition which passes for apostolic is acknowledged to be in conformity with this rule, the Church has the right to make use of it and even to proclaim it to be authentic on the same grounds as the written rule – and this is *because it is the same Magisterium which had previously fixed the written rule,* and which has not 'abdicated' after fixing it, as Cullmann himself says (p. 45). The Church always enjoys this right which it received from Christ in the person of St Peter (*Mt* 16:18f; *Lk* 22:32; *Jn* 21:15–17; cf. *RBibl* 1953, p. 575f; above p. 168f), and if it made use of this right in the second century to decide which of its writings were truly apostolic[1], it can still make use of it in succeeding centuries to pronounce that such and such an oral tradition also has an apostolic value that imposes it on faith. When the Roman Church proclaims a dogma, it in no way intends to 'juxtapose' beside the Canon of the Scriptures 'later traditions' upon which, by an abuse, it confers '*equal normative authority*' (p. 46); on the contrary it claims that these traditions (concerning, for example, the privileges of Mary) are themselves of apostolic origin and authority, that even if they are not contained explicitly in the sacred writings, they at least conform to this norm and are contained implicitly in the living faith which the Church received from Christ and which precedes, carries and extends beyond these writings themselves. The Church intends in no way to limit itself to a task of scriptural exegesis, according to a 'fiction' which it tends little by little to abandon (p. 38); it knows itself superior to all exegetes, as to all private theologians, because it possesses something they do not, the official deposit of the rule of faith.

This 'rule of faith' which accompanies and forms a commentary on the Scriptures, and has done since the beginning of the Church, finds striking expression in the Apostles' Creed. Cullmann himself acknowledges the normative value of this fixed formula which is yet not Scripture, but he claims that it is a unique exception and one which cannot be reproduced, since this formula, differing from all others which the Church might afterwards elaborate, goes back in practice to the apostles (p. 49). In fact this is not so, as P. Daniélou has rightly pointed out when he emphasises the decisive importance

---

[1] I would not say, either, as Cullmann does (p. 48), that the Church 'gave' a normative authority to the Canon, but rather that it acknowledged it. Before being listed in an official catalogue, the writings of the New Testament already, of themselves, that is through their apostolic origins, had a normative authority. Cf. LAGRANGE, *Histoire Ancienne du Canon du Nouveau Testament,* Paris, 1933, pp. 11, 179 and *passim.*

of this precedent (*Dieu Vivant*, 24, p. 115f)[1]. In reality this formula does not go back to the apostles, it represents a first elaboration, a 'development', 'the expression of the Church's official interpretation of the written revelation' (*ibid.*). If the Christians of the second century thought that the Creed had been effectively composed by the apostles, it was not only because of this belief (the legendary nature of which would gravely compromise their decision)[2] that they received it as a text having authority, but because they recognised in it an authentic expression of the faith. Through them then the Magisterium recognised itself as possessing the right to establish a rule of faith which was not the inspired scripture; has it since lost this right it possessed then? Yes, if we admit, as Cullmann seems often to do, that the Church is no longer the same after its famous decision in the middle of the second century: no, if we acknowledge, as Catholic tradition relying on the promises of Christ asserts, that the Church is always the same, founded by the Lord, responsible since Peter for the deposit of the living faith, acting since the apostolic age and continuing the exercise of this Magisterium until the end of the world.

At the basis of Cullmann's thinking there is in fine the Protestant principle of Scripture as the decisive and unique expression of the Word of God. And beneath this principle I believe we can discern a narrow and inexact idea of Inspiration, which is shared also by many Catholic theologians, although they do not draw the same consequences from it. So I would like, before I finish, to draw attention to this last point. Inspiration is a very rich charisma and analogous in its extent; scriptural inspiration is only a particular, and not the most elevated, case of it. Beside it, and no doubt, above it are prophetic inspiration, apostolic inspiration, etc., charismas which were not ordered directly to this final end, that revelation should be recorded in writing, but much rather to the efflorescence of this revelation in all the richness of its first oral formulation and to its multiform development in the living community chosen by God to receive, elaborate and transmit the Word[3]. This is an infinitely supple and

---

[1] P. 49, n. 3, Cullmann paraphrases this objection, but does not refute it in a satisfactory fashion. It is precisely the '*principle* of an apostolic creed' distinct from Scripture and formulated by the Church which appears to us to be of such decisive importance, whatever the precise formulation itself may be.

[2] Similarly, to suggest an analogous case, the affirmation by the early Fathers of the inspiration of the Septuagint has a foundation quite other than their belief in the seventy elders and is not to be compromised by the legendary character of this belief.

[3] Cf. 'La Prophétie' (*Somme Théologique, Revue des Jeunes*, Paris, 1947) pp. 313–324; 332–5.

varied action of the Spirit in the whole of the human milieu in which it operates, first in the people of the Old Covenant, then in the apostolic community which is the nascent Church; an action which although it may be exercised above all through certain more outstanding personalities such as the prophets and the apostles, is no less at work in the anonymous numbers who in various ways contribute to the conception and the formulation of the message. The Sacred Book in which, as criticism is better able to recognise today, the extreme complexity of this living, oral and written preparation, with its multiple currents, is reflected, is only the result of this long gestation, a result guaranteed of course by the charisma granted to those who received the actual charge to write it down. But their 'scriptural' inspiration must not make us forget all the preceding inspirations of which it is the last echo. The charisma of the apostles as witnesses of Christ is indeed at the origin of the whole fermentation of the faith which took place in the apostolic generation; but the Holy Spirit worked outside them also, in all those believers who were already the Church, especially in those leaders called by God to construct the Church and who, acting under the guidance and the influence of the apostles, already constituted its first Magisterium. Once we become aware of this situation in the concrete, we shall avoid making the New Testament merely the written witness of the apostles, just as we shall understand on the other hand that this text could not enclose all the potentialities of their witnessing in its living richness. Lastly perhaps we shall be daring enough to speak of a continuation of inspiration in the Church. In the same way that the Spirit acted in the former chosen people by a kind of collective inspiration[1], so he pursues his action in the new Israel. The difference, which is certainly essential, is that the coming of Christ has brought 'revelation' to its fulfilment, that the latter came to a close with the end of the apostolic age and cannot progress substantially. But, without bringing fresh 'revelation', the Spirit continues to 'inspire' the Church by giving it the power ever to understand and explicate better the deposit entrusted to it. It is this permanent assistance from the Spirit of Christ which gives the Magisterium of the Church its infallible authority, and that not only by a 'negative assistance', as it is often called, which preserves it from error in making solemn definitions, but also by a positive charisma which helps it to perceive and declare the truths

---

[1] P. Daniélou (*Dieu Vivant*, 24, p. 112), restricting 'inspiration properly so-called' to its scriptural aspect, speaks in this sense of a more 'general assistance'.

contained implicitly in the apostolic rule of faith better as time goes on. If the Spirit inspired the authors of Scripture, he also inspired the authors of the living Tradition, and he is still present in the Church authorising it to declare the true sense of both.

This long review of a short work demonstrates well enough the interest it deserves; and the frankness of this discussion responds, I hope, to the desire expressed by the author for a fruitful dialogue between the servants of Christ.